SELECTED POEMS

Thomas Hardy
Selected Poems

Including the complete text of
Chosen Poems of Thomas Hardy

Edited by

David Bromwich

Yale UNIVERSITY PRESS

NEW HAVEN AND LONDON

Published with assistance from the Kingsley Trust Association
Publication Fund established by the Scroll and Key Society
of Yale College, and from the Louis Stern Memorial Fund.
Introduction and annotations copyright © 2023
by David Bromwich.

Yale University Press books may be purchased in quantity for
educational, business, or promotional use. For information, please
e-mail sales.press@yale.edu (U.S. office) or sales@yaleup.co.uk
(U.K. office).

Designed by Mary Valencia
Set in Janson type by Newgen North America, Inc.
Printed in the United States of America.

Library of Congress Control Number: 2023931274
ISBN 978-0-300-09528-9 (hardcover : alk. paper)

A catalogue record for this book is available from
the British Library.

This paper meets the requirements of ANSI/NISO Z39.48-1992
(Permanence of Paper).

10 9 8 7 6 5 4 3 2 1

CONTENTS

Chosen Poems of Thomas Hardy

Part I. Poems Chiefly Lyrical

PART II. POEMS NARRATIVE AND REFLECTIVE

PART III. WAR POEMS, AND LYRICS FROM "THE DYNASTS"

FROM "THE DYNASTS"

Additional Poems

FROM WESSEX POEMS

FROM MOMENTS OF VISION

FROM LATE LYRICS AND EARLIER

FROM HUMAN SHOWS

FROM WINTER WORDS

INTRODUCTION

Thomas Hardy had attained an unrivaled eminence as a novelist before he published his first volume of poems. Yet poetry was his first love, and praise of his new work was only intermittently dulled by officious questions about the author venturing outside his métier. Hardy's frankness regarding the complexities of social class and sexual relationships had also given him the public character of a rebel against convention, though this was a description he neither sought nor embraced. At all events, the emotional and generic variety of his poems would soon take him beyond any simple classification. An early piece like "The Ivy-Wife" may seem to betray the author's quaintness, with archaisms such as "therewith" and "afterhaps," yet it startles by the freshness of its closing image of a man who, "Being bark-bound, flagged, snapped, fell outright, / And in his fall felled me." Generationally, as well as stylistically, Hardy was to remain an outlier: a situation that suited him.

Ever since his poetic debut on the eve of the twentieth century, his stature has been a puzzle to commentators. To call him a minor poet seems absurd. On the other hand, the great modernists, Yeats and Stevens preeminently, created the expectation that a poetic career should advance through distinct eras or phases of self-invention. Hence the modern fascination with "origins" and "poetic influence" and "late style." By contrast, an early and a late poem by Hardy cannot easily be distinguished; their only obvious common trait is a certain consistency of temperament. Should we therefore read him as a displaced Victorian? But that will not do, either. His poems about the First World War—above all, "And There Was a Great Calm"—show the hollowness of such a supposition. Seldom in Hardy's poetry is there an impression of the florid, the affected, or any artifice that depends on the prestige of a period manner. He has an integrity that cannot be counterfeited.

The timelessness of his language, a Shakespearean quality, has made his poems a rallying point for the survival of an English idiom based in common speech and capable of surprising renewals. However one judges this claim—sharply formulated by Donald Davie in *Thomas Hardy and British Poetry*—Hardy's poems have held a wide audience among discerning readers for a century. Something of their attractiveness can be gauged by the progress from Yeats's choice, in his *Oxford Book of Modern Verse* (1936), of just four poems by Hardy to Philip Larkin's selection of twenty-seven in his *Oxford Book of Twentieth-Century English Verse* (1973). It is normally the first posthumous decades that adjust the general sense of the esteem owed to an author; and the adjustment tends to be downward. With Hardy the reverse has happened. His poems offer a landscape filled with people; there are characters in it, and voices other than the author's; there is the music of personality, from more than one person. Hardy can employ, as Wordsworth thought a poet should do, "the real language of men in a state of vivid sensation," but he has equally at his command the language of reverie, of meditation, of metaphysical perplexity. With impressive frequency, his poetry expands to encompass a drama of dialogue, occasionally incorporating the antiphonal effects of multiple speakers and a chorus. The characters of his poetry are as various as people can be, each possessed of a separate self.

Hardy was born in 1840, two years after the coronation of Queen Victoria, and died in 1928, the year before the onset of the Great Depression—an exceptional span of history and experience. He grew up in Higher Bockhampton, in the parish of Stinsford, in Dorset. His father had set out in life as a self-employed stonemason, and within a few years attained the status of master-mason. By 1860, when young Thomas was twenty, Thomas Hardy senior employed six men under him; but he was known as well for his avocation, playing violin-cello and singing tenor at country dances. This was a love that Thomas, who played the fiddle, would inherit and render unmistakable in songlike poems such as "Great Things," the novel *Under the Greenwood Tree*, and one of his best stories, "The Fiddler of the Reels." Hardy's mother, Jemima, came from a family of pauper children; she had worked as a maidservant and cook before marrying—a point of reticence for Hardy, who could bring himself to refer only to his mother's "distressful experiences." Jemima Hardy was in fact a woman of serious intelligence and taste, a dedicated reader and educationally ambitious for her eldest son. After two years at a local school, she enrolled him in a Nonconformist academy in Dorchester, where he learned French and Latin. Hardy's formal education stopped at sixteen, but he immersed himself in the Bible (and may have augmented it with his mother's favorite book, *The Divine Comedy*), along with Greek and Latin authors in translation. A measure of supererogatory learning would become a marked trait of his poetry and fiction: you see it in the unexpected erudite detail, the carefully noted historical fact, or the far-fetched word. Such curiosities, however, are brought in by Hardy for the purpose of precise registration. The central idiom of English poetry was his largest resource: Shakespeare, Milton, Wordsworth, and Shelley, but with tributaries as diverse as John Keble's *Christian Year* and the Dorset dialect poems of William Barnes.

When, in his early twenties, Hardy took up a junior position in a London firm as a draftsman for church restoration and design, his studious habits found a new field of exercise. He would visit the National Gallery in his spare hours and look at a single painting long enough to commit it to memory. He pursued his self-education as a faithful reader of the *Saturday Review*, and had the luck to encounter, early on, two of the leading intellectual spirits of the mid-Victorian generation. George Meredith was the publisher's reader for Hardy's first submitted manuscript, *The Poor Man and the Lady*, a "socialistic novel" (as Hardy described it) whose energy the older writer praised while detecting the thinness of its self-imposed sophistication. He advised Hardy to try something of narrower scope; the result was the "sensation novel" *Desperate Remedies*. A later and more important preceptor, Leslie Stephen, admired Hardy's second novel, *Under the Greenwood Tree*, and invited him to publish its successor in the prestigious magazine he edited, the *Cornhill*. After completing an already commissioned novel, *A Pair of Blue Eyes*, Hardy accepted the offer. He would receive from Stephen a depth and tact of guidance that make *Far from the Madding Crowd* the first of his books to exhibit a commanding gift for realism. His gratitude to these slightly older mentors is memorialized in poems that appear on adjacent pages of his *Chosen Poems*. "The Shreckhorn" (the Matterhorn) honors Stephen's moral courage as an avowed agnostic, and his physical courage as a mountain-climber, seeking a "semblance to his personality" in "quaint glooms, keen lights, and rugged trim." The compact elegy "George Meredith" praises the stamina with which Meredith's poetry and fiction exposed "The counterfeits that Time will break," and concludes with a peerless compliment: "His words wing on—as live words will."

In his thirtieth year, Hardy received an assignment from his new employer, the Weymouth architect G. R. Crickmay: "Can you go into Cornwall for me, to take a plan and particulars of a church I am about to rebuild there?" It was the Church of St. Juliot; and in those environs, Hardy would catch his first glimpse of Emma Gifford, against a background she later described in her diary: "the wild Atlantic Ocean rolling in with its magnificent waves and spray, its white gulls, and black choughs and grey puffins, its cliffs and rocks and gorgeous sunsettings." He saw her riding along the cliffs, "an unforgettable experience to me," as she called it, "scampering up and down the hills on my beloved mare alone, wanting no protection, the rain going down my back often, and my hair floating on the wind." Soon they were taking all-day walks together. Hardy would recall their courtship in a poem written half a century later:

> She opened the door of the West to me,
>   With its loud sea-lashings,
>   And cliff-side clashings
> Of waters rife with revelry.

Emma Gifford and Thomas Hardy were married four years later; and the history of their love would come back unforgettably in the poems that flooded Hardy's imagination at the time of her death. He printed together a central group, *Poems of 1912–13*, about those first meetings and the romance and marriage that followed; but enchantment is far from the only note of these elegies. "Summer gave us sweets, but autumn wrought division"—that, too, was part of their story, and so was this: "All's past amend, / Unchangeable. It must go."

Hardy had worked at poems from his earliest writing days. In the *Life of Thomas Hardy*—the biography he ghost-wrote under the signature of his second wife, Florence Emily Hardy—he said he had "mostly aimed at keeping his narratives close to natural life and as near to poetry in their subject as the conditions would allow, and had often regretted that those conditions would not let him keep them nearer still." Yet he launched his poetic career in late middle age: *Wessex Poems, Poems of the Past and the Present*, and *Time's Laughingstocks* came out close together in 1898, 1901, and 1909. Why the sudden flowering? Hardy felt he had been released into poetry by the scandalized public reaction to *Jude the Obscure* in 1895.

The hero's broken relationships with two women, the effects of his life on his children, the narrative exposure of the illusiveness of the "career open to talents," all conspired to render *Jude* the most painfully searching of Hardy's novels and in many ways the most courageous. The sense of a dead weight of circumstance that defeats all human purpose would again suffuse his poem of the Napoleonic wars, *The Dynasts*, published in three parts in 1904, 1906, and 1908. This was at once an epic on the Homeric model, and—since it contains historical characters who make speeches and a chorus that comments on the action—a closet drama in 130 scenes, which for reasons of both length and interest was hardly susceptible of performance on the English stage. This extraordinary work had no prototype in its chosen form. Nor was there any precursor for its moral stance, except, perhaps, Shelley's "Lines Written on Hearing the News of the Death of Napoleon," where the reader is offered an ironic commentary on the fallible doings of men and women by a character named Earth.

The Dynasts reflects Hardy's belief in Necessity, or what we would now call a deterministic view of human will. One can feel this in the tone of the poem and even, at times, its grammar. Yet Hardy resisted the temptation to personify Necessity by an abstract character who utters hermetic and riddling lines—the function that Shelley had assigned to Demogorgon in *Prometheus Unbound*. The closest approximation is Hardy's idea of the Immanent Will (which will appear again in his poem on the sinking of the *Titanic*). His dramatis personae are either confined by the historical data of their lives or else quite lacking in the human attribute of will. The supra-personal entities of *The Dynasts* (the Ancient Spirit of the Years and Chorus of the Years, the Spirit and Chorus of the Pities, Spirits Sinister and Ironic, and so on) seem often more individuated than the people, and they embody a version of fate as easily recognized by readers of Ibsen as of Aeschylus. The non-moral interests of these metaphysical agents resemble those of the capricious gods of the *Iliad* in one important respect. They are *entertained* by the spectacle of the "human shows" beneath them.

The Dynasts evinces an impartial skepticism regarding the great powers that dominated Europe in the early 1800s, an anti-sentimental refusal that may recall the Tolstoy of *War and Peace*. But Hardy's epic claims a taxonomist's rather than a novelist's relationship to human life; and though his *Chosen Poems* included some songs and choruses from *The Dynasts*, he wisely refrained from reprinting any of the speeches. And yet, for all its encumbering machinery and its longueurs, Hardy's epic remains readable. A canny review by the great drama critic of the age, Max Beerbohm, spoke of the challenge the author had set himself: "Impossible his task certainly is. To do perfectly what he essays would need a syndicate of much greater poets than ever were born into the world, working in an age of miracles." Nevertheless, Beerbohm judged it "a great book. It is absolutely new in that it is the first modern work of dramatic fiction in which free-will is denied to the characters."

Hardy came to maturity in an England marked by political anxiety at the coming of democracy, and by religious doubt at the discovery that human beings had descended from animals. The widening of the franchise in the Reform Bills of 1832 and 1867 meant that the old system of manners and deference would give way to an ever-increasing degree of popular representation. Meanwhile, the "Higher Criticism" of religion was epitomized by the collective volume *Essays and Reviews* (1860), which treated the Bible as a historical document whose wisdom and narratives alike were a human creation. Hardy was an active partisan of the great secularists of the age, Huxley, Mill, and Darwin; and all his work testifies to the limits placed on human desire by nature and society. Accordingly, his poems sometimes seem to carry a ground note of more-than-personal resignation. To say it another way, the rhetoric of his poetry, as it prepares a clinching final line, sometimes seems fashioned to administer a doctrinal sting. This tendency earned Hardy the name of *pessimist*—a description congenial to Victorian mores on other grounds, since Hardy, as much as Meredith and Stephen, declined to profess his belief in a personal God. The poems are visibly the work of the same author who announced his heroine's fate in the last paragraph of *Tess of the D'Urbervilles:* "the President of the Immortals, in Æschylean phrase, had ended his sport with Tess."

A characteristic poem in this anti-moralistic vein, "The Burghers," works up a doom-laden argument suitable to its temper. A jealous lover meditates revenge on the treacherous pair who have betrayed him, but, seeing them embrace with a love he was denied, and knowing he can either tyrannize over them or let them flee with scant resources, he abandons them to their love and time's revenges: the "wounds that none can cicatrize" will be worse than any a knife could make. So, too, in "The Subalterns," the leaden sky, the North, and a personified "Sickness" and "Death" disclaim responsibility for human misfortunes: they are (they say) secondary causes, ignorant of any prior design; and having conversed with them and learned that they never intended harm, the poet confesses himself reconciled: life thereafter "had less / Of that fell look it wore ere when / They owned their passiveness." Another poem remarkable both for its affection and for its lack of sentimentality, "The Souls of the Slain," grants to soldiers who died for their country nothing but the dignity they owned as persons; after death, they are remembered in their households for things they did *before* going off to war. "Alas!" say the souls, "our glory / Weighs less in their thought / Than our old homely acts, / And the long-ago commonplace facts / Of our lives." But the poem reproves the vanity lurking beneath their surprise and disappointment. It is wrong to suppose that life holds a glory superior to the daily decencies we show toward those we love.

What, then, of "our common hope," the Christian promise of an afterlife? "I have been looking for God 50 Years," Hardy declared in his journal in 1890, "and I think that if he had existed I should have discovered him." He thought no institution could redeem the passions he alluded to in a famous episode of *The Dynasts*, where Napoleon accepts the crown of Lombardy from the Cardinal Archbishop Caprara and, far above, the Spirit of the Pities asks: "What is the creed that these rich rites disclose?" The Spirit of the Years replies:

> A local cult, called Christianity,
> Which the wild dramas of the wheeling spheres
> Include, with divers other such, in dim
> Pathetical and brief parentheses,
> Beyond whose span, uninfluenced, unconcerned,
> The systems of the suns go sweeping on
> With all their many-mortaled planet train
> In mathematic roll unceasingly.

Often in Hardy's shorter poems, as much as in *The Dynasts*, human concerns are viewed from afar and it can seem that people have dwindled to the size of atoms. The author invites the reader to share a perspective that is essentially astronomical. Yet the preface of his last book, *Winter Words*, went to some lengths to deny that Hardy's unbelief was systematic. No "harmonious philosophy" was to be found in his latest volume, or "in any bygone pages of mine, for that matter."

His continuous lyric power, his sensitivity to fugitive and delicate gradations of feeling, is so plain a strength that, for illustration, one is tempted merely to quote such poems as "He Abjures Love," "Shut Out That Moon," "Transformations," or "I Look into My Glass." A poem of renunciation might be expected to end where "He Abjures Love" begins—

> At last I put off love,
> > For twice ten years
> The daysman of my thought

—but Hardy goes on to say that he had grown accustomed to the "disquietings" of love. The plural noun is almost a new word, and true to his experience. He was drawn to women, older women when he was still a boy, younger women in his last years, with a desire that mattered to him more than fulfillment. Still, the speaker's disavowal of love at the end of this poem is not quite believable. Perhaps it is not meant to be believed. Having talked himself into the wisdom of a relinquished search, he bids the reader an extravagant farewell:

> —I speak as one who plumbs
> > Life's dim profound,
> One who at length can sound
> > Clear views and certain.
> But—after love what comes?
> > A scene that lours,
> A few sad vacant hours,
> > And then, the Curtain.

The tone is chastened, but there is a grim humor in the theatrical gesture, the author pulling down the coffin-lid and at the same time saluting an imagined audience as he exits the stage.

"I Look into My Glass" imparts a similar disenchantment in a setting that is personal rather than public. It tells of the regret of encroaching age and a wish for reciprocal feeling that can no longer be requited. The speaker sees in the mirror "wasting skin" but a heart that has not "shrunk as thin"; so the fact of old age itself becomes a source of immedicable woes:

But Time, to make me grieve,
Part steals, lets part abide;
And shakes this fragile frame at eve
With throbbings of noontide.

Soft-spoken as it is—muttered, almost, rather than spoken—the lament of "I Look into My Glass" carries equal force and pathos whether one pictures it as delivered by a man or a woman.

The moods of the mind, for Hardy, show tremendous consistency from youth to age. The happiness that time steals from the lovers in "Neutral Tones" brings an acute impression of loss, a possible feeling even at the "noontide" of youth. From its opening words, the poem matches inward emotion to corresponding details of the landscape:

We stood by a pond that winter day,
And the sun was white, as though chidden of God,
And a few leaves lay on the starving sod;
 —They had fallen from an ash, and were gray.

The bitter memory of a depleted love is signaled with Hardy's usual fearlessness: "The smile on your mouth was the deadest thing / Alive enough to have strength to die." But with a narrative authority equal to its reserve, the description leaves the unhappy couple at a standoff—the very attitude with which the poem began, seen from a slightly different angle: "Your face, and the God-curst sun, and a tree, / And a pond edged with grayish leaves." The implied underlying sentiment may be explained by "Hap," a more abstract and quasi-didactic poem which survives on the strength of its final pardon to the gods of affliction: "These purblind Doomsters had as readily strown / Blisses about my pilgrimage as pain."

As the longest surviving of the great Victorian chroniclers of manners and morals, Hardy would have felt the propriety of offering commemorations or verse commentaries on large matters of state, but he was notably sparing of such attentions. He has nothing to show on the order of Tennyson's "Bury the Great Duke" or Kipling's "Recessional." Yet in its way, "The Darkling Thrush"—his poem on the last day of the nineteenth century—responds to a comparable demand. "I leant upon a coppice gate / When Frost was spectre-gray": as the poem begins, he is resting in the

middle of a journey, uncertain of his forward path; the clouded sky is de-
scribed with a Shakespearean dignity that Hardy commands like no other
modern poet: "And Winter's dregs made desolate / The weakening eye of
day." He projects on the dismal scene the image of the poet as an aeolian
harp, now stripped of its music: "The tangled bine-stems scored the sky /
Like strings of broken lyres"; and the ominous exordium concludes in the
same key: "And every spirit upon earth / Seemed fervourless as I." How
much of Hardy's temperament is present is in that single word *fervourless*.

The voice that rouses him from a settled despair is a bird so human it
might be a knobby-legged older neighbor:

> An aged thrush, frail, gaunt, and small,
>   In blast-beruffled plume,
> Had chosen thus to fling his soul
>   Upon the growing gloom.

Flinging his soul: the bird throws down the gauntlet to the poet as if to say,
"Do you dare to be cheerless while I sing?" This challenge breaks through
the oppressive mood of the time of day, as well as the time in history, a cen-
tury's exhaustion; so the surprising notes, "carolings" as Hardy calls them,
tease him out of thought. The sentiment on which the poem concludes—
the fancy that this thrush knows (or the poet "could think" he knows) what
the human listener cannot fathom—may seem a willful consolation. Yet the
fastidious drab naturalism of Hardy's description overrules any impatience
at the design of his argument. The bird refuses to mourn "the century's
corpse outleant." To him, it is just the moment for a last tune of the day.

"The Convergence of the Twain" marks a less ordinary encounter.
The iceberg that will sink the *Titanic* shares a tendency common to life-
less things in Hardy's poetry. It is as if these shapes, created outside the
existence of human time, wanted to be human and alive. Thus, even if
"salamandrine fires" no longer burn in the sunk ship's engine, something
like a salamander will outlast its fires:

> Over the mirrors meant
>   To glass the opulent
> The sea-worm crawls—grotesque, slimed, dumb, indifferent.

The Immanent Will was aware of the pride that fashioned the ship and
"Prepared a sinister mate / For her—so gaily great—/ A Shape of Ice, for

the time far and dissociate." The partners, fated to be "anon twin halves of one august event," are locked in a kind of marriage: "And consummation comes, and jars two hemispheres."

What are we meant to feel in reading such a poem? The event is terrible and momentous, but it is not, for Hardy, an occasion for mourning; a lesson, rather, in not being wrongly moved. Can the poet be accused of heartlessness? (a complaint familiar to the creator of Tess and Jude). Probably Hardy's reply would be that he was dealing with an inanimate *thing*, a gigantic artifice whose pretensions had made it an advertisement for the modern age itself. There is an unexpected valor, after all, in having conceived and executed a poem about the disaster without the slightest pretense of ceremonial emotion.

The more one reads and looks back on Hardy's poems, the more they astonish by their sheer variety, in treatment as well as genre. There are short stories accidentally cast in verse ("Her Death and After"), ventriloquized memoirs ("Reminiscences of a Dancing Man"), "satires of circumstance" (anecdotes based on ironic juxtapositions, too small for a story but big enough for a sonnet). There are songs, dreams, ballads ("A Trampwoman's Tragedy"), protests against the universe, poems of revisited places or persons ("Epeisodia"), elegies ("Thoughts of Phena"), almost-random notations on the ephemerality of desire ("On the Departure Platform"). There are also "sketches," in frank imitation of paintings or of charcoal or pencil sketches; and there are church poems (behavior in churches, exteriors of churches, burial mounds, headstone inscriptions). At times, it is enough for Hardy to trace the bare record of an affinity or attachment ("The Roman Road").

Whenever the mood strikes him, to freshen the worldly scene Hardy may turn and write about animals. His reverence—and more than reverence, respect—for all of animate creation shows even in a childhood memory like "The Oxen." The poem is based on a country legend he used to hear about oxen kneeling on Christmas Eve; an appealing fancy for a child, but the poem makes it more than that. If someone should beckon him even now to "Come; see the oxen kneel," Hardy says, "I should go with him in the gloom, / Hoping it might be so." A perceptive remark by Charles Lamb about Wordsworth's "Old Cumberland Beggar" affords a clue to his procedure: "The mind knowingly passes a fiction upon herself . . . and, in the same breath detecting the fallacy, will not part with the wish." Many of Hardy's best and most characteristic poems will be found to obey this psychological pattern.

"I Watched a Blackbird" deals with another fellow creature, without any background in myth or fantasy—a glimpse of the beak, a swoop for a twig, and a lift to its nest. By contrast, the witness of the ugly utilitarian scene in "Horses Aboard" responds with sympathy and horror as the unknowing animals are loaded onto a ship and made to stand in a row:

> They are horses of war,
> And are going to where there is fighting afar;
> But they gaze through their eye-holes unwitting they are,
> And that in some wilderness, gaunt and ghast,
> Their bones will bleach ere a year has passed,
> And the item be as "war-waste" classed.

Their pathetic docility makes these creatures, for Hardy, almost human, almost like the soldiers who will be shipped abroad to a similar fate; but the complete innocence of the horses suggests a whole different scale of injustice.

"A Sheep Fair" presents a commonplace scene of Hardy's Dorset where the farmers come to sell their sheep on a day of drenching rain. The auctioneer intones his dreary "Going—going," and the poet, as a curious spectator, notices things the breeders and sellers neglect:

> Jammed tight, to turn, or lie, or lunge,
> They strive in vain.
> Their horns are soft as finger-nails,
> Their shepherds reek against the rails,
> The tied dogs soak with tucked-in tails.

A continuous gnawing discomfort pervades the two stanzas of description; only in the final stanza, under the heading "Postscript," are we reminded that the sheep, raised and cared for by their shepherds, are sold to be slaughtered. The "Going—going" of the auctioneer takes on a separate meaning, a death sentence that is the more affecting for its commonness.

Elsewhere, having passed from people to animals, Hardy retreats further to a form of life that might seem incapable of provoking indignation or remorse. "In a Wood" discovers a Darwinian moral in the com-

petition of trees for limited space, a brute fact that convicts and exoner-
ates all earth's inhabitants equally. Being human through no choice of his
own, Hardy turns back half-gratefully to his own kind, because he belongs
to them:

> There at least smiles abound,
> There discourse trills around,
> There, now and then, are found
>   Life-loyalties.

More gravely, "Yell'ham-Wood's Story" asks what wisdom the wood itself
might impart if it could. "It says," Hardy reports, "that Life would signify /
A thwarted purposing: / That we come to live, and are called to die." From
one point of view, Hardy's ecumenical spirit offers a prospect of utter deso-
lation: human actors are here no different from the rest of nature. But why
(he asks) should things be otherwise?

Given this emphasis in so many poems, Hardy's inclusion of "The Eve
of Waterloo" in *Chosen Poems* tells much about his motive for writing *The
Dynasts*; much, too, about his disgust at the apparently incurable predilec-
tion for war as a proof of human efficacy. "The Man He Killed" and "In
Time of 'the Breaking of Nations'" might be cited to the same effect; but
"The Eve of Waterloo" shocks by its lacerating image of the waste to which
we subject the creatures with whom we share the earth. War is sometimes
pictured by its celebrants as a kind of sport and a collective test of national
substance. Hardy never thought so. He did not forget the soldiers who die
or are ruined for life by the injuries of war. Yet it was like him to go a step
further—only his plodding conscientiousness could have done it—and to
count the dumb creatures on the battlefield among the sufferers:

> Yea, the coneys are scared by the thud of hoofs,
> And their white scuts flash at their vanishing heels,
> And swallows abandon the hamlet-roofs.
>
> The mole's tunnelled chambers are crushed by wheels,
> The lark's eggs scattered, their owners fled;
> And the hedgehog's household the sapper unseals.
>
> The snail draws in at the terrible tread,
> But in vain; he is crushed by the felloe-rim;
> The worm asks what can be overhead,

And wriggles deep from a scene so grim,
And guesses him safe; for he does not know
What a foul red flood will be soaking him!

The greatest atrocities reveal their scope in the smallest of the casualties. It would not have been beyond Hardy to imagine a larger planetary devastation occurring as a result of the same indifference.

Pet birds, in Hardy's time, were sometimes blinded on the theory that this improved their singing, but the practice also expunged the temptation of flight, and a proud owner could claim to have made the creature happier in its subjugation to human possessiveness and affection. "The Blinded Bird" knows that such things are done for reasons that claim to be generous. The Christian heart of this poem belongs, however, not to the rationalizer of a benevolent order but to the sufferer, and the stirring conclusion is at once a prayer and a sermon delivered by the poet:

Who hath charity? This bird.
Who suffereth long and is kind,
Is not provoked, though blind
And alive ensepulchred?
Who hopeth, endureth all things?
Who thinketh no evil, but sings?
Who is divine? This bird.

Hardy's favorite passages from the Bible were 1 Kings 19 ("but the Lord was not in the wind: and after the wind an earthquake; but the Lord was not in the earthquake: and after the earthquake a fire; but the Lord was not in the fire: and after the fire a still small voice") and 1 Corinthians 13 and 15 ("now abideth faith, hope, charity, these three; but the greatest of these is charity. . . . I say, brethren, that flesh and blood cannot inherit the kingdom of God; neither doth corruption inherit incorruption. Behold, I shew you a mystery; We shall not all sleep, but we shall all be changed"). "The Blinded Bird" carries into the reader's heart a truth about faith and charity that is deeper than doctrine.

Humanity, as Hardy understands it, is best regarded now and then from a height, or from the long perspective of memory. The opening of *The Return of the Native*, "the nightly roll into darkness" of the landscape of

Egdon Heath, exemplifies that wide-angle approach, but in Hardy's poems it is not always followed by a gradual movement closer in. Indeed, the poet may be happiest where his physical distance from his subject belongs to the very geography of the poem. "Wessex Heights" was written in 1896, soon after Hardy dedicated himself entirely to poetry, and it finds him carefree in his solitude:

> There are some heights in Wessex, shaped as if by a kindly hand
> For thinking, dreaming, dying on, and at crises when I stand,
> Say, on Ingpen Beacon eastward, or on Wylls-Neck westwardly,
> I seem where I was before my birth, and after death may be.

His freedom to stand and watch alone is all the more complete because the place-names are his invention (though they correspond to real places he knew). He goes on to admit his aversion to the towns, where he is "tracked by phantoms having weird detective ways" and where he seems "false to myself"; likewise the plains, where he is haunted by "a figure against the moon"; and again, Yell'ham Bottom or Froom-side Vale, where other ghosts abide. Even the memory of "one rare fair woman" offers no comfort beyond the thought that "time cures hearts of tenderness." Still, as Hardy confides to the reader, he will continue to walk freely and gaze down from the heights, where no memory or importunity can assail him:

> So I am found on Ingpen Beacon, or on Wylls-Neck to the west,
> Or else on homely Bulbarrow, or little Pilsdon Crest,
> Where men have never cared to haunt, nor women have walked with me,
> And ghosts then keep their distance; and I know some liberty.

It is a curious secret he confesses, namely that he has a real need of human company, but it must not come too close. A comparison with his novels will confirm this truth. Far from being a native drawn irresistibly back to his origins, Hardy never felt at home for long anywhere. Happy though his childhood seems to have been, he was not bound by the fidelities of local patriotism. Nor was he altogether comfortable in later years as the dignified presider at Max Gate—the house on the outskirts of Dorchester which he designed and built himself, and where he lived from 1885 until his death.

An inveterate elusiveness defines his poetry in other ways. A prominent charge against Hardy by those who dismiss him as something less than a master poet is that his diction is often impure: he does not deny admission to clichés and pet words, and he shows an undisciplined attraction to archaisms and recondite usage. It is also said—a more serious fault, from the high modernist point of view—that an element of preaching seems inseparable from his poetry. Both criticisms are fair. One comes to recognize the occasionally makeshift character of Hardy's idiom when one recalls his fondness for an adjective like *sere*, a noun like *casement*, a verb like *conned*. Well, but what of it? The best defense of his practice came from another idiosyncratic genius, the American poet and critic John Crowe Ransom: "There is too much force in his representations . . . to have them set aside for finicky reasons. And there is too much greatness of heart." By greatness of heart, Ransom surely meant Hardy's unbetrayable affection for the things and people he knew well; and they cover pretty much the range of humanity. The finest discoveries in his poetry involve the capture of familiar objects across a wide separation of time and space. So "A Commonplace Day" situates him at an hour of fading sunlight when "The day is turning ghost." He pushes the logs in the fireplace close together to catch a flame from the embers, as "beamless black impends." It is raining outside, and as "Day's presence wanes," Hardy says, "He wakens my regret." Day is personified, himself a bearer of regret; and the poem verges on self-parody (as Hardy often does). Yet he pulls back and makes room for an exception to his mood; a possibility that

> maybe, in some soul,
> In some spot undiscerned on sea or land, some impulse rose,
> Or some intent upstole
> Of that enkindling ardency from whose maturer glows
> The world's amendment flows.

The intimation of a still undiscernible hope—even a past hope, unfulfilled—by its "undervoicings" (says Hardy) "May wake regret in me." Yet this second regret is different from the first. It is free of self-pity and speaks not of a personal loss but rather the inevitable wastage in most lives, a sense of the luck or "hap" that renders every happiness provisional.

"During Wind and Rain" is a touchstone of that feeling. Though its texture and songlike cadences are unique to Hardy, it is one of the rare English lyrics that aspire to and achieve a superb anonymity. The poem recounts a series of scenes in the history of a family: singing together in the first stanza and, in the second, clearing and improving their modest estate; the younger generation, grown-up in the third stanza, are seen breakfasting together; finally, we witness their move to "a high new house." The surface of the story thus tells of the apparent rise, growth, and unhindered satisfaction of the characters. A counter-current appears only in the last two lines of each stanza—the first line is a pitying refrain at the mere fact of the passage of time ("Ah, no; the years O" and "Ah, no; the years, the years"); the second line, to close each stanza, is a darker omen that breaks upon the tune that sang of promises fulfilled. "How the sick leaves reel down in throngs!" "See, the white storm-birds wing across." "And the rotten rose is ript from the wall" (with its suggestion of romantic disaster or infidelity). And the last of the stanza-settling lines is delivered with a concussion: "Down their carved names the rain-drop ploughs"—an effect both hyperbolic and, in the scheme of centuries, oddly precise. The design of the poem calls for narrative action in the first five lines of each stanza and a comment in the last two lines. Hardy, an accomplished fiddler, would have known a good many tunes superficially organized like this one; but the words "during wind and rain" deepen the perspective. They allude to Feste's song in *Twelfth Night* and its double refrain, "With a hey ho, the wind and the rain" and "The rain it raineth every day." The title thereby evokes an irony that the poem can observe without having to formulate. Every event of our lives—the warmest success as much as the direst catastrophe—takes place as if during wind and rain.

"Great Things" is another poem that sounds as if it were built to accompany an unwritten tune. Hardy omits the conventional great things, the crowned heads of powerful nations, the grandees with their trophies and shining deeds. Instead, he takes to heart the smaller things that keep their tang from childhood to old age: sweet cyder, an all-night dance, the half-detected shadow of a new young love—a tryst where "A figure flits like one a-wing / Out from the nearest tree." The same miniature focus on *moments* is deployed with startling condensation in the war poem "In Time of 'the Breaking of Nations,'" published in 1915 but written forty-five years earlier, at the time of the Franco-Prussian War. It is one of the great short poems in English, not least for the way it stands apart from any circumstantial excuse regarding the reasons for war. Hardy's tableaux are picked for their remoteness from the fighting: "Only a man harrowing clods / In a slow silent walk," "Only thin smoke without flame / From the heaps of couch-grass," and, to close the meditation:

> Yonder a maid and her wight
> Come whispering by:
> War's annals will cloud into night
> Ere their story die.

The greatest of Hardy's achievements in the eyes of later commentators, and perhaps of Hardy himself, are the *Poems of 1912–13*. This sequence of twenty-one elegies was written for, and about, Emma Hardy, reflecting on a marriage that had lapsed almost insensibly into estrangement. One of the uncanny resonances of the poems is that they seem to refer to a woman far off or long removed from sight. *We were together for years and loved each other, somehow we parted ways, and suddenly you have died*—such is likely to be a reader's initial impression. The truth is that at the time of her death, they were living in the same house but almost separately. "At the Word 'Farewell,'" a poem about Emma that Hardy placed outside the 1912–13 group, sketches what one might call his theory of the accidental moment. In a doorway once, they almost parted forever, and "Even then the scale might have been turned / Against love by a feather." Just a turn of the scale, one way or the other, would join or hold them back. Their union, he came to think, happened by a chance that scarcely knew its name. Yet there is magic in such accidents. "I have no right to disturb you so," says the protagonist of *A Laodician*, Paula Power, to her supplicant George Somerset, after he admits that time away from her has made him miserable. "But I have given you some pleasure," she adds, "have I not? A little more pleasure than pain, perhaps?"—and with those words the scale is turned. Hardy wrote more than a dozen poems on this theory of the accidental moment. Closely related are his many poems about women just glimpsed or fleetingly embraced, or else thought about for an age after a chance encounter, or consciously befriended with a feeling deeper than friendship.

The *Poems of 1912–13*, however, belong to a different category of intensity and depth. Their internal echoes are purposeful; the poems, in fact, add up to a kind of musical "theme and variations"—or rather, we hear a theme that comes to be known only through its variations. "When I Set Out for Lyonnesse" (again, a poem dealing with the same events though nominally distinct from the group) was Hardy's favorite among all his "chiefly lyrical" poems. New readers may prefer "The Going" or "I Found Her Out There." But through the entire sequence, one notices a marked difference between his reliance on memory and that of his exemplar Wordsworth. Memory, for Wordsworth, is stored up as a blessing, a reserve against ignorance or loss, which identifies the poet with his indelible experience. By contrast, Hardy portrays memory as a compulsion, a not always welcome mediator of experience, a burden at times and even an encumbrance. A journal note he made in 1866 betrays the peculiarity of this blend of emotions. On a visit to the town of Hatfield, he finds it "changed since my early visit" and "I regretted," he explains, "that the beautiful sunset did not occur in a place of no reminiscences, that I might have enjoyed it without their tinge." He does not imply that the memories were unhappy, only that his joy would have been purer without them. Hardy was unusual in soliciting inspiration from a power of mind about which he was guarded to the point of aversion.

"When I Set Out for Lyonnesse" affords the unofficial entry to the sequence. It is an exhilarated elegy without a trace of mourning, simple in structure and unadorned, and it glories in the fact that the time it speaks of ever was. Maybe it is truer to say that the person and the time have fused for Hardy in a single thought:

> When I set out for Lyonnesse
> A hundred miles away,
> The rime was on the spray,
> And starlight lit my lonesomeness.

On his return to London, everyone saw that he had changed forever:

> When I came back from Lyonnesse
> With magic in my eyes,
> All marked with mute surmise
> My radiance rare and fathomless.

The difference between his feelings then and now is an insoluble perplexity. It makes Hardy's memory as "fathomless" as he must have seemed to those who witnessed his transformation those many years ago.

"Where the Picnic Was" remembers a gathering of Hardy and three friends; but he stands alone now, seeing the "burnt circle" of the fire they made, with "stick-ends, charred." He is himself like those remnants, "Last relic of the band / Who came that day." A cold wind stops him, and he is baffled at his survival where others have vanished:

> Yes, I am here
> Just as last year,
> And the sea breathes brine
> From its strange straight line.

One of them, Emma, is dead now and two others "have wandered far / From this grassy rise / Into urban roar / Where no picnics are." The final note, here, is of his lost love—it was her eyes sharing these sights that sanctified the memory. The place where the friends met, and the brine from the sea below, recall to his mind the enchantment and the finiteness of the moment.

Romantic love for Hardy was a myth that could override the ordinary motives and deeds of a life. His personal myth held that he had stolen Emma from nature; and in that light, the memorials of 1912–13 were his return of nature's gift. "I found her out there," he says about the Cornwall coast, and "I brought her here," to Dorchester. It was the magic of his storytelling that lured her: she would listen to his tales "As a wind-tugged tress / Flapped her cheek like a flail." He speaks (as if he were Prospero and she were Ariel) of having freed but also trapped her, far from "her loamy cell / By the waves long heard / And loved so well." Her consolation, in the delicate close of the poem, is that her spirit may now pass to the ocean by a hidden stream:

> Yet her shade, maybe,
> Will creep underground
> Till it catch the sound
> Of that western sea
> As it swells and sobs
> Where she once domiciled,
> And joy in its throbs
> With the heart of a child.

Having domesticated her spirit and compelled it to live in a world far from romance, the poet imagines Emma restored at her death to the freedom of her ocean home.

In "The Voice," he is more urgently haunted by her spirit, troubled at once by its beckoning and the memories it may summon:

> Woman much missed, how you call to me, call to me,
> Saying that now you are not as you were
> When you had changed from the one who was all to me,
> But as at first, when our day was fair.

He struggles to interpret her message, and is the more grieved to think that her ghost may be only his fancy, an illusion conjured from the sound of the wind, a projection of his love and his remorse:

> Thus I; faltering forward,
> Leaves around me falling,
> Wind oozing thin through the thorn from norward,
> And the woman calling.

"The Voice" is among the most subtly musical poems in English, not least in the pulling-up-short of this ending: a finer imaginative effect than any calculated crescendo or dying fall.

Recurrent in Hardy's elegies is the idea that inanimate things *remember us*. And it is true that our memories are mingled with an awareness of non-human things—a selection we make of them, which is both arbitrary and final. Hardy was strangely comforted by this thought, as he remarks in a journal entry of 1876: "I sometimes look upon all things in inanimate Nature as pensive mutes." The sentiment may recall Wordsworth's fascination with "mute insensate things"; but for Hardy the things aspire to humanity, and they take an added luster by being mixed with human cares. He said this plainly in "Old Furniture":

> I see the hands of the generations
>   That owned each shiny familiar thing
> In play on its knobs and indentations,
>   And with its ancient fashioning
>   Still dallying.

The same thought makes its way into several of the *Poems of 1912–13*, as in "At Castle Boterel":

> What we did as we climbed, and what we talked of
>   Matters not much, nor to what it led,—
> Something that life will not be balked of
>   Without rude reason till hope is dead,
>   And feeling fled.
>
> It filled but a minute. But was there ever
>   A time of such quality, since or before,
> In that hill's story? To one mind never,
>   Though it has been climbed, foot-swift, foot-sore,
>   By thousands more.
>
> Primaeval rocks form the road's steep border,
>   And much have they faced there, first and last,
> Of the transitory in Earth's long order;
>   But what they record in colour and cast
>   Is—that we two passed.

The present *Selected Poems* reprints approximately one-third of Hardy's *Collected Poems*. It includes the complete text of *Chosen Poems of Thomas Hardy*—the last of several personal selections made by the poet himself—along with my choice of additional poems. The principles guiding the result are partly explained by Hardy's evident inclinations in picking his *Chosen Poems* and partly by a necessary economy in adding to that volume. Hardy seems to have felt that readers would want to see a healthy preponderance of short poems. Why? They have a handsome look, nicely filling a page in the pocket-size format his *Chosen Poems* has sometimes been given. My own rule was to avoid redundancy. Accordingly, I have tried to omit poems that follow a design or argument that Hardy used elsewhere to better effect. He wrote "The Haunter" many times, for example, though the other versions do not always refer to Emma Gifford or for that matter to Hardy himself.

A pervasive tendency of his judgment in anthologizing himself becomes apparent when you read his *Collected Poems*. Hardy, I think, was concerned in *Chosen Poems* to present himself as a romantic; a lyric poet;

a Shelleyan, if one must give it a name. His inclusion of the poem on Shelley's skylark makes that point, as does the poem on the death of Swinburne and "Rome: At the Pyramid of Cestius near the Graves of Shelley and Keats" (with its memory of "Ozymandias"). He omitted "The Last Signal," his wonderful elegy on the death of William Barnes, a more individual poem than either of the above. Judged against the background of his *Collected Poems*, a somewhat misleading impression also comes from his decision to place only lyrics and songs in the first half of *Chosen Poems*.

Hardy was certainly influenced by a desire to include poems that he knew many people had liked: a legitimate consideration for an author making the selection for readers of his time. My additions to the *Chosen Poems* must answer to readers who have had almost a century to sift the possibilities. I suspect that Hardy felt duty-bound to exhibit conventional forms and subjects, even if they had not always prompted his best writing. He reprinted a fair number of sonnets and occasional poems, especially poems about war, somber and evocative statements-in-verse that often lack a strong personal motive. One thinks well of Hardy after reading them; and compared to dutiful national prophets like Hugo and Tolstoy, he must have felt himself a free man. He resembled those titans in the length of his life and the ever-increasing proportions of his fame, but he carried the torch for no idealism that can be compared to the Republican zeal of Hugo or the Christian radicalism of Tolstoy. Hardy saw himself as a representative member of his society, and at the same time a dignified skeptic and outsider. He had no revolutionary pretensions and it was impossible that a cult should gather around him. Even so, he was a public figure, and this sense of obligation exacted a toll as obvious as its rewards.

The self-doubting hero of *Desperate Remedies*, Edward Springrove, confesses early in his flirtation with the heroine Cytherea Graye that "poetical days are getting past with me, according to the usual rule"; to which she responds, "Then the difference between a common man and a recognized poet is, that one has been deluded, and cured of his delusion, and the other continues deluded all his days." Hardy, in this sense, was never free of delusion, never undeceived—and so much the better for his poetry. Never was there a poet whose loves were so plainly patterned and yet so inscrutable to himself; never a person in the world of whom it could be said less truly that he "abjured love." His steady voice of feeling would have been remarkable at any time; but if he had not existed, no one could have predicted the survival of this author whose work spans six decades from the prime of Dickens, Thackeray, and George Eliot to the maturity of Yeats, Woolf, and T. S. Eliot. Yet at no time was it possible for Hardy's contemporaries to regard him chiefly as a link to the past. He was the peer of the artists of three generations: a fact memorialized by the touching tribute he received on his eighty-first birthday from "your younger comrades in the craft of letters. . . . You have inspired us both by your work and by the manner in which it was done." They had in mind his dedication, his persistence, his detachment from any orthodoxy or coterie, and perhaps above all (in an age of public moralists and holders-forth) his privacy. "The business of the poet and novelist," he observed in his journal after finishing *The Mayor of Casterbridge*, "is to show the sorriness underlying the grandest things, and the grandeur underlying the sorriest things." No other English writer has aimed for quite this complex effect, but it is the sort of recognition that great art may be known by, and Hardy, in his poems as well as his fiction, will be found to have accomplished his intent.

Note on the Text

The text of *Chosen Poems* is taken from the Macmillan edition of 1929. Additional poems are from the fourth edition of Hardy's *Collected Poems* (Macmillan, 1930). All the *Poems of 1912–13* are reprinted here, each of them once: those that Hardy omitted from *Chosen Poems* appear below among the Additional Poems, and their original order is shown in Appendix B. Where Hardy altered the title of a selection for *Chosen Poems*, its original title is given in brackets. The endnotes gloss unusual words or out-of-the-way references that may raise a question in the reader's mind in the course of a given poem. They eschew interpretation and the back-loading of historical or biographical data that are easily available elsewhere. All notes accompanying poems in the body of the text are Hardy's own.

SELECTED POEMS

Chosen Poems of Thomas Hardy

PART I

Poems Chiefly Lyrical

AFTER THE VISIT
(To F. E. D.)

Come again to the place
Where your presence was as a leaf that skims
Down a drouthy way whose ascent bedims
    The bloom on the farer's face.

Come again, with the feet
That were light on the green as a thistledown ball,
And those mute ministrations to one and to all
    Beyond a man's saying sweet.

Until then the faint scent
Of the bordering flowers swam unheeded away,
And I marked not the charm in the changes of day
    As the cloud-colours came and went.

Through the dark corridors
Your walk was so soundless I did not know
Your form from a phantom's of long ago
    Said to pass on the ancient floors,

Till you drew from the shade,
And I saw the large luminous living eyes
Regard me in fixed inquiring-wise
    As those of a soul that weighed,

Scarce consciously,
The eternal question of what Life was,
And why we were there, and by whose strange laws
    That which mattered most could not be.

TO MEET, OR OTHERWISE

Whether to sally and see thee, girl of my dreams,
    Or whether to stay
And see thee not! How vast the difference seems
    Of Yea from Nay
Just now. Yet this same sun will slant its beams
    At no far day
On our two mounds, and then what will the difference weigh!

Yet I will see thee, maiden dear, and make
    The most I can
Of what remains to us amid this brake
    Cimmerian
Through which we grope, and from whose thorns we ache,
    While still we scan
Round our frail faltering progress for some path or plan.

By briefest meeting something sure is won;
    It will have been:
Nor God nor Demon can undo the done,
    Unsight the seen,
Make muted music be as unbegun,
    Though things terrene
Groan in their bondage till oblivion supervene.

So, to the one long-sweeping symphony
    From times remote
Till now, of human tenderness, shall we
    Supply one note,
Small and untraced, yet that will ever be
    Somewhere afloat
Amid the spheres, as part of sick Life's antidote.

THE DIFFERENCE

I

Sinking down by the gate I discern the thin moon,
And a blackbird tries over old airs in the pine,
But the moon is a sorry one, sad the bird's tune,
For this spot is unknown to that Heartmate of mine.

II

Did my Heartmate but haunt here at times such as now,
The song would be joyous and cheerful the moon;
But she will see never this gate, path, or bough,
Nor I find a joy in the scene or the tune.

ON THE DEPARTURE PLATFORM

We kissed at the barrier; and passing through
She left me, and moment by moment got
Smaller and smaller, until to my view
    She was but a spot;

A wee white spot of muslin fluff
That down the diminishing platform bore
Through hustling crowds of gentle and rough
    To the carriage door.

Under the lamplight's fitful glowers,
Behind dark groups from far and near,
Whose interests were apart from ours,
    She would disappear,

Then show again, till I ceased to see
That flexible form, that nebulous white;
And she who was more than my life to me
    Had vanished quite. . . .

We have penned new plans since that fair fond day,
And in season she will appear again—
Perhaps in the same soft white array—
    But never as then!

—"And why, young man, must eternally fly
A joy you'll repeat, if you love her well?"
—O friend, nought happens twice thus; why,
    I cannot tell!

IN A CATHEDRAL CITY

These people have not heard your name;
No loungers in this placid place
Have helped to bruit your beauty's fame.

The grey Cathedral, towards whose face
Bend eyes untold, has met not yours;
Your shade has never swept its base,

Your form has never darked its doors,
Nor have your faultless feet once thrown
A pensive pit-pat on its floors.

Along the street to maids well known
Blithe lovers hum their tender airs,
But in your praise voice not a tone. . . .

—Since nought bespeaks you here, or bears,
As I, your imprint through and through,
Here might I rest, till my heart shares
The spot's unconsciousness of you!

Salisbury.

"I SAY I'LL SEEK HER"

I say, "I'll seek her side
    Ere hindrance interposes";
    But eve in midnight closes,
And here I still abide.

When darkness wears I see
    Her sad eyes in a vision;
    They ask, "What indecision
Detains you, Love, from me?—

"The creaking hinge is oiled,
    I have unbarred the backway,
    But you tread not the trackway;
And shall the thing be spoiled?

"Far cockcrows echo shrill,
    The shadows are abating,
    And I am waiting, waiting;
But O, you tarry still!"

SONG OF HOPE

O sweet To-morrow!—
    After to-day
    There will away
This sense of sorrow.
Then let us borrow
Hope, for a gleaming
Soon will be streaming,
    Dimmed by no gray—
      No gray!

While the winds wing us
    Sighs from The Gone,
    Nearer to dawn
Minute-beats bring us;
When there will sing us
Larks, of a glory
Waiting our story
    Further anon—
      Anon!

Doff the black token,
    Don the red shoon,
    Right and retune
Viol-strings broken;
Null the words spoken
In speeches of rueing,
The night cloud is hueing,
    To-morrow shines soon—
      Shines soon!

BEFORE AND AFTER SUMMER

I

Looking forward to the spring
One puts up with anything.
On this February day
Though the winds leap down the street
Wintry scourgings seem but play,
And these later shafts of sleet
—Sharper pointed than the first—
And these later snows—the worst—
Are as a half-transparent blind
Riddled by rays from sun behind.

II

Shadows of the October pine
Reach into this room of mine:
On the pine there swings a bird;
He is shadowed with the tree.
Mutely perched he bills no word;
Blank as I am even is he.
For those happy suns are past,
Fore-discerned in winter last.
When went by their pleasure, then?
I, alas, perceived not when.

FIRST SIGHT OF HER AND AFTER

A day is drawing to its fall
   I had not dreamed to see;
The first of many to enthrall
   My spirit, will it be?
Or is this eve the end of all
   Such new delight for me?

I journey home: the pattern grows
   Of moonshades on the way:
"Soon the first quarter, I suppose,"
   Sky-glancing travellers say;
I realize that it, for those,
   Has been a common day.

THE SUN ON THE BOOKCASE
(*Student's Love-song:* 1870)

Once more the cauldron of the sun
Smears the bookcase with winy red,
And here my page is, and there my bed,
And the apple-tree shadows travel along.
Soon their intangible track will be run,
   And dusk grow strong
   And they have fled.

Yes: now the boiling ball is gone,
And I have wasted another day. . . .
But wasted—*wasted*, do I say?
Is it a waste to have imaged one
Beyond the hills there, who, anon,
   My great deeds done,
   Will be mine alway?

"WHEN I SET OUT FOR LYONNESSE"
(1870)

When I set out for Lyonnesse,
  A hundred miles away,
  The rime was on the spray,
And starlight lit my lonesomeness
When I set out for Lyonnesse
  A hundred miles away.

What would bechance at Lyonnesse
  While I should sojourn there
  No prophet durst declare,
Nor did the wisest wizard guess
What would bechance at Lyonnesse
  While I should sojourn there.

When I came back from Lyonnesse
  With magic in my eyes,
  All marked with mute surmise
My radiance rare and fathomless,
When I came back from Lyonnesse
  With magic in my eyes!

AT THE WORD "FAREWELL"

She looked like a bird from a cloud
    On the clammy lawn,
Moving alone, bare-browed
    In the dim of dawn.
The candles alight in the room
    For my parting meal
Made all things withoutdoors loom
    Strange, ghostly, unreal.

The hour itself was a ghost,
    And it seemed to me then
As of chances the chance furthermost
    I should see her again.
I beheld not where all was so fleet
    That a Plan of the past
Which had ruled us from birthtime to meet
    Was in working at last:

No prelude did I there perceive
    To a drama at all,
Or foreshadow what fortune might weave
    From beginnings so small;
But I rose as if quicked by a spur
    I was bound to obey,
And stepped through the casement to her
    Still alone in the gray.

"I am leaving you. . . . Farewell!" I said,
    As I followed her on
By an alley bare boughs overspread;
    "I soon must be gone!"
Even then the scale might have been turned
    Against love by a feather,
—But crimson one cheek of hers burned
    When we came in together.

DITTY

(E. L. G.)

Beneath a knap where flown
    Nestlings play,
Within walls of weathered stone,
    Far away
From the files of formal houses,
By the bough the firstling browses,
Lives a Sweet: no merchants meet,
No man barters, no man sells
    Where she dwells.

Upon that fabric fair
    "Here is she!"
Seems written everywhere
    Unto me.
But to friends and nodding neighbours,
Fellow-wights in lot and labours,
Who descry the times as I,
No such lucid legend tells
    Where she dwells.

Should I lapse to what I was
    Ere we met;
(Such will not be, but because
    Some forget
Let me feign it)—none would notice
That where she I know by rote is
Spread a strange and withering change,
Like a drying of the wells
    Where she dwells.

To feel I might have kissed—
    Loved as true—
Otherwhere, nor Mine have missed
    My life through,
Had I never wandered near her,

Is a smart severe—severer
In the thought that she is nought,
Even as I, beyond the dells
    Where she dwells.

And Devotion droops her glance
    To recall
What bond-servants of Chance
    We are all.
I but found her in that, going
On my errant path unknowing,
I did not out-skirt the spot
That no spot on earth excels,
    —Where she dwells!

1870.

THE NIGHT OF THE DANCE

The cold moon hangs to the sky by its horn,
    And centres its gaze on me;
The stars, like eyes in reverie,
Their westering as for a while forborne,
    Quiz downward curiously.

Old Robert draws the backbrand in,
    The green logs steam and spit;
The half-awakened sparrows flit
From the riddled thatch; and owls begin
    To whoo from the gable-slit.

Yes; far and nigh things seem to know
    Sweet scenes are impending here;
That all is prepared; that the hour is near
For welcomes, fellowships, and flow
    Of sally, song, and cheer;

That spigots are pulled and viols strung;
    That soon will arise the sound
Of measures trod to tunes renowned;
That She will return in Love's low tongue
    My vows as we wheel around.

TO LIZBIE BROWNE

I

Dear Lizbie Browne,
Where are you now?
In sun, in rain?—
Or is your brow
Past joy, past pain,
Dear Lizbie Browne?

II

Sweet Lizbie Browne,
How you could smile,
How you could sing!—
How archly wile
In glance-giving,
Sweet Lizbie Browne!

III

And, Lizbie Browne,
Who else had hair
Bay-red as yours,
Or flesh so fair
Bred out of doors,
Sweet Lizbie Browne?

IV

When, Lizbie Browne,
You had just begun
To be endeared
By stealth to one,
You disappeared
My Lizbie Browne!

V

Ay, Lizbie Browne,
So swift your life,
And mine so slow,
You were a wife

Ere I could show
Love, Lizbie Browne.

VI

Still, Lizbie Browne,
You won, they said,
The best of men
When you were wed. . . .
Where went you then,
O Lizbie Browne?

VII

Dear Lizbie Browne,
I should have thought,
"Girls ripen fast,"
And coaxed and caught
You ere you passed,
Dear Lizbie Browne!

VIII

But, Lizbie Browne,
I let you slip;
Shaped not a sign;
Touched never your lip
With lip of mine,
Lost Lizbie Browne!

IX

So, Lizbie Browne,
When on a day
Men speak of me
As not, you'll say,
"And who was he?"—
Yes, Lizbie Browne!

LET ME ENJOY

I

Let me enjoy the earth no less
Because the all-enacting Might
That fashioned forth its loveliness
Had other aims than my delight.

II

About my path there flits a Fair,
Who throws me not a word or sign;
I'll charm me with her ignoring air,
And laud the lips not meant for mine.

III

From manuscripts of moving song
Inspired by scenes and dreams unknown
I'll pour out raptures that belong
To others, as they were my own.

IV

And some day hence, toward Paradise
And all its blest—if such should be—
I will lift glad, afar-off eyes,
Though it contain no place for me.

THE BALLAD-SINGER

Sing, Ballad-singer, raise a hearty tune;
Make me forget that there was ever a one
I walked with in the meek light of the moon
    When the day's work was done.

Rhyme, Ballad-rhymer, start a country song;
Make me forget that she whom I loved well
Swore she would love me dearly, love me long,
    Then—what I cannot tell!

Sing, Ballad-singer, from your little book;
Make me forget those heart-breaks, achings, fears;
Make me forget her name, her sweet sweet look—
    Make me forget her tears.

THE DIVISION

Rain on the windows, creaking doors,
    With blasts that besom the green,
And I am here, and you are there,
    And a hundred miles between!

O were it but the weather, Dear,
    O were it but the miles
That summed up all our severance,
    There might be room for smiles.

But that thwart thing betwixt us twain,
    Which nothing cleaves or clears,
Is more than distance, Dear, or rain,
    And longer than the years!

1893.

YELL'HAM-WOOD'S STORY

Coomb-Firtrees say that Life is a moan,
    And Clyffe-hill Clump says "Yea!"
But Yell'ham says a thing of its own:
      It's not "Gray, gray
      Is Life alway!"
      That Yell'ham says,
    Nor that Life is for ends unknown.

It says that Life would signify
    A thwarted purposing:
That we come to live, and are called to die.
      Yes, that's the thing
      In fall, in spring,
      That Yell'ham says:—
    "Life offers—to deny!"

1902.

HER INITIALS

Upon a poet's page I wrote
Of old two letters of her name;
Part seemed she of the effulgent thought
Whence that high singer's rapture came.
—When now I turn the leaf the same
Immortal light illumes the lay,
But from the letters of her name
The radiance has waned away!

1869.

THE WOUND

I climbed to the crest,
  And, fog-festooned,
The sun lay west
  Like a crimson wound:

Like that wound of mine
  Of which none knew,
For I'd given no sign
  That it pierced me through.

HAP

If but some vengeful god would call to me
From up the sky, and laugh: "Thou suffering thing,
Know that thy sorrow is my ecstasy,
That thy love's loss is my hate's profiting!"

Then would I bear it, clench myself, and die,
Steeled by the sense of ire unmerited;
Half-eased in that a Powerfuller than I
Had willed and meted me the tears I shed.

But not so. How arrives it joy lies slain,
And why unblooms the best hope ever sown?
—Crass Casualty obstructs the sun and rain,
And dicing Time for gladness casts a moan. . . .
These purblind Doomsters had as readily strown
Blisses about my pilgrimage as pain.

1866.

A MERRYMAKING IN QUESTION

"I will get a new string for my fiddle,
    And call to the neighbours to come,
And partners shall dance down the middle
    Until the old pewter-wares hum:
    And we'll sip the mead, cyder, and rum!"

From the night came the oddest of answers:
    A hollow wind, like a bassoon,
And headstones all ranged up as dancers,
    And cypresses droning a croon,
    And gurgoyles that mouthed to the tune.

"HOW GREAT MY GRIEF"
(Triolet)

How great my grief, my joys how few,
    Since first it was my fate to know thee!
—Have the slow years not brought to view
How great my grief, my joys how few,
Nor memory shaped old times anew,
    Nor loving-kindness helped to show thee
How great my grief, my joys how few,
    Since first it was my fate to know thee?

AT AN INN

When we as strangers sought
    Their catering care,
Veiled smiles bespoke their thought
    Of what we were.
They warmed as they opined
    Us more than friends—
That we had all resigned
    For love's dear ends.

And that swift sympathy
    With living love
Which quicks the world—maybe
    The spheres above,
Made them our ministers,
    Moved them to say,
"Ah, God, that bliss like theirs
    Would flush our day!"

And we were left alone
    As Love's own pair;
Yet never the love-light shone
    Between us there!
But that which chilled the breath
    Of afternoon,
And palsied unto death
    The pane-fly's tune.

The kiss their zeal foretold,
    And now deemed come,
Came not: within his hold
    Love lingered numb.
Why cast he on our port
    A bloom not ours?
Why shaped us for his sport
    In after-hours?

As we seemed we were not
That day afar,
And now we seem not what
We aching are.
O severing sea and land,
O laws of men,
Ere death, once let us stand
As we stood then!

A BROKEN APPOINTMENT

You did not come,
And marching Time drew on, and wore me numb.—
Yet less for loss of your dear presence there
Than that I thus found lacking in your make
That high compassion which can overbear
Reluctance for pure lovingkindness' sake
Grieved I, when, as the hope-hour stroked its sum,
You did not come.

You love not me,
And love alone can lend you loyalty;
—I know and knew it. But, unto the store
Of human deeds divine in all but name,
Was it not worth a little hour or more
To add yet this: Once you, a woman, came
To soothe a time-torn man; even though it be
You love not me?

THOUGHTS OF PHENA

AT NEWS OF HER DEATH

Not a line of her writing have I,
 Not a thread of her hair,
No mark of her late time as dame in her dwelling, whereby
 I may picture her there;
 And in vain do I urge my unsight
 To conceive my lost prize
At her close, whom I knew when her dreams were upbrimming with light,
 And with laughter her eyes.

What scenes spread around her last days,
 Sad, shining, or dim?
Did her gifts and compassions enray and enarch her sweet ways
 With an aureate nimb?
 Or did life-light decline from her years,
 And mischances control
Her full day-star; unease, or regret, or forebodings, or fears
 Disennoble her soul?

Thus I do but the phantom retain
 Of the maiden of yore
As my relic; yet haply the best of her—fined in my brain
 It may be the more
 That no line of her writing have I,
 Nor a thread of her hair,
No mark of her late time as dame in her dwelling, whereby
 I may picture her there.

March 1890.

IN A EWELEAZE NEAR WEATHERBURY

The years have gathered grayly
   Since I danced upon this leaze
With one who kindled gaily
   Love's fitful ecstasies!
But despite the term as teacher,
   I remain what I was then
In each essential feature
   Of the fantasies of men.

Yet I note the little chisel
   Of never-napping Time
Defacing wan and grizzel
   The blazon of my prime.
When at night he thinks me sleeping
   I feel him boring sly
Within my bones, and heaping
   Quaintest pains for by-and-by.

Still, I'd go the world with Beauty,
   I would laugh with her and sing,
I would shun divinest duty
   To resume her worshipping.
But she'd scorn my brave endeavour,
   She would not balm the breeze
By murmuring "Thine for ever!"
   As she did upon this leaze.

1890.

A SPOT

In years defaced and lost,
Two sat here, transport-tossed,
Lit by a living love
The wilted world knew nothing of:
　　Scared momently
　　By gaingivings,
　　Then hoping things
　　That could not be. . . .

Of love and us no trace
Abides upon the place;
The sun and shadows wheel,
Season and season sereward steal;
　　Foul days and fair
　　Here, too, prevail,
　　And gust and gale
　　As everywhere.

But lonely shepherd souls
Who bask amid these knolls
May catch a faery sound
On sleepy noontides from the ground:
　　"O not again
　　Till Earth outwears
　　Shall love like theirs
　　Suffuse this glen!"

THE DARKLING THRUSH

I leant upon a coppice gate
    When Frost was spectre-gray,
And Winter's dregs made desolate
    The weakening eye of day.
The tangled bine-stems scored the sky
    Like strings of broken lyres,
And all mankind that haunted nigh
    Had sought their household fires.

The land's sharp features seemed to be
    The Century's corpse outleant,
His crypt the cloudy canopy,
    The wind his death-lament.
The ancient pulse of germ and birth
    Was shrunken hard and dry,
And every spirit upon earth
    Seemed fervourless as I.

At once a voice arose among
    The bleak twigs overhead
In a full-hearted evensong
    Of joy illimited;
An aged thrush, frail, gaunt, and small,
    In blast-beruffled plume,
Had chosen thus to fling his soul
    Upon the growing gloom.

So little cause for carolings
    Of such ecstatic sound
Was written on terrestrial things
    Afar or nigh around,
That I could think there trembled through
    His happy good-night air
Some blessed Hope, whereof he knew
    And I was unaware.

31st December 1900.

THE TEMPORARY THE ALL
(Sapphics)

Change and chancefulness in my flowering youthtime
Set me sun by sun near to one unchosen;
Wrought us fellowlike, and despite divergence,
      Fused us in friendship.

"Cherish him can I while the true one forthcome—
Come the rich fulfiller of my prevision;
Life is roomy yet, and the odds unbounded."
      So self-communed I.

'Thwart my wistful way did a damsel saunter,
Fair, albeit unformed to be all-eclipsing;
"Maiden meet," held I, "till arise my forefelt
      Wonder of women."

Long a visioned hermitage deep desiring,
Tenements uncouth I was fain to house in:
"Let such lodging be for a breath-while," thought I,
      "Soon a more seemly.

"Then high handiwork will I make my life-deed,
Truth and Light outshow; but the ripe time pending,
Intermissive aim at the thing sufficeth."
      Thus I. . . . But lo, me!

Mistress, friend, place, aims to be bettered straightway,
Bettered not has Fate or my hand's achievement;
Sole the showance those of my onward earth-track—
      Never transcended!

THE GHOST OF THE PAST

We two kept house, the Past and I,
    The Past and I;
Through all my tasks it hovered nigh,
    Leaving me never alone.
It was a spectral housekeeping
    Where fell no jarring tone,
As strange, as still a housekeeping
    As ever has been known.

As daily I went up the stair
    And down the stair,
I did not mind the Bygone there—
    The Present once to me;
Its moving meek companionship
    I wished might ever be,
There was in that companionship
    Something of ecstasy.

It dwelt with me just as it was,
    Just as it was
When first its prospects gave me pause
    In wayward wanderings,
Before the years had torn old troths
    As they tear all sweet things,
Before gaunt griefs had torn old troths
    And dulled old rapturings.

And then its form began to fade,
    Began to fade,
Its gentle echoes faintlier played
    At eves upon my ear
Than when the autumn's look embrowned
    The lonely chambers here,
When autumn's settling shades embrowned
    Nooks that it haunted near.

And so with time my vision less,
    Yea, less and less
Makes of that Past my housemistress,
    It dwindles in my eye;
It looms a far-off skeleton
    And not a comrade nigh,
A fitful far-off skeleton
    Dimming as days draw by.

THE SELF-UNSEEING

Here is the ancient floor,
Footworn and hollowed and thin,
Here was the former door
Where the dead feet walked in.

She sat here in her chair,
Smiling into the fire;
He who played stood there,
Bowing it higher and higher.

Childlike, I danced in a dream;
Blessings emblazoned that day;
Everything glowed with a gleam;
Yet we were looking away!

TO LIFE

O Life with the sad seared face,
  I weary of seeing thee,
And thy draggled cloak, and thy hobbling pace,
  And thy too-forced pleasantry!

I know what thou would'st tell
  Of Death, Time, Destiny—
I have known it long, and know, too, well
  What it all means for me.

But canst thou not array
  Thyself in rare disguise,
And feign like truth, for one mad day,
  That Earth is Paradise?

I'll tune me to the mood,
  And mumm with thee till eve
And maybe what as interlude
  I feign, I shall believe!

UNKNOWING

When, soul in soul reflected,
We breathed an æthered air,
    When we neglected
    All things elsewhere,
And left the friendly friendless
To keep our love aglow,
    We deemed it endless . . .
    —We did not know!

When panting passion-goaded,
We planned to hie away,
    But, unforeboded,
    All the long day
The storm so pierced and pattered
That none could up and go,
    Our lives seemed shattered . . .
    —We did not know!

When I found you helpless lying,
And you waived my long misprise,
    And swore me, dying,
    In phantom-guise
To wing to me when grieving,
And touch away my woe,
    We kissed, believing . . .
    —We did not know!

But though, your powers outreckoning,
You tarry dead and dumb,
    Or scorn my beckoning,
    And will not come:
And I say, "Why thus inanely
Brood on her memory so!"
    I say it vainly—
    I feel and know!

SHE AT HIS FUNERAL

They bear him to his resting-place—
In slow procession sweeping by;
I follow at a stranger's space;
His kindred they, his sweetheart I.
Unchanged my gown of garish dye,
Though sable-sad is their attire;
But they stand round with griefless eye,
Whilst my regret consumes like fire!

187–.

THE FIDDLER

The fiddler knows what's brewing
    To the lilt of his lyric wiles:
The fiddler knows what rueing
    Will come of this night's smiles!

He sees couples join them for dancing,
    And afterwards joining for life,
He sees them pay high for their prancing
    By a welter of wedded strife.

He twangs: "Music hails from the devil,
    Though vaunted to come from heaven
For it makes people do at a revel
    What multiplies sins by seven.

"There's many a heart now mangled,
    And waiting its time to go,
Whose tendrils were first entangled
    By my sweet viol and bow!"

LOST LOVE

I play my sweet old airs—
    The airs he knew
    When our love was true—
    But he does not balk
    His determined walk,
And passes up the stairs.

I sing my songs once more,
    And presently hear
    His footstep near
    As if it would stay;
    But he goes his way,
And shuts a distant door.

So I wait for another morn,
    And another night
    In this soul-sick blight;
    And I wonder much
    As I sit, why such
A woman as I was born!

THE GOING

Why did you give no hint that night
That quickly after the morrow's dawn,
And calmly, as if indifferent quite,
You would close your term here, up and be gone
         Where I could not follow
         With wing of swallow
To gain one glimpse of you ever anon!

         Never to bid good-bye,
         Or lip me the softest call,
Or utter a wish for a word, while I
Saw morning harden upon the wall,
         Unmoved, unknowing
         That your great going
Had place that moment, and altered all.

Why do you make me leave the house
And think for a breath it is you I see
At the end of the alley of bending boughs
Where so often at dusk you used to be;
         Till in darkening dankness
         The yawning blankness
Of the perspective sickens me!

         You were she who abode
         By those red-veined rocks far West,
You were the swan-necked one who rode
Along the beetling Beeny Crest,
         And, reining nigh me,
         Would muse and eye me,
While Life unrolled us its very best.

Why, then, latterly did we not speak,
Did we not think of those days long dead,
And ere your vanishing strive to seek

PART I. POEMS CHIEFLY LYRICAL

That time's renewal? We might have said,
     "In this bright spring weather
     We'll visit together
Those places that once we visited."

     Well, well! All's past amend,
     Unchangeable. It must go.
I seem but a dead man held on end
To sink down soon. . . . O you could not know
     That such swift fleeing
     No soul foreseeing—
Not even I—would undo me so!

        December 1912.

"I FOUND HER OUT THERE"

I found her out there
On a slope few see,
That falls westwardly
To the salt-edged air,
Where the ocean breaks
On the purple strand,
And the hurricane shakes
The solid land.

I brought her here,
And have laid her to rest
In a noiseless nest
No sea beats near.
She will never be stirred
In her loamy cell
By the waves long heard
And loved so well.

So she does not sleep
By those haunted heights
The Atlantic smites
And the blind gales sweep,
Whence she often would gaze
At Dundagel's famed head,
While the dipping blaze
Dyed her face fire-red;

And would sigh at the tale
Of sunk Lyonnesse,
As a wind-tugged tress
Flapped her cheek like a flail;
Or listen at whiles
With a thought-bound brow
To the murmuring miles
She is far from now.

Yet her shade, maybe,
Will creep underground
Till it catch the sound
Of that western sea
As it swells and sobs
Where she once domiciled,
And joy in its throbs
With the heart of a child.

THE VOICE

Woman much missed, how you call to me, call to me,
Saying that now you are not as you were
When you had changed from the one who was all to me,
But as at first, when our day was fair.

Can it be you that I hear? Let me view you, then,
Standing as when I drew near to the town
Where you would wait for me: yes, as I knew you then,
Even to the original air-blue gown!

Or is it only the breeze, in its listlessness
Travelling across the wet mead to me here,
You being ever dissolved to wan wistlessness,
Heard no more again far or near?

Thus I; faltering forward,
Leaves around me falling,
Wind oozing thin through the thorn from norward,
And the woman calling.

December 1912.

AFTER A JOURNEY

Hereto I come to view a voiceless ghost;
   Whither, O whither will its whim now draw me?
Up the cliff, down, till I'm lonely, lost,
   And the unseen waters' ejaculations awe me.
Where you will next be there's no knowing,
   Facing round about me everywhere,
      With your nut-coloured hair,
And gray eyes, and rose-flush coming and going.

Yes: I have re-entered your olden haunts at last;
   Through the years, through the dead scenes I have tracked you;
What have you now found to say of our past—
   Scanned across the dark space wherein I have lacked you?
Summer gave us sweets, but autumn wrought division?
   Things were not lastly as firstly well
      With us twain, you tell?
But all's closed now, despite Time's derision.

I see what you are doing: you are leading me on
   To the spots we knew when we haunted here together,
The waterfall, above which the mist-bow shone
   At the then fair hour in the then fair weather,
And the cave just under, with a voice still so hollow
   That it seems to call out to me from forty years ago,
      When you were all aglow,
And not the thin ghost that I now frailly follow!

Ignorant of what there is flitting here to see,
   The waked birds preen and the seals flop lazily,
Soon you will have, Dear, to vanish from me,
   For the stars close their shutters and the dawn whitens hazily.
Trust me, I mind not, though Life lours,
   The bringing me here; nay, bring me here again!
      I am just the same as when
Our days were a joy, and our paths through flowers.

                Pentargan Bay.

BEENY CLIFF
March 1870–March 1913

I

O the opal and the sapphire of that wandering western sea,
And the woman riding high above with bright hair flapping free—
The woman whom I loved so, and who loyally loved me.

II

The pale mews plained below us, and the waves seemed far away
In a nether sky, engrossed in saying their ceaseless babbling say,
As we laughed light-heartedly aloft on that clear-sunned March day.

III

A little cloud then cloaked us, and there flew an irised rain,
And the Atlantic dyed its levels with a dull misfeatured stain,
And then the sun burst out again, and purples prinked the main.

IV

—Still in all its chasmal beauty bulks old Beeny to the sky,
And shall she and I not go there once again now March is nigh,
And the sweet things said in that March say anew there by and by?

V

What if still in chasmal beauty looms that wild weird western shore,
The woman now is—elsewhere—whom the ambling pony bore,
And nor knows nor cares for Beeny, and will laugh there nevermore.

AT CASTLE BOTEREL

As I drive to the junction of lane and highway.
  And the drizzle bedrenches the waggonette,
I look behind at the fading byway,
  And see on its slope, now glistening wet,
    Distinctly yet

Myself and a girlish form benighted
  In dry March weather. We climb the road
Beside a chaise. We had just alighted
  To ease the sturdy pony's load
    When he sighed and slowed.

What we did as we climbed, and what we talked of
  Matters not much, nor to what it led,—
Something that life will not be balked of
  Without rude reason till hope is dead,
    And feeling fled.

It filled but a minute. But was there ever
  A time of such quality, since or before,
In that hill's story? To one mind never,
  Though it has been climbed, foot-swift, foot-sore,
    By thousands more.

Primaeval rocks form the road's steep border,
  And much have they faced there, first and last,
Of the transitory in Earth's long order;
  But what they record in colour and cast
    Is—that we two passed.

And to me, though Time's unflinching rigour,
   In mindless rote, has ruled from sight
The substance now, one phantom figure
    Remains on the slope, as when that night
      Saw us alight.

I look and see it there, shrinking, shrinking,
   I look back at it amid the rain
For the very last time; for my sand is sinking,
    And I shall traverse old love's domain
      Never again.

March 1913.

THE PHANTOM HORSEWOMAN

I

Queer are the ways of a man I know:
>> He comes and stands
>> In a careworn craze,
>> And looks at the sands
>> And the seaward haze
>> With moveless hands
>> And face and gaze,
>> Then turns to go . . .
And what does he see when he gazes so?

II

They say he sees as an instant thing
>> More clear than to-day,
>> A sweet soft scene
>> That was once in play
>> By that briny green;
>> Yes, notes alway
>> Warm, real, and keen,
>> What his back years bring—
A phantom of his own figuring.

III

Of this vision of his they might say more:
>> Not only there
>> Does he see this sight,
>> But everywhere
>> In his brain—day, night,
>> As if on the air
>> It were drawn rose-bright—
>> Yea, far from that shore
Does he carry this vision of heretofore:

IV

A ghost-girl-rider. And though, toil-tried
    He withers daily,
    Time touches her not,
    But she still rides gaily
    In his rapt thought
    On that shagged and shaly
    Atlantic spot,
    And as when first eyed
Draws rein and sings to the swing of the tide.

1913.

WHERE THE PICNIC WAS

Where we made the fire
In the summer time
Of branch and briar
On the hill to the sea.
I slowly climb
Through winter mire,
And scan and trace
The forsaken place
Quite readily.

Now a cold wind blows,
And the grass is gray,
But the spot still shows
As a burnt circle—aye,
And stick-ends, charred,
Still strew the sward
Whereon I stand,
Last relic of the band
Who came that day!

Yes, I am here
Just as last year,
And the sea breathes brine
From its strange straight line
Up hither, the same
As when we four came.
—But two have wandered far
From this grassy rise
Into urban roar
Where no picnics are,
And one—has shut her eyes
For evermore.

ON A MIDSUMMER EVE

I idly cut a parsley stalk,
And blew therein towards the moon;
I had not thought what ghosts would walk
With shivering footsteps to my tune.

I went, and knelt, and scooped my hand
As if to drink, into the brook,
And a faint figure seemed to stand
Above me, with the bygone look.

I lipped rough rhymes of chance, not choice,
I thought not what my words might be;
There came into my ear a voice
That turned a tenderer verse for me.

"MY SPIRIT WILL NOT HAUNT THE MOUND"

My spirit will not haunt the mound
      Above my breast,
But travel, memory-possessed,
To where my tremulous being found
      Life largest, best.

My phantom-footed shape will go
      When nightfall grays
Hither and thither along the ways
I and another used to know
      In backward days.

And there you'll find me, if a jot
      You still should care
For me, and for my curious air;
If otherwise, then I shall not,
      For you, be there.

THE HOUSE OF HOSPITALITIES

Here we broached the Christmas barrel,
   Pushed up the charred log-ends;
Here we sang the Christmas carol,
     And called in friends.

Time has tired me since we met here
   When the folk now dead were young,
Since the viands were outset here
     And quaint songs sung.

And the worm has bored the viol
   That used to lead the tune,
Rust eaten out the dial
     That struck night's noon.

Now no Christmas brings in neighbours,
   And the New Year comes unlit;
Where we sang the mole now labours,
     And spiders knit.

Yet at midnight if here walking,
   When the moon sheets wall and tree,
I see forms of old time talking,
     Who smile on me.

SHUT OUT THAT MOON

Close up the casement, draw the blind,
    Shut out that stealing moon,
She wears too much the guise she wore
    Before our lutes were strewn
With years-deep dust, and names we read
    On a white stone were hewn.

Step not forth on the dew-dashed lawn
    To view the Lady's Chair,
Immense Orion's glittering form,
    The Less and Greater Bear:
Stay in; to such sights we were drawn
    When faded ones were fair.

Brush not the bough for midnight scents
    That come forth lingeringly,
And wake the same sweet sentiments
    They breathed to you and me
When living seemed a laugh, and love
    All it was said to be.

Within the common lamp-lit room
    Prison my eyes and thought;
Let dingy details crudely loom,
    Mechanic speech be wrought:
Too fragrant was Life's early bloom
    Too tart the fruit it brought!

1904.

"REGRET NOT ME"

Regret not me;
Beneath the sunny tree
I lie uncaring, slumbering peacefully

Swift as the light
I flew my faery flight;
Ecstatically I moved, and feared no night.

I did not know
That heydays fade and go,
But deemed that what was would be always so

I skipped at morn
Between the yellowing corn,
Thinking it good and glorious to be born.

I ran at eves
Among the piled-up sheaves,
Dreaming, "I grieve not, therefore nothing grieves."

Now soon will come
The apple, pear, and plum,
And hinds will sing, and autumn insects hum.

Again you will fare
To cider-makings rare,
And junketings; but I shall not be there.

Yet gaily sing
Until the pewter ring
Those songs we sang when we went gipsying.

And lightly dance
Some triple-timed romance
In coupled figures, and forget mischance;

And mourn not me
Beneath the yellowing tree;
For I shall mind not, slumbering peacefully.

IN THE MIND'S EYE

That was once her casement,
　And the taper nigh,
Shining from within there,
　Beckoned, "Here am I!"

Now, as then, I see her
　Moving at the pane;
Ah; 'tis but her phantom
　Borne within my brain!—

Foremost in my vision
　Everywhere goes she;
Change dissolves the landscapes,
　She abides with me.

Shape so sweet and shy, Dear,
　Who can say thee nay?
Never once do I, Dear,
　Wish thy ghost away.

AMABEL

I marked her ruined hues,
Her custom-straitened views,
And asked, "Can there indwell
    My Amabel?"

I looked upon her gown,
Once rose, now earthen brown;
The change was like the knell
    Of Amabel.

Her step's mechanic ways
Had lost the life of May's;
Her laugh, once sweet in swell,
    Spoilt Amabel.

I mused: "Who sings the strain
I sang ere warmth did wane?
Who thinks its numbers spell
    His Amabel?"—

Knowing that, though Love cease,
Love's race shows no decrease;
All find in dorp or dell
    An Amabel.

—I felt that I could creep
To some housetop, and weep
That Time the tyrant fell
    Ruled Amabel!

I said (the while I sighed
That love like ours had died),
"Fond things I'll no more tell
    To Amabel,

"But leave her to her fate,
And fling across the gate,
'Till the Last Trump, farewell,
    O Amabel!'"

1865.

"I SAID TO LOVE"

I said to Love,
"It is not now as in old days
When men adored thee and thy ways
    All else above;
Named thee the Boy, the Bright, the One
Who spread a heaven beneath the sun,"
    I said to Love.

I said to him,
"We now know more of thee than then;
We were but weak in judgment when,
    With hearts abrim,
We clamoured thee that thou would'st please
Inflict on us thine agonies,"
    I said to him.

I said to Love,
"Thou art not young, thou art not fair,
No elfin darts, no cherub air,
    Nor swan, nor dove
Are thine; but features pitiless,
And iron daggers of distress,"
    I said to Love.

"Depart then, Love! . . .
—Man's race shall perish, threatenest thou,
Without thy kindling coupling-vow?
    The age to come the man of now
    Know nothing of?—
We fear not such a threat from thee;
We are too old in apathy!
Mankind shall cease.—So let it be,"
    I said to Love.

REMINISCENCES OF A DANCING MAN

I

Who now remembers Almack's balls—
    Willis's sometime named—
In those two smooth-floored upper halls
    For faded ones so famed?
Where as we trod to trilling sound
The fancied phantoms stood around,
    Or joined us in the maze,
Of the powdered Dears from Georgian years.
Whose dust lay in sightless sealed-up biers,
    The fairest of former days.

II

Who now remembers gay Cremorne,
    And all its jaunty jills,
And those wild whirling figures born
    Of Jullien's grand quadrilles?
With hats on head and morning coats
There footed to his prancing notes
    Our partner-girls and we;
And the gas-jets winked, and the lustres clinked,
And the platform throbbed as with arms enlinked
    We moved to the minstrelsy.

III

Who now recalls those crowded rooms
    Of old yclept "The Argyle,"
Where to the deep Drum-polka's booms
    We hopped in standard style?
Whither have danced those damsels now!
Is Death the partner who doth moue
    Their wormy chaps and bare?
Do their spectres spin like sparks within
The smoky halls of the Prince of Sin
    To a thunderous Jullien air?

IN A WOOD

Pale beech and pine so blue,
    Set in one clay,
Bough to bough cannot you
    Live out your day?
When the rains skim and skip,
Why mar sweet comradeship,
Blighting with poison-drip
    Neighbourly spray?

Heart-halt and spirit-lame,
    City-opprest,
Unto this wood I came
    As to a nest,
Dreaming that sylvan peace
Offered the harrowed ease—
Nature a soft release
    From men's unrest.

But, having entered in,
    Great growths and small
Show them to men akin—
    Combatants all!
Sycamore shoulders oak,
Bines the slim sapling yoke,
Ivy-spun halters choke
    Elms stout and tall.

Touches from ash, O wych,
    Sting you like scorn!
You, too, brave hollies, twitch
    Sidelong from thorn.
Even the rank poplars bear
Lothly a rival's air,

Cankering in blank despair
        If overborne.

Since, then, no grace I find
        Taught me of trees,
Turn I back to my kind,
        Worthy as these.
There at least smiles abound,
There discourse trills around,
There, now and then, are found
        Life-loyalties.

1887 : 1896.

HE ABJURES LOVE

At last I put off love,
  For twice ten years
The daysman of my thought,
  And hope, and doing;
Being ashamed thereof,
  And faint of fears
And desolations, wrought
  In his pursuing,

Since first in youthtime those
  Disquietings
That heart-enslavement brings
  To hale and hoary,
Became my housefellows,
  And, fool and blind,
I turned from kith and kind
  To give him glory.

I was as children be
  Who have no care;
I did not shrink or sigh,
  I did not sicken;
But lo, Love beckoned me,
  And I was bare,
And poor, and starved, and dry,
  And fever-stricken.

Too many times ablaze
  With fatuous fires,
Enkindled by his wiles
  To new embraces,
Did I, by wilful ways
  And baseless ires,
Return the anxious smiles
  Of friendly faces.

No more will now rate I
 The common rare,
The midnight drizzle dew,
 The gray hour golden,
The wind a yearning cry.
 The faulty fair,
Things dreamt, of comelier hue
 Than things beholden! . . .

—I speak as one who plumbs
 Life's dim profound,
One who at length can sound
 Clear views and certain.
But—after love what comes?
 A scene that lours,
A few sad vacant hours,
 And then, the Curtain.

  1883.

THE DREAM-FOLLOWER

A dream of mine flew over the mead
    To the halls where my old Love reigns;
And it drew me on to follow its lead:
    And I stood at her window-panes;

And I saw but a thing of flesh and bone
    Speeding on to its cleft in the clay;
And my dream was scared, and expired on a moan,
    And I whitely hastened away.

WESSEX HEIGHTS
(1896)

There are some heights in Wessex, shaped as if by a kindly hand
For thinking, dreaming, dying on, and at crises when I stand,
Say, on Ingpen Beacon eastward, or on Wylls-Neck westwardly,
I seem where I was before my birth, and after death may be.

In the lowlands I have no comrade, not even the lone man's friend—
Her who suffereth long and is kind; accepts what he is too weak to mend:
Down there they are dubious and askance; there nobody thinks as I,
But mind-chains do not clank where one's next neighbour is the sky.

In the towns I am tracked by phantoms having weird detective ways—
Shadows of beings who fellowed with myself of earlier days:
They hang about at places, and they say harsh heavy things—
Men with a wintry sneer, and women with tart disparagings.

Down there I seem to be false to myself, my simple self that was,
And is not now, and I see him watching, wondering what crass cause
Can have merged him into such a strange continuator as this,
Who yet has something in common with himself, my chrysalis.

I cannot go to the great grey Plain; there's a figure against the moon,
Nobody sees it but I, and it makes my breast beat out of tune;
I cannot go to the tall-spired town, being barred by the forms now passed
For everybody but me, in whose long vision they stand there fast.

There's a ghost at Yell'ham Bottom chiding loud at the fall of the night,
There's a ghost in Froom-side Vale, thin-lipped and vague, in a shroud of white,
There is one in the railway-train whenever I do not want it near,
I see its profile against the pane, saying what I would not hear.

As for one rare fair woman, I am now but a thought of hers,
I enter her mind and another thought succeeds me that she prefers;
Yet my love for her in its fulness she herself even did not know;
Well, time cures hearts of tenderness, and now I can let her go.

So I am found on Ingpen Beacon, or on Wylls-Neck to the west,
Or else on homely Bulbarrow, or little Pilsdon Crest,
Where men have never cared to haunt, nor women have walked with me,
And ghosts then keep their distance; and I know some liberty.

TO A MOTHERLESS CHILD

Ah, child, thou art but half thy darling mother's:
    Hers couldst thou wholly be,
My light in thee would outglow all in others;
    She would relive to me.
But niggard Nature's trick of birth
    Bars, lest she overjoy,
Renewal of the loved on earth
    Save with alloy.

The Dame has no regard, alas, my maiden,
    For love and loss like mine—
No sympathy with mindsight memory-laden;
    Only with fickle eyne.
To her mechanic artistry
    My dreams are all unknown,
And why I wish that thou couldst be
    But One's alone!

"I NEED NOT GO"

I need not go
Through sleet and snow
To where I know
She waits for me;
She will tarry me there
Till I find it fair,
And have time to spare
From company.

When I've overgot
The world somewhat,
When things cost not
Such stress and strain,
Is soon enough
By cypress sough
To tell my Love
I am come again.

And if some day,
When none cries nay,
I still delay
To seek her side,
(Though ample measure
Of fitting leisure
Await my pleasure)
She will not chide.

What—not upbraid me
That I delayed me,
Nor ask what stayed me
So long? Ah, no!—
New cares may claim me,
New loves inflame me,
She will not blame me,
But suffer it so.

SHELLEY'S SKYLARK
(*The neighbourhood of Leghorn: March* 1887)

Somewhere afield here something lies
In Earth's oblivious eyeless trust
That moved a poet to prophecies—
A pinch of unseen, unguarded dust:

The dust of the lark that Shelley heard,
And made immortal through times to be;—
Though it only lived like another bird,
And knew not its immortality:

Lived its meek life; then, one day, fell—
A little ball of feather and bone;
And how it perished, when piped farewell,
And where it wastes, are alike unknown.

Maybe it rests in the loam I view,
Maybe it throbs in a myrtle's green,
Maybe it sleeps in the coming hue
Of a grape on the slopes of yon inland scene.

Go find it, faeries, go and find
That tiny pinch of priceless dust,
And bring a casket silver-lined,
And framed of gold that gems encrust;

And we will lay it safe therein,
And consecrate it to endless time;
For it inspired a bard to win
Ecstatic heights in thought and rhyme.

WIVES IN THE SERE

I

Never a careworn wife but shows,
    If a joy suffuse her,
Something beautiful to those
    Patient to peruse her,
Some one charm the world unknows,
    Precious to a muser,
Haply what, ere years were foes,
    Moved her mate to choose her.

II

But, be it a hint of rose
    That an instant hues her,
Or some early light or pose
    Wherewith thought renews her—
Seen by him at full, ere woes
    Practised to abuse her—
Sparely comes it, swiftly goes,
    Time again subdues her.

WEATHERS

I

This is the weather the cuckoo likes,
    And so do I;
When showers betumble the chestnut spikes,
    And nestlings fly:
And the little brown nightingale bills his best,
And they sit outside at "The Travellers' Rest,"
And maids come forth sprig-muslin drest,
And citizens dream of the south and west,
    And so do I.

II

This is the weather the shepherd shuns,
    And so do I;
When beeches drip in browns and duns,
    And thresh, and ply;
And hill-hid tides throb, throe on throe,
And meadow rivulets overflow,
And drops on gate-bars hang in a row,
And rooks in families homeward go,
    And so do I.

EPEISODIA

I

Past the hills that peep
Where the leaze is smiling,
On and on beguiling
Crisply-cropping sheep;
Under boughs of brushwood
Linking tree and tree
In a shade of lushwood,
    There caressed we!

II

Hemmed by city walls
That outshut the sunlight,
In a foggy dun light,
Where the footstep falls
With a pit-pat wearisome
In its cadency
On the flagstones drearisome
    There pressed we!

III

Where in wild-winged crowds
Blown birds show their whiteness
Up against the lightness
Of the clammy clouds;
By the random river
Pushing to the sea,
Under bents that quiver
    There shall rest we.

JOYS OF MEMORY

When the spring comes round, and a certain day
Looks out from the brume by the eastern copsetrees
    And says, Remember,
  I begin again, as if it were new,
  A day of like date I once lived through,
  Whiling it hour by hour away;
    So shall I do till my December,
      When spring comes round.

  I take my holiday then and my rest
Away from the dun life here about me,
    Old hours re-greeting
  With the quiet sense that bring they must
  Such throbs as at first, till I house with dust,
  And in the numbness my heartsome zest
    For things that were, be past repeating
      When spring comes round.

TO THE MOON

"What have you looked at, Moon,
     In your time,
  Now long past your prime?"
"O, I have looked at, often looked at
     Sweet, sublime,
Sore things, shudderful, night and noon
     In my time."

  "What have you mused on, Moon,
     In your day,
  So aloof, so far away?"
"O, I have mused on, often mused on
     Growth, decay,
Nations alive, dead, mad, aswoon,
     In my day!"

  "Have you much wondered, Moon,
     On your rounds,
  Self-wrapt, beyond Earth's bounds?"
"Yea, I have wondered, often wondered
     At the sounds
Reaching me of the human tune
     On my rounds."

  "What do you think of it, Moon,
     As you go?
  Is Life much, or no?"
"O, I think of it, often think of it
     As a show
God ought surely to shut up soon,
     As I go."

TIMING HER
(Written to an old folk-tune)

Lalage's coming:
Where is she now, O?
Turning to bow, O,
And smile, is she,
Just at parting,
Parting, parting,
As she is starting
To come to me?

Where is she now, O,
Now, and now, O,
Shadowing a bough, O,
Of hedge or tree
As she is rushing,
Rushing, rushing,
Gossamers brushing
To come to me?

Lalage's coming;
Where is she now, O;
Climbing the brow, O,
Of hills I see?
Yes, she is nearing,
Nearing, nearing,
Weather unfearing
To come to me.

Near is she now, O,
Now, and now, O;
Milk the rich cow, O,
Forward the tea;
Shake the down bed for her,
Linen sheets spread for her,
Drape round the head for her
Coming to me.

Lalage's coming,
She's nearer now, O,
End anyhow, O,
To-day's husbandry!
Would a gilt chair were mine,
Slippers of vair were mine,
Brushes for hair were mine
Of ivory!

What will she think, O,
She who's so comely,
Viewing how homely
A sort are we!
Nothing resplendent,
No prompt attendant,
Not one dependent
Pertaining to me!

Lalage's coming;
Where is she now, O?
Fain I'd avow, O,
Full honestly
Nought here's enough for her,
All is too rough for her,
Even my love for her
Poor in degree.

She's nearer now, O,
Still nearer now, O,
She 'tis, I vow, O,
Passing the lea.
Rush down to meet her there,
Call out and greet her there,
Never a sweeter there
Crossed to me!

Lalage's come; aye,
Come is she now, O! . . .
Does Heaven allow, O,

A meeting to be?
Yes, she is here now,
Here now, here now,
Nothing to fear now,
Here's Lalage!

"THE CURTAINS NOW ARE DRAWN"
(Song)

I

The curtains now are drawn,
And the spindrift strikes the glass,
Blown up the jaggèd pass
By the surly salt sou'-west,
And the sneering glare is gone
Behind the yonder crest,
    While she sings to me:
"O the dream that thou art my Love, be it thine,
And the dream that I am thy Love, be it mine,
And death may come, but loving is divine."

II

I stand here in the rain,
With its smite upon her stone,
And the grasses that have grown
Over women, children, men,
And their texts that "Life is vain";
But I hear the notes as when
    Once she sang to me:
"O the dream that thou art my Love, be it thine,
And the dream that I am thy Love, be it mine,
And death may come, but loving is divine."

1913.

76

"AS 'TWERE TO-NIGHT"
(Song)

As 'twere to-night, in the brief space
    Of a far eventime,
    My spirit rang achime
At vision of a girl of grace;
As 'twere to-night, in the brief space
    Of a far eventime.

As 'twere at noontide of to-morrow
    I airily walked and talked,
    And wondered as I walked
What it could mean, this soar from sorrow;
As 'twere at noontide of to-morrow
    I airily walked and talked.

As 'twere at waning of this week
    Broke a new life on me;
    Trancings of bliss to be
In some dim dear land soon to seek;
As 'twere at waning of this week
    Broke a new life on me!

SAYING GOOD-BYE
(Song)

We are always saying
  "Good-bye, good-bye!"
In work, in playing,
In gloom, in gaying:
    At many a stage
    Of pilgrimage
    From youth to age
    We say, "Good-bye.
      Good-bye!"

We are undiscerning
    Which go to sigh.
Which will be yearning
For soon returning;
    And which no more
    Will dark our door
    Or tread our shore
    But go to die,
      To die.

Some come from roaming
    With joy again;
Some, who come homing
By stealth at gloaming,
    Had better have stopped
    Till death, and dropped
    By strange hands propped,
    Than come so fain,
      So fain.

So, with this saying,
    "Good-bye, good-bye,"
We speed their waying

Without betraying
    Our grief, our fear
    No more to hear
    From them, close, clear,
    Again: "Good-bye,
        Good-bye!"

"ANY LITTLE OLD SONG"

Any little old song
    Will do for me,
Tell it of joys gone long,
    Or joys to be,
Or friendly faces best
    Loved to see.

Newest themes I want not
    On subtle strings,
And for thrillings pant not
    That new song brings:
I only need the homeliest
    Of heartstirrings.

LOVER TO MISTRESS
(Song)

Beckon to me to come
With handkerchief or hand,
Or finger mere or thumb;
Let forecasts be but rough,
Parents more bleak than bland,
   'Twill be enough,
     Maid mine,
   'Twill be enough!

Two fields, a wood, a tree,
Nothing now more malign
Lies between you and me;
But were they bysm, or bluff,
Or snarling sea, one sign,
   Would be enough,
     Maid mine,
   Would be enough!

From an old copy.

COME NOT; YET COME!
(Song)

In my sage moments I can say,
        Come not near,
But far in foreign regions stay,
        So that here
A mind may grow again serene and clear.

But the thought withers. Why should I
        Have fear to earn me
Fame from your nearness, though thereby
        Old fires new burn me,
And lastly, maybe, tear and overturn me!

So I say, Come: deign again shine
        Upon this place,
Even if unslackened smart be mine
        From that sweet face,
And I faint to a phantom past all trace.

"LET ME BELIEVE"
(Song)

Let me believe it, dearest,
 Let it be
As just a dream—the merest—
 Haunting me,
That a frank full-souled sweetness
 Warmed your smile
And voice, to indiscreetness
 Once, awhile!

And I will fondly ponder
 Till I lie
Earthed up with others yonder
 Past a sigh,
That you may name at stray times
 With regret
One whom through green and gray times
 You forget!

LAST LOVE-WORD
(Song)

This is the last; the very, very last!
    Anon, and all is dead and dumb,
    Only a pale shroud over the past,
        That cannot be
    Of value small or vast,
        Love, then to me!

I can say no more: I have even said too much.
    I did not mean that this should come:
    I did not know 'twould swell to such—
        Nor, perhaps, you—
    When that first look and touch,
        Love, doomed us two!

189–.

SINGING LOVERS

I rowed: the dimpled tide was at the turn,
And mirth and moonlight spread upon the bay:
There were two singing lovers in the stern;
    But mine had gone away,—
    Whither, I shunned to say!

The houses stood confronting us afar,
A livid line against the evening glare;
The small lamps livened; then out-stole a star;
    But my Love was not there,—
    Vanished, I sorrowed where!

His arm was round her, both full facing me
With no reserve. Theirs was not love to hide;
He held one tiller-rope, the other she;
    I pulled—the merest glide,—
    Looked on at them, and sighed.

The moon's glassed glory heaved as we lay swinging
Upon the undulations. Shoreward, slow,
The plash of pebbles joined the lovers' singing,
    But she of a bygone vow
    Joined in the song not now!

Weymouth.

"SOMETHING TAPPED"

Something tapped on the pane of my room
　　When there was never a trace
Of wind or rain, and I saw in the gloom
　　My weary Belovéd's face.

"O I am tired of waiting," she said,
　　"Night, morn, noon, afternoon;
So cold it is in my lonely bed,
　　And I thought you would join me soon!"

I rose and neared the window-glass,
　　But vanished thence had she:
Only a pallid moth, alas,
　　Tapped at the pane for me.

August 1913.

GREAT THINGS

Sweet cyder is a great thing,
  A great thing to me,
Spinning down to Weymouth town
  By Ridgway thirstily,
And maid and mistress summoning
  Who tend the hostelry:
O cyder is a great thing,
  A great thing to me!

The dance it is a great thing,
  A great thing to me,
With candles lit and partners fit
  For night-long revelry;
And going home when day-dawning
  Peeps pale upon the lea:
O dancing is a great thing,
  A great thing to me!

Love is, yea, a great thing,
  A great thing to me,
When, having drawn across the lawn
  In darkness silently,
A figure flits like one a-wing
  Out from the nearest tree:
O love is, yes, a great thing,
  A great thing to me!

Will these be always great things,
  Great things to me? . . .
Let it befall that One will call,
  "Soul, I have need of thee":
What then? Joy-jaunts, impassioned flings
  Love, and its ecstasy,
Will always have been great things,
  Great things to me!

THE SINGING WOMAN

There was a singing woman
    Came riding across the mead
At the time of the mild May weather,
    Tameless, tireless;
This song she sung: "I am fair, I am young!"
    And many turned to heed.

And the same singing woman
    Sat crooning in her need
At the time of the winter weather;
    Friendless, fireless,
She sang this song: "Life, thou'rt too long!"
    And there was none to heed.

THE LAST TIME

The kiss had been given and taken,
    And gathered to many past:
It never could reawaken;
    But I heard none say: "It's the last!"

The clock showed the hour and the minute
    But I did not turn and look:
I read no finis in it,
    As at closing of a book.

But I read it all too rightly
    When, at a time anon,
A figure lay stretched out whitely,
    And I stood looking thereon.

TWO LIPS

I kissed them in fancy as I came
          Away in the morning glow:
I kissed them through the glass of her picture-frame:
          She did not know.

I kissed them in love, in troth, in laughter,
          When she knew all; long so!
That I should kiss them in a shroud thereafter
          She did not know.

JUST THE SAME

I sat. It all was past;
Hope never would hail again;
Fair days had ceased at a blast,
The world was a darkened den.

The beauty and dream were gone,
And the halo in which I had hied
So gaily gallantly on
Had suffered blot and died!

I went forth, heedless whither,
In a cloud too black for name:
—People frisked, hither and thither;
The world was just the same.

THE BLINDED BIRD

So zestfully canst thou sing?
And all this indignity,
With God's consent, on thee!
Blinded ere yet a-wing
By the red-hot needle thou,
I stand and wonder how
So zestfully thou canst sing!

Resenting not such wrong,
Thy grievous pain forgot,
Eternal dark thy lot,
Groping thy whole life long,
After that stab of fire;
Enjailed in pitiless wire;
Resenting not such wrong!

Who hath charity? This bird.
Who suffereth long and is kind,
Is not provoked, though blind
And alive ensepulchred?
Who hopeth, endureth all things?
Who thinketh no evil, but sings?
Who is divine? This bird.

THE CHIMES PLAY "LIFE'S A BUMPER!"

"Awake! I'm off to cities far away,"
I said; and rose on peradventures bent.
The chimes played "Life's a Bumper!" long that day
To the measure of my walking as I went:
Their sweetness frisked and floated on the lea,
As they played out "Life's a Bumper!" there to me.

"Awake!" I said. "I go to take a bride!"
—The sun arose behind me ruby-red
As I journeyed townwards from the countryside,
The chiming bells saluting near ahead.
Their sweetness swelled in tripping tings of glee
As they played out "Life's a Bumper!" there to me.

"Again arise." I seek a turfy slope,
And go forth slowly on an autumn noon,
And there I lay her who has been my hope,
And think, "O may I follow hither soon!"
While on the wind the chimes come cheerily,
Playing out "Life's a Bumper!" there to me.

1913.

THE MONUMENT-MAKER

I chiselled her monument
    To my mind's content,
  Took it to the church by night,
  When her planet was at its height,
And set it where I had figured the place in the daytime.
    Having niched it there
I stepped back, cheered, and thought its outlines fair,
    And its marbles rare.

Then laughed she over my shoulder as in our Maytime:
    "It spells not me!" she said:
"Tells nothing about my beauty, wit, or gay time
    With all those, quick and dead,
    Of high or lowlihead,
      That hovered near,
Including you, who carve there your devotion;
    But you felt none, my dear!"

And then she vanished. Checkless sprang my emotion,
    And forced a tear
At seeing I'd not been truly known by her,
And never prized!—that my memorial here,
    To consecrate her sepulchre,
      Was scorned, almost,
      By her sweet ghost:
Yet I hoped not quite, in her very innermost!

1916.

"COULD HE BUT LIVE FOR ME"
(Iseult's Song: Queen of Cornwall)

Could he but live for me
A day, yea, even an hour,
Its petty span would be
Steeped in felicity
Passing the price of Heaven's held-dearest dower:
Could he but live, could *he*
But live for me!

Could he but come to me
Amid these murks that lour,
My hollow life would be
So brimmed with ecstasy
As heart-dry honeysuck by summer shower:
Could he but come, could he
But come to me!

"LET'S MEET AGAIN TO-NIGHT, MY FAIR"
(*Tristram's Song: Queen of Cornwall*)

Let's meet again to-night, my Fair,
    Let's meet unseen of all;
The day-god labours to his lair,
    And then the evenfall!

O living lute, O lily-rose,
    O form of fantasie,
When torches waste and warders doze
    Steal to the stars will we!

While nodding knights carouse at meat
    And shepherds shamble home,
We'll cleave in close embracements—sweet
    As honey in the comb!

Till crawls the dawn from Condol's crown,
    And over Neitan's Kieve,
As grimly ghosts we conjure down
    And hopes still weave and weave!

SONG TO AN OLD BURDEN

The feet have left the wormholed flooring,
    That danced to the ancient air,
    The fiddler, all-ignoring,
Sleeps by the gray-grassed 'cello player:
Shall I then foot around around around,
    As once I footed there!

The voice is heard in the room no longer
    That trilled, none sweetlier,
    To gentle stops or stronger,
Where now the dust-draped cobwebs stir:
Shall I then sing again again again,
    As once I sang with her!

The eyes that beamed out rapid brightness
    Have longtime found their close,
    The cheeks have wanned to whiteness
That used to sort with summer rose:
Shall I then joy anew anew anew,
    As once I joyed in those!

O what's to me this tedious Maying,
    What's to me this June?
    O why should viols be playing
To catch and reel and rigadoon?
Shall I sing, dance around around around,
    When phantoms call the tune!

"WHY DO I?"

Why do I go on doing these things?
    Why not cease?—
Is it that you are yet in this world of welterings
    And unease,
And that, while so, mechanic repetitions please?

When shall I leave off doing these things?—
    When I hear
You have dropped your dusty cloak and taken you wondrous wings
    To another sphere,
Where no pain is: Then shall I hush this dinning gear.

TO AN UNBORN PAUPER CHILD

I

Breathe not, hid Heart: cease silently,
And though thy birth-hour beckons thee,
   Sleep the long sleep:
   The Doomsters heap
Travails and teens around us here,
And Time-wraiths turn our songsingings to fear.

II

Hark, how the peoples surge and sigh,
And laughters fail, and greetings die:
   Hopes dwindle; yea,
   Faiths waste away,
Affections and enthusiasms numb;
Thou canst not mend these things if thou dost come.

III

Had I the ear of wombèd souls
Ere their terrestrial chart unrolls,
   And thou wert free
   To cease, or be,
Then would I tell thee all I know,
And put it to thee: Wilt thou take Life so?

IV

Vain vow! No hint of mine may hence
To theeward fly: to thy locked sense
   Explain none can
   Life's pending plan:
Thou wilt thy ignorant entry make
Though skies spout fire and blood and nations quake.

V

Fain would I, dear, find some shut plot
Of earth's wide wold for thee, where not
   One tear, one qualm,
   Should break the calm.
But I am weak as thou and bare;
No man can change the common lot to rare.

VI

Must come and bide. And such are we—
Unreasoning, sanguine, visionary—
   That I can hope
   Health, love, friends, scope
In full for thee; can dream thou'lt find
Joys seldom yet attained by humankind!

THE DEAD MAN WALKING

They hail me as one living,
    But don't they know
That I have died of late years,
    Untombed although?

I am but a shape that stands here,
    A pulseless mould,
A pale past picture, screening
    Ashes gone cold.

Not at a minute's warning,
    Not in a loud hour,
For me ceased Time's enchantments
    In hall and bower.

There was no tragic transit,
    No catch of breath,
When silent seasons inched me
    On to this death. . . .

—A Troubadour-youth I rambled
    With Life for lyre,
The beats of being raging
    In me like fire.

But when I practised eyeing
    The goal of men,
It iced me, and I perished
    A little then.

When passed my friend, my kinsfolk
    Through the Last Door,
And left me standing bleakly,
    I died yet more;

And when my Love's heart kindled
    In hate of me,
Wherefore I knew not, died I
    One more degree.

And if when I died fully
    I cannot say,
And changed into the corpse-thing
    I am to-day,

Yet is it that, though whiling
    The time somehow
In walking, talking, smiling,
    I live not now.

"I LOOK INTO MY GLASS"

I look into my glass,
And view my wasting skin,
And say, "Would God it came to pass
My heart had shrunk as thin!"

For then, I, undistrest
By hearts grown cold to me,
Could lonely wait my endless rest
With equanimity.

But Time, to make me grieve,
Part steals, lets part abide;
And shakes this fragile frame at eve
With throbbings of noontide.

EXEUNT OMNES

I

Everybody else, then, going,
And I still left where the fair was? . . .
Much have I seen of neighbour loungers
    Making a lusty showing,
    Each now past all knowing.

II

There is an air of blankness
In the street and the littered spaces;
Thoroughfare, steeple, bridge and highway
    Wizen themselves to lankness;
    Kennels dribble dankness.

III

Folk all fade. And whither,
As I wait alone where the fair was?
Into the clammy and numbing night-fog
    Whence they entered hither.
    Soon one more goes thither.

June 2, 1913.

AFTERWARDS

When the Present has latched its postern behind my tremulous stay,
　And the May month flaps its glad green leaves like wings,
Delicate-filmed as new-spun silk, will the neighbours say,
　"He was a man who used to notice such things"?

If it be in the dusk when, like an eyelid's soundless blink,
　The dewfall-hawk comes crossing the shades to alight
Upon the wind-warped upland thorn, a gazer may think,
　"To him this must have been a familiar sight."

If I pass during some nocturnal blackness, mothy and warm,
　When the hedgehog travels furtively over the lawn,
One may say, "He strove that such innocent creatures should come to no harm,
　But he could do little for them; and now he is gone."

If, when hearing that I have been stilled at last, they stand at the door,
　Watching the full-starred heavens that winter sees,
Will this thought rise on those who will meet my face no more,
　"He was one who had an eye for such mysteries"?

And will any say when my bell of quittance is heard in the gloom,
　And a crossing breeze cuts a pause in its outrollings,
Till they rise again, as they were a new bell's boom,
　"He hears it not now, but used to notice such things"?

PART II

Poems Narrative and Reflective

PAYING CALLS

I went by footpath and by stile
 Beyond where bustle ends,
Strayed here a mile and there a mile,
 And called upon some friends.

On certain ones I had not seen
 For years past did I call,
And then on others who had been
 The oldest friends of all.

It was the time of midsummer
 When they had used to roam;
But now, though tempting was the air,
 I found them all at home.

I spoke to one and other of them
 By mound and stone and tree
Of things we had done ere days were dim,
 But they spoke not to me.

FRIENDS BEYOND

William Dewy, Tranter Reuben, Farmer Ledlow late at plough,
    Robert's kin, and John's, and Ned's,
And the Squire, and Lady Susan, lie in Mellstock churchyard now!

"Gone," I call them, gone for good, that group of local hearts and heads;
    Yet at mothy curfew-tide,
And at midnight when the noon-heat breathes it back from walls and leads,

They've a way of whispering to me—fellow-wight who yet abide—
    In the muted, measured note
Of a ripple under archways, or a lone cave's stillicide:

"We have triumphed: this achievement turns the bane to antidote,
    Unsuccesses to success,
Many thought-worn eves and morrows to a morrow free of thought.

"No more need we corn and clothing, feel of old terrestrial stress;
    Chill detraction stirs no sigh;
Fear of death has even bygone us: death gave all that we possess."

W. D.—"Ye mid burn the old bass-viol that I set such value by."
Squire—"You may hold the manse in fee,
    You may wed my spouse, may let my children's memory of me die."

Lady S.—"You may have my rich brocades, my laces; take each household key;
    Ransack coffer, desk, bureau;
Quiz the few poor treasures hid there, con the letters kept by me."

Far.—"Ye mid zell my favourite heifer, ye mid let the charlock grow,
    Foul the grinterns, give up thrift."
Far. Wife—"If ye break my best blue china, children, I shan't care or ho."

All—"We've no wish to hear the tidings, how the people's fortunes shift;
    What your daily doings are;
Who are wedded, born, divided; if your lives beat slow or swift.

"Curious not the least are we if our intents you make or mar,
    If you quire to our old tune,
If the City stage still passes, if the weirs still roar afar."

—Thus, with very gods' composure, freed those crosses late and soon
    Which, in life, the Trine allow
(Why, none witteth), and ignoring all that haps beneath the moon,

William Dewy, Tranter Reuben, Farmer Ledlow late at plough,
    Robert's kin, and John's, and Ned's,
And the Squire, and Lady Susan, murmur mildly to me now.

IN FRONT OF THE LANDSCAPE

Plunging and labouring on in a tide of visions,
    Dolorous and dear,
Forward I pushed my way as amid waste waters
    Stretching around,
Through whose eddies there glimmered the customed landscape
    Yonder and near

Blotted to feeble mist. And the coomb and the upland
    Coppice-crowned,
Ancient chalk-pit, milestone, rills in the grass-flat
    Stroked by the light,
Seemed but a ghost-like gauze, and no substantial
    Meadow or mound.

What were the infinite spectacles featuring foremost
    Under my sight,
Hindering me to discern my paced advancement,
    Lengthening to miles;
What were the re-creations killing the daytime
    As by the night?

O they were speechful faces, gazing insistent,
    Some as with smiles,
Some as with slow-born tears that brinily trundled
    Over the wrecked
Cheeks that were fair in their flush-time, ash now with anguish,
    Harrowed by wiles.

Yes, I could see them, feel them, hear them, address them—
    Halo-bedecked—
And, alas, onwards, shaken by fierce unreason,
    Rigid in hate,
Smitten by years-long wryness born of misprision,
    Dreaded, suspect.

Then there would breast me shining sights, sweet seasons
    Further in date;
Instruments of strings with the tenderest passion
    Vibrant, beside
Lamps long extinguished, robes, cheeks, eyes with the earth's crust
    Now corporate.

Also there rose a headland of hoary aspect
    Gnawed by the tide,
Frilled by the nimb of the morning as two friends stood there
    Guilelessly glad—
Wherefore they knew not—touched by the fringe of an ecstasy
    Scantly descried.

Later images too did the day unfurl me,
    Shadowed and sad,
Clay cadavers of those who had shared in the dramas,
    Laid now at ease,
Passions all spent, chiefest the one of the broad brow
    Sepulture-clad.

So did beset me scenes, miscalled of the bygone,
    Over the leaze,
Past the clump, and down to where lay the beheld ones;
    —Yea, as the rhyme
Sung by the sea-swell, so in their pleading dumbness
    Captured me these.

For, their lost revisiting manifestations
    In their live time
Much had I slighted, caring not for their purport,
    Seeing behind
Things more coveted, reckoned the better worth calling
    Sweet, sad, sublime.

Thus do they now show hourly before the intenser
    Stare of the mind
As they were ghosts avenging their slights by my bypast
    Body-borne eyes,

Show, too, with fuller translation than rested upon them
    As living kind.

  Hence wag the tongues of the passing people, saying
    In their surmise,
"Ah—whose is this dull form that perambulates, seeing nought
    Round him that looms
Whithersoever his footsteps turn in his farings,
    Save a few tombs?"

THE CONVERGENCE OF THE TWAIN
(Lines on the loss of the "Titanic")

I

In a solitude of the sea
Deep from human vanity,
And the Pride of Life that planned her, stilly couches she.

II

Steel chambers, late the pyres
Of her salamandrine fires,
Cold currents thrid, and turn to rhythmic tidal lyres.

III

Over the mirrors meant
To glass the opulent
The sea-worm crawls—grotesque, slimed, dumb, indifferent.

IV

Jewels in joy designed
To ravish the sensuous mind
Lie lightless, all their sparkles bleared and black and blind.

V

Dim moon-eyed fishes near
Gaze at the gilded gear
And query: "What does this vaingloriousness down here?" . . .

VI

Well: while was fashioning
This creature of cleaving wing,
The Immanent Will that stirs and urges everything

VII

Prepared a sinister mate
For her—so gaily great—
A Shape of Ice, for the time far and dissociate.

VIII

And as the smart ship grew
In stature, grace, and hue,
In shadowy silent distance grew the Iceberg too.

IX

Alien they seemed to be:
No mortal eye could see
The intimate welding of their later history,

X

Or sign that they were bent
By paths coincident
On being anon twin halves of one august event,

XI

Till the Spinner of the Years
Said "Now!" And each one hears,
And consummation comes, and jars two hemispheres.

THE SCHRECKHORN

(With thoughts of Leslie Stephen)
(June 1897)

Aloof, as if a thing of mood and whim;
Now that its spare and desolate figure gleams
Upon my nearing vision, less it seems
A looming Alp-height than a guise of him
Who scaled its horn with ventured life and limb,
Drawn on by vague imaginings, maybe,
Of semblance to his personality
In its quaint glooms, keen lights, and rugged trim.

At his last change, when Life's dull coils unwind,
Will he, in old love, hitherward escape,
And the eternal essence of his mind
Enter this silent adamantine shape,
And his low voicing haunt its slipping snows
When dawn that calls the climber dyes them rose?

GEORGE MEREDITH
(1828–1909)

Forty years back, when much had place
That since has perished out of mind,
I heard that voice and saw that face.

He spoke as one afoot will wind
A morning horn ere men awake;
His note was trenchant, turning kind.

He was of those whose wit can shake
And riddle to the very core
The counterfeits that Time will break.

Of late, when we two met once more,
The luminous countenance and rare
Shone just as forty years before.

So that, when now all tongues declare
His shape unseen by his green hill,
I scarce believe he sits not there.

No matter. Further and further still
Through the world's vaporous vitiate air
His words wing on—as live words will.

May 1909.

A SINGER ASLEEP

(Algernon Charles Swinburne, 1837–1909)

I

In this fair niche above the unslumbering sea,
That sentrys up and down all night, all day,
From cove to promontory, from ness to bay,
The Fates have fitly bidden that he should be
    Pillowed eternally.

II

—It was as though a garland of red roses
Had fallen about the hood of some smug nun
When irresponsibly dropped as from the sun,
In fulth of numbers freaked with musical closes,
Upon Victoria's formal middle time
    His leaves of rhythm and rhyme.

III

O that far morning of a summer day
When, down a terraced street whose pavements lay
Glassing the sunshine into my bent eyes,
I walked and read with a quick glad surprise
    New words, in classic guise,—

IV

The passionate pages of his earlier years,
Fraught with hot sighs, sad laughters, kisses, tears;
Fresh-fluted notes, yet from a minstrel who
Blew them not naïvely, but as one who knew
    Full well why thus he blew.

V

I still can hear the brabble and the roar
At those thy tunes, O still one, now passed through
That fitful fire of tongues then entered new!
Their power is spent like spindrift on this shore;
    Thine swells yet more and more.

VI

—His singing-mistress verily was no other
Than she the Lesbian, she the music-mother

Of all the tribe that feel in melodies;
Who leapt, love-anguished, from the Leucadian steep
Into the rambling world-encircling deep
    Which hides her where none sees.

VII

And one can hold in thought that nightly here
His phantom may draw down to the water's brim,
And hers come up to meet it, as a dim
Lone shine upon the heaving hydrosphere,
And mariners wonder as they traverse near,
    Unknowing of her and him.

VIII

One dreams him sighing to her spectral form:
"O teacher, where lies hid thy burning line;
Where are those songs, O poetess divine
Whose very orts are love incarnadine?"
And her smile back: "Disciple true and warm,
    Sufficient now are thine." . . .

IX

So here, beneath the waking constellations,
Where the waves peal their everlasting strains,
And their dull subterrene reverberations
Shake him when storms make mountains of their plains—
Him once their peer in sad improvisations,
And deft as wind to cleave their frothy manes—
I leave him, while the daylight gleam declines
    Upon the capes and chines.

Bonchurch, 1910.

IN THE MOONLIGHT

"O lonely workman, standing there
In a dream, why do you stare and stare
At her grave, as no other grave there were?

"If your great gaunt eyes so importune
Her soul by the shine of this corpse-cold moon,
Maybe you'll raise her phantom soon!"

"Why, fool, it is what I would rather see
Than all the living folk there be;
But alas, there is no such joy for me!"

"Ah—she was one you loved, no doubt,
Through good and evil, through rain and drought,
And when she passed, all your sun went out?"

"Nay: she was the woman I did not love,
Whom all the others were ranked above,
Whom during her life I thought nothing of."

A CHURCH ROMANCE
(Mellstock, *circa* 1835)

She turned in the high pew, until her sight
Swept the west gallery, and caught its row
Of music-men with viol, book, and bow
Against the sinking sad tower-window light.

She turned again; and in her pride's despite
One strenuous viol's inspirer seemed to throw
A message from his string to her below,
Which said: "I claim thee as my own forthright!"

Thus their hearts' bond began, in due time signed.
And long years thence, when Age had scared Romance,
At some old attitude of his or glance
That gallery-scene would break upon her mind,
With him as minstrel, ardent, young, and trim,
Bowing "New Sabbath" or "Mount Ephraim."

THE ROMAN ROAD

The Roman Road runs straight and bare
As the pale parting-line in hair
Across the heath. And thoughtful men
Contrast its days of Now and Then,
And delve, and measure, and compare;

Visioning on the vacant air
Helmed legionaries, who proudly rear
The Eagle, as they pace again
        The Roman Road.

But no tall brass-helmed legionnaire
Haunts it for me. Uprises there
A mother's form upon my ken,
Guiding my infant steps, as when
We walked that ancient thoroughfare,
        The Roman Road.

THE OXEN

Christmas Eve, and twelve of the clock.
  "Now they are all on their knees,"
An elder said as we sat in a flock
  By the embers in hearthside ease.

We pictured the meek mild creatures where
  They dwelt in their strawy pen,
Nor did it occur to one of us there
  To doubt they were kneeling then.

So fair a fancy few would weave
  In these years! Yet, I feel,
If some one said on Christmas Eve,
  "Come; see the oxen kneel

"In the lonely barton by yonder coomb
  Our childhood used to know,"
I should go with him in the gloom,
  Hoping it might be so.

1915.

SHE HEARS THE STORM

There was a time in former years—
    While my roof-tree was his—
When I should have been distressed by fears
    At such a night as this!

I should have murmured anxiously,
    "The pricking rain strikes cold;
His road is bare of hedge or tree,
    And he is getting old."

But now the fitful chimney-roar,
    The drone of Thorncombe trees,
The Froom in flood upon the moor,
    The mud of Mellstock Leaze,

The candle slanting sooty wick'd,
    The thuds upon the thatch,
The eaves-drops on the window flicked,
    The clacking garden-hatch,

And what they mean to wayfarers,
    I scarcely heed or mind;
He has won that storm-tight roof of hers
    Which Earth grants all her kind.

AFTER THE LAST BREATH
(J. H. 1813–1904)

There's no more to be done, or feared, or hoped;
None now need watch, speak low, and list, and tire;
No irksome crease outsmoothed, no pillow sloped
    Does she require.

Blankly we gaze. We are free to go or stay;
Our morrow's anxious plans have missed their aim;
Whether we leave to-night or wait till day
    Counts as the same.

The lettered vessels of medicaments
Seem asking wherefore we have set them here;
Each palliative its silly face presents
    As useless gear.

And yet we feel that something savours well;
We note a numb relief withheld before;
Our well-beloved is prisoner in the cell
    Of Time no more.

We see by littles now the deft achievement
Whereby she has escaped the Wrongers all,
In view of which our momentary bereavement
    Outshapes but small.

1904.

NIGHT IN THE OLD HOME

When the wasting embers redden the chimney-breast,
And Life's bare pathway looms like a desert track to me,
And from hall and parlour the living have gone to their rest,
My perished people who housed them here come back to me.

They come and seat them around in their mouldy places,
Now and then bending towards me a glance of wistfulness,
A strange upbraiding smile upon all their faces,
And in the bearing of each a passive tristfulness.

"Do you uphold me, lingering and languishing here,
A pale late plant of your once strong stock?" I say to them;
"A thinker of crooked thoughts upon Life in the sere,
And on That which consigns men to night after showing the day to them?"

"—O let be the Wherefore! We fevered our years not thus:
Take of Life what it grants, without question!" they answer me seemingly.
"Enjoy, suffer, wait: spread the table here freely like us,
And, satisfied, placid, unfretting, watch Time away beamingly!"

NEUTRAL TONES

We stood by a pond that winter day,
And the sun was white, as though chidden of God,
And a few leaves lay on the starving sod;
    —They had fallen from an ash, and were gray.

Your eyes on me were as eyes that rove
Over tedious riddles of years ago;
And some words played between us to and fro
    On which lost the more by our love.

The smile on your mouth was the deadest thing
Alive enough to have strength to die;
And a grin of bitterness swept thereby
    Like an ominous bird a-wing. . . .

Since then, keen lessons that love deceives,
And wrings with wrong, have shaped to me
Your face, and the God-curst sun, and a tree,
    And a pond edged with grayish leaves.

1867.

TO HIM

Perhaps, long hence, when I have passed away,
Some other's feature, accent, thought like mine,
Will carry you back to what I used to say,
And bring some memory of your love's decline.

Then you may pause awhile and think, "Poor jade!"
And yield a sigh to me—as ample due,
Not as the tittle of a debt unpaid
To one who could resign her all to you—

And thus reflecting, you will never see
That your thin thought, in two small words conveyed,
Was no such fleeting phantom-thought to me,
But the Whole Life wherein my part was played;
And you amid its fitful masquerade
A Thought—as I in your life seem to be!

1866.

ROME

THE VATICAN: SALA DELLE MUSE
(1887)

I sat in the Muses' Hall at the mid of the day,
And it seemed to grow still, and the people to pass away,
And the chiselled shapes to combine in a haze of sun,
Till beside a Carrara column there gleamed forth One.

She looked not this nor that of those beings divine,
But each and the whole—an essence of all the Nine;
With tentative foot she neared to my halting-place,
A pensive smile on her sweet, small, marvellous face.

"Regarded so long, we render thee sad?" said she.
"Not you," sighed I, "but my own inconstancy!
I worship each and each; in the morning one,
And then, alas! another at sink of sun.

"To-day my soul clasps Form; but where is my troth
Of yesternight with Tune: can one cleave to both?"
—"Be not perturbed," said she. "Though apart in fame,
As I and my sisters are one, those, too, are the same."

—"But my love goes further—to Story, and Dance, and Hymn,
The lover of all in a sun-sweep is fool to whim—
Is swayed like a river-weed as the ripples run!"
—"Nay, wooer, thou sway'st not. These are but phases of one;

"And that one is I; and I am projected from thee,
One that out of thy brain and heart thou causest to be—
Extern to thee nothing. Grieve not, nor thyself becall,
Woo where thou wilt; and rejoice thou canst love at all!"

ROME

AT THE PYRAMID OF CESTIUS NEAR THE
GRAVES OF SHELLEY AND KEATS
(1887)

Who, then, was Cestius,
        And what is he to me?—
Amid thick thoughts and memories multitudinous
        One thought alone brings he.

I can recall no word
        Of anything he did;
For me he is a man who died and was interred
        To leave a pyramid

Whose purpose was exprest
        Not with its first design,
Nor till, far down in Time, beside it found their rest
        Two countrymen of mine.

Cestius in life, maybe,
        Slew, breathed out threatening;
I know not. This I know: in death all silently
        He does a finer thing,

In beckoning pilgrim feet
        With marble finger high
To where, by shadowy wall and history-haunted street,
        Those matchless singers lie. . . .

—Say, then, he lived and died
        That stones which bear his name
Should mark through Time, where two immortal Shades abide;
        It is an ample fame.

ON AN INVITATION TO THE UNITED STATES

I

My ardours for emprize nigh lost
Since Life has bared its bones to me,
I shrink to seek a modern coast
Whose riper times have yet to be;
Where the new regions claim them free
From that long drip of human tears
Which peoples old in tragedy
Have left upon the centuried years.

II

For, wonning in these ancient lands,
Enchased and lettered as a tomb,
And scored with prints of perished hands,
And chronicled with dates of doom,
Though my own Being bear no bloom
I trace the lives such scenes enshrine,
Give past exemplars present room,
And their experience count as mine.

AT A LUNAR ECLIPSE

Thy shadow, Earth, from Pole to Central Sea,
Now steals along upon the Moon's meek shine
In even monochrome and curving line
Of imperturbable serenity.

How shall I link such sun-cast symmetry
With the torn troubled form I know as thine,
That profile, placid as a brow divine,
With continents of moil and misery?

And can immense Mortality but throw
So small a shade, and Heaven's high human scheme
Be hemmed within the coasts yon arc implies?

Is such the stellar gauge of earthly show,
Nation at war with nation, brains that teem,
Heroes, and women fairer than the skies?

THE SUBALTERNS

I

"Poor wanderer," said the leaden sky,
    "I fain would lighten thee,
But there are laws in force on high
    Which say it must not be."

II

—"I would not freeze thee, shorn one," cried
    The North, "knew I but how
To warm my breath, to slack my stride;
    But I am ruled as thou."

III

—"To-morrow I attack thee, wight,"
    Said Sickness. "Yet I swear
I bear thy little ark no spite,
    But am bid enter there."

IV

—"Come hither, Son," I heard Death say;
    "I did not will a grave
Should end thy pilgrimage to-day,
    But I, too, am a slave!"

V

We smiled upon each other then,
    And life to me had less
Of that fell look it wore ere when
    They owned their passiveness.

THE SLEEP-WORKER

When wilt thou wake, O Mother, wake and see—
As one who, held in trance, has laboured long
By vacant rote and prepossession strong—
The coils that thou hast wrought unwittingly;

Wherein have place, unrealized by thee,
Fair growths, foul cankers, right enmeshed with wrong,
Strange orchestras of victim-shriek and song,
And curious blends of ache and ecstasy?—

Should that morn come, and show thy opened eyes
All that Life's palpitating tissues feel,
How wilt thou bear thyself in thy surprise?—

Wilt thou destroy, in one wild shock of shame,
Thy whole high heaving firmamental frame,
Or patiently adjust, amend, and heal?

BEYOND THE LAST LAMP
(*Near Tooting Common*)

I

While rain, with eve in partnership,
Descended darkly, drip, drip, drip,
Beyond the last lone lamp I passed
    Walking slowly, whispering sadly,
    Two linked loiterers, wan, downcast:
Some heavy thought constrained each face,
And blinded them to time and place.

II

The pair seemed lovers, yet absorbed
In mental scenes no longer orbed
By love's young rays. Each countenance
    As it slowly, as it sadly
    Caught the lamplight's yellow glance,
Held in suspense a misery
At things which had been or might be.

III

When I retrod that watery way
Some hours beyond the droop of day,
Still I found pacing there the twain
    Just as slowly, just as sadly,
    Heedless of the night and rain.
One could but wonder who they were
And what wild woe detained them there.

IV

Though thirty years of blur and blot
Have slid since I beheld that spot,
And saw in curious converse there
    Moving slowly, moving sadly
    That mysterious tragic pair,
Its olden look may linger on—
All but the couple; they have gone.

V

Whither? Who knows, indeed. . . . And yet
To me, when nights are weird and wet,
Without those comrades there at tryst
   Creeping slowly, creeping sadly,
   That lone lane does not exist.
There they seem brooding on their pain,
And will, while such a lane remain.

THE DEAD QUIRE

I

Beside the Mead of Memories,
Where Church-way mounts to Moaning Hill,
The sad man sighed his phantasies:
    He seems to sigh them still.

II

"'Twas the Birth-tide Eve, and the hamleteers
Made merry with ancient Mellstock zest,
But the Mellstock quire of former years
    Had entered into rest.

III

"Old Dewy lay by the gaunt yew tree,
And Reuben and Michael a pace behind,
And Bowman with his family
    By the wall that the ivies bind.

IV

"The singers had followed one by one,
Treble, and tenor, and thorough-bass;
And the worm that wasteth had begun
    To mine their mouldering place.

V

"For two-score years, ere Christ-day light,
Mellstock had throbbed to strains from these;
But now there echoed on the night
    No Christmas harmonies.

VI

"Three meadows off, at a dormered inn,
The youth had gathered in high carouse,
And, ranged on settles, some therein
    Had drunk them to a drowse.

VII

"Loud, lively, reckless, some had grown.
Each dandling on his jigging knee
Eliza, Dolly, Nance, or Joan—
    Livers in levity.

VIII

"The taper flames and hearthfire shine
Grew smoke-hazed to a lurid light,
And songs on subjects not divine
    Were warbled forth that night.

IX

"Yet many were sons and grandsons here
Of those who, on such eves gone by,
At that still hour had throated clear
    Their anthems to the sky.

X

"The clock belled midnight; and ere long
One shouted, 'Now 'tis Christmas morn;
Here's to our women old and young,
    And to John Barleycorn!'

XI

"They drink the toast and shout again:
The pewter-ware rings back the boom,
And for a breath-while follows then
    A silence in the room.

XII

"When nigh without, as in old days,
The ancient quire of voice and string
Seemed singing words of prayer and praise
    As they had used to sing:

XIII

"While shepherds watch'd their flocks by night,—
Thus swells the long familiar sound
In many a quaint symphonic flight
    To, *Glory shone around.*

XIV

"The sons defined their fathers' tones,
The widow his whom she had wed,
And others in the minor moans
    The viols of the dead.

XV

"Something supernal has the sound
As verse by verse the strain proceeds,

And stilly staring on the ground
    Each roysterer holds and heeds.

XVI

"Towards its chorded closing bar
Plaintively, thinly, waned the hymn,
Yet lingered, like the notes afar
    Of banded seraphim.

XVII

"With brows abashed, and reverent tread,
The hearkeners sought the tavern door:
But nothing, save wan moonlight, spread
    The empty highway o'er.

XVIII

"While on their hearing fixed and tense
The aerial music seemed to sink,
As it were gently moving thence
    Along the river brink.

XIX

"Then did the Quick pursue the Dead
By crystal Froom that crinkles there;
And still the viewless quire ahead
    Voiced the old holy air.

XX

"By Bank-walk wicket, brightly bleached,
It passed, and 'twixt the hedges twain,
Dogged by the living; till it reached
    The bottom of Church Lane.

XXI

"There, at the turning, it was heard
Drawing to where the churchyard lay:
But when they followed thitherward
    It smalled, and died away.

XXII

"Each headstone of the quire, each mound,
Confronted them beneath the moon;
But no more floated therearound
    That ancient Birth-night tune.

135

XXIII

"There Dewy lay by the gaunt yew tree,
There Reuben and Michael, a pace behind,
And Bowman with his family
    By the wall that the ivies bind. . . .

XXIV

"As from a dream each sobered son
Awoke, and musing reached his door:
'Twas said that of them all, not one
    Sat in a tavern more."

XXV

—The sad man ceased; and ceased to heed
His listener, and crossed the leaze
From Moaning Hill towards the mead—
    The Mead of Memories.

1897.

THE BURGHERS
(17-)

The sun had wheeled from Grey's to Dammer's Crest,
And still I mused on that Thing imminent:
At length I sought the High-street to the West.

The level flare raked pane and pediment
And my wrecked face, and shaped my nearing friend
Like one of those the Furnace held unshent.

"I've news concerning her," he said. "Attend.
They fly to-night at the late moon's first gleam:
Watch with thy steel: two righteous thrusts will end

Her shameless visions and his passioned dream.
I'll watch with thee, to testify thy wrong—
To aid, maybe.—Law consecrates the scheme."

I started, and we paced the flags along
Till I replied: "Since it has come to this
I'll do it! But alone. I can be strong."

Three hours past Curfew, when the Froom's mild hiss
Reigned sole, undulled by whirr of merchandize,
From Pummery-Tout to where the Gibbet is,

I crossed my pleasaunce hard by Glyd'path Rise,
And stood beneath the wall. Eleven strokes went,
And to the door they came, contrariwise,

And met in clasp so close I had but bent
My lifted blade on either to have let
Their two souls loose upon the firmament.

But something held my arm. "A moment yet
As pray-time ere you wantons die!" I said;
And then they saw me. Swift her gaze was set

With eye and cry of love illimited
Upon her Heart-king. Never upon me
Had she thrown look of love so thorough-sped! . . .

At once she flung her faint form shieldingly
On his, against the vengeance of my vows;
The which o'erruling, her shape shielded he.

Blanked by such love, I stood as in a drowse,
And the slow moon edged from the upland nigh,
My sad thoughts moving thuswise: "I may house

And I may husband her, yet what am I
But licensed tyrant to this bonded pair?
Says Charity, Do as ye would be done by." . . .

Hurling my iron to the bushes there
I bade them stay. And, as if brain and breast
Were passive, they walked with me to the stair.

Inside the house none watched; and on we prest
Before a mirror, in whose gleam I read
Her beauty, his,—and mine own mien unblest;

Till at her room I turned. "Madam," I said,
"Have you the wherewithal for this? Pray speak.
Love fills no cupboard. You'll need daily bread."

"We've nothing, sire," she lipped; "and nothing seek.
'Twere base in me to rob my lord unware;
Our hands will earn a pittance week by week."

And next I saw she had piled her raiment rare
Within the garde-robes, and her household purse,
Her jewels, her least lace of personal wear,

And stood in homespun. Now grown wholly hers,
I handed her the gold, her jewels all,
And him the choicest of her robes diverse.

"I'll take you to the doorway in the wall,
And then adieu," I told them. "Friends, withdraw."
They did so; and she went—beyond recall.

And as I paused beneath the arch I saw
Their moonlit figures—slow, as in surprise—
Descend the slope, and vanish on the haw.

"'Fool,' some will say," I thought—"But who is wise,
Save God alone, to weigh my reasons why?"
—"Hast thou struck home?" came with the boughs' night-sighs.

It was my friend. "I have struck well. They fly,
But carry wounds that none can cicatrize."
—"Not mortal?" said he. "Lingering—worse," said I.

THE CORONATION

At Westminster, hid from the light of day,
Many who once had shone as monarchs lay.

Edward the Pious, and two Edwards more,
The second Richard, Henrys three or four;

That is to say, those who were called the Third,
Fifth, Seventh, and Eighth (the much self-widowered);

And James the Scot, and near him Charles the Second,
And, too, the second George could there be reckoned.

Of women, Mary and Queen Elizabeth,
And Anne, all silent in a musing death;

And William's Mary, and Mary, Queen of Scots,
And consort-queens whose names oblivion blots;

And several more whose chronicle one sees
Adorning ancient royal pedigrees.

—Now, as they drowsed on, freed from Life's old thrall,
And heedless, save of things exceptional,

Said one: "What means this throbbing thudding sound
That reaches to us here from overground;

"A sound of chisels, augers, planes, and saws,
Infringing all ecclesiastic laws?

"And these tons-weight of timber on us pressed,
Unfelt here since we entered into rest?

"Surely, at least to us, being corpses royal,
A meet repose is owing by the loyal?"

"—Perhaps a scaffold!" Mary Stuart sighed,
"If such still be. It was that way I died."

"—Ods! Far more like," said he the many-wived,
"That for a wedding 'tis this work's contrived.

"Ha-ha! I never would bow down to Rimmon,
But I had a rare time with those six women!"

"Not all at once?" gasped he who loved confession.
"Nay, nay!" said Hal. "That would have been transgression."

"—They build a catafalque here, black and tall,
Perhaps," mused Richard, "for some funeral?"

And Anne chimed in: "Ah, yes: it may be so!"
"Nay!" squeaked Eliza. "Little you seem to know—

"Clearly 'tis for some crowning here in state,
As they crowned us at our long bygone date;

"Though we'd no such a power of carpentry,
But let the ancient architecture be;

"If I were up there where the parsons sit,
In one of my gold robes, I'd see to it!"

"But you are not," Charles chuckled. "You are here,
And never will know the sun again, my dear!"

"Yea," whispered those whom no one had addressed;
"With slow, sad march, amid a folk distressed,
We were brought here, to take our dusty rest.

"And here, alas, in darkness laid below,
We'll wait and listen, and endure the show. . . .
Clamour dogs kingship; afterwards not so!"

1911.

A COMMONPLACE DAY

The day is turning ghost,
And scuttles from the kalendar in fits and furtively,
To join the anonymous host
Of those that throng oblivion; ceding his place, maybe,
To one of like degree.

I part the fire-gnawed logs,
Rake forth the embers, spoil the busy flames, and lay the ends
Upon the shining dogs;
Further and further from the nooks the twilight's stride extends,
And beamless black impends.

Nothing of tiniest worth
Have I wrought, pondered, planned; no one thing asking blame or praise,
Since the pale corpse-like birth
Of this diurnal unit, bearing blanks in all its rays—
Dullest of dull-hued Days!

Wanly upon the panes
The rain slides, as have slid since morn my colourless thoughts; and yet
Here, while Day's presence wanes,
And over him the sepulchre-lid is slowly lowered and set,
He wakens my regret.

Regret—though nothing dear
That I wot of, was toward in the wide world at his prime,
Or bloomed elsewhere than here,
To die with his decease, and leave a memory sweet, sublime,
Or mark him out in Time. . . .

—Yet, maybe, in some soul,
In some spot undiscerned on sea or land, some impulse rose,
Or some intent upstole
Of that enkindling ardency from whose maturer glows
The world's amendment flows;

But which, benumbed at birth
By momentary chance or wile, has missed its hope to be
Embodied on the earth;
And undervoicings of this loss to man's futurity
May wake regret in me.

HER DEATH AND AFTER

The summons was urgent: and forth I went—
By the way of the Western Wall, so drear
On that winter night, and sought a gate,
    Where one, by Fate,
    Lay dying that I held dear.

And there, as I paused by her tenement,
And the trees shed on me their rime and hoar,
I thought of the man who had left her lone—
    Him who made her his own
    When I loved her, long before.

The rooms within had the piteous shine
That home-things wear when there's aught amiss;
From the stairway floated the rise and fall
    Of an infant's call,
    Whose birth had brought her to this.

Her life was the price she would pay for that whine—
For a child by the man she did not love.
"But let that rest for ever," I said,
    And bent my tread
    To the bedchamber above.

She took my hand in her thin white own,
And smiled her thanks—though nigh too weak—
And made them a sign to leave us there,
    Then faltered, ere
    She could bring herself to speak.

"Just to see you—before I go—he'll condone
Such a natural thing now my time's not much—
When Death is so near it hustles hence
    All passioned sense
    Between woman and man as such!

"My husband is absent. As heretofore
The City detains him. But, in truth,

He has not been kind. . . . I will speak no blame,
  But—the child is lame;
   O, I pray she may reach his ruth!

"Forgive past days—I can say no more—
Maybe had we wed you would now repine! . . .
But I treated you ill. I was punished. Farewell!
  —Truth shall I tell?
   Would the child were yours and mine!

"As a wife I was true. But, such my unease
That, could I insert a deed back in Time,
I'd make her yours, to secure your care;
  And the scandal bear,
   And the penalty for the crime!"

—When I had left, and the swinging trees
Rang above me, as lauding her candid say,
Another was I. Her words were enough:
  Came smooth, came rough,
   I felt I could live my day.

Next night she died; and her obsequies
In the Field of Tombs where the earthworks frowned
Had her husband's heed. His tendance spent,
  I often went
   And pondered by her mound.

All that year and the next year whiled,
And I still went thitherward in the gloam;
But the Town forgot her and her nook,
  And her husband took
   Another Love to his home.

And the rumour flew that the lame lone child
Whom she wished for its safety child of mine,
Was treated ill when offspring came
  Of the new-made dame,
   And marked a more vigorous line.

A smarter grief within me wrought
Than even at loss of her so dear—

That the being whose soul my soul suffused
    Had a child ill-used,
      While I dared not interfere!

One eve as I stood at my spot of thought
In the white-stoned Garth, brooding thus her wrong,
Her husband neared; and to shun his nod
    By her hallowed sod
      I went from the tombs among

To the Cirque of the Gladiators which faced—
That haggard mark of Imperial Rome,
Whose Pagan echoes mock the chime
    Of our Christian time
      From its hollows of chalk and loam.

The sun's gold touch was scarce displaced
From the vast Arena where men once bled,
When her husband followed; bowed; half-passed
    With lip upcast;
      Then halting sullenly said:

"It is noised that you visit my first wife's tomb.
Now, I gave her an honoured name to bear
While living, when dead. So I've claim to ask
    By what right you task
      My patience by vigiling there?

"There's decency even in death, I assume;
Preserve it, sir, and keep away;
For the mother of my first-born you
    Show mind undue!
      —Sir, I've nothing more to say."

A desperate stroke discerned I then—
God pardon—or pardon not—the lie;
She had sighed that she wished (lest the child should pine
    Of slights) 'twere mine,
      So I said: "But the father I.

"That you thought it yours is the way of men;
But I won her troth long ere your day:

You learnt how, in dying, she summoned me?
    'Twas in fealty.
    —Sir, I've nothing more to say,

"Save that, if you'll hand me my little maid,
I'll take her, and rear her, and spare you toil.
Think it more than a friendly act none can;
    I'm a lonely man,
    While you've a large pot to boil.

"If not, and you'll put it to ball or blade—
To-night, to-morrow night, anywhen—
I'll meet you here. . . . But think of it,
    And in season fit
    Let me hear from you again."

—Well, I went away, hoping; but nought I heard
Of my stroke for the child, till there greeted me
A little voice that one day came
    To my window-frame
    And babbled innocently:

"My father who's not my own, sends word
I'm to stay here, sir, where I belong!"
Next a writing came: "Since the child was the fruit
    Of your lawless suit,
    Pray take her, to right a wrong."

And I did. And I gave the child my love,
And the child loved me, and estranged us none.
But compunctions loomed; for I'd harmed the dead
    By what I said
    For the good of the living one.

—Yet though, God wot, I am sinner enough
And unworthy the woman who drew me so,
Perhaps this wrong for her darling's good
    She forgives, or would,
    If only she could know!

A TRAMPWOMAN'S TRAGEDY
(182–)

I

From Wynyard's Gap the livelong day,
    The livelong day,
We beat afoot the northward way
    We had travelled times before.
The sun-blaze burning on our backs,
Our shoulders sticking to our packs,
By fosseway, fields, and turnpike tracks
    We skirted sad Sedge-Moor.

II

Full twenty miles we jaunted on,
    We jaunted on,—
My fancy-man, and jeering John,
    And Mother Lee, and I.
And, as the sun drew down to west,
We climbed the toilsome Poldon crest,
And saw, of landskip sights the best,
    The inn that beamed thereby.

III

For months we had padded side by side,
    Ay, side by side
Through the Great Forest, Blackmoor wide,
    And where the Parret ran.
We'd faced the gusts on Mendip ridge,
Had crossed the Yeo unhelped by bridge,
Been stung by every Marshwood midge,
    I and my fancy-man.

IV

Lone inns we loved, my man and I,
    My man and I;
"King's Stag," "Windwhistle" high and dry,
    "The Horse" on Hintock Green,
The cosy house at Wynyard's Gap,

"The Hut" renowned on Bredy Knap,
And many another wayside tap
    Where folk might sit unseen.

V

Now as we trudged—O deadly day,
    O deadly day!—
I teased my fancy-man in play
    And wanton idleness.
I walked alongside jeering John,
I laid his hand my waist upon;
I would not bend my glances on
    My lover's dark distress

VI

Thus Poldon top at last we won,
    At last we won,
And gained the inn at sink of sun
    Far-famed as "Marshal's Elm."
Beneath us figured tor and lea,
From Mendip to the western sea—
I doubt if finer sight there be
    Within this royal realm.

VII

Inside the settle all a-row—
    All four a-row
We sat, I next to John, to show
    That he had wooed and won.
And then he took me on his knee,
And swore it was his turn to be
My favoured mate, and Mother Lee
    Passed to my former one.

VIII

Then in a voice I had never heard,
    I had never heard,
My only Love to me: "One word,
    My lady, if you please!
Whose is the child you are like to bear?—
His? After all my months o' care?"

God knows 'twas not! But, O despair!
    I nodded—still to tease.

IX

Then up he sprung, and with his knife—
    And with his knife
He let out jeering Johnny's life,
    Yes; there, at set of sun.
The slant ray through the window nigh
Gilded John's blood and glazing eye,
Ere scarcely Mother Lee and I
    Knew that the deed was done.

X

The taverns tell the gloomy tale,
    The gloomy tale,
How that at Ivel-chester jail
    My Love, my sweetheart swung;
Though stained till now by no misdeed
Save one horse ta'en in time o'need;
(Blue Jimmy stole right many a steed
    Ere his last fling he flung.)

XI

Thereaft I walked the world alone,
    Alone, alone!
On his death-day I gave my groan
    And dropt his dead-born child.
'Twas nigh the jail, beneath a tree,
None tending me; for Mother Lee
Had died at Glaston, leaving me
    Unfriended on the wild.

XII

And in the night as I lay weak,
    As I lay weak,
The leaves a-falling on my cheek,
    The red moon low declined—
The ghost of him I'd die to kiss
Rose up and said: "Ah, tell me this!
Was the child mine, or was it his?
    Speak, that I rest may find!"

XIII

O doubt not but I told him then,
I told him then,
That I had kept me from all men
Since we joined lips and swore.
Whereat he smiled, and thinned away
As the wind stirred to call up day . . .
—'Tis past! And here alone I stray
Haunting the Western Moor.

Notes:—"Windwhistle" (Stanza IV.). The highness and dryness of Windwhistle Inn was impressed upon the writer two or three years ago, when, after climbing on a hot afternoon to the beautiful spot near which it stands and entering the inn for tea, he was informed by the landlady that none could be had, unless he would fetch water from a valley half a mile off, the house containing not a drop, owing to its situation. However, a tantalizing row of full barrels behind her back testified to a wetness of a certain sort, which was not at that time desired.

"Marshal's Elm" (Stanza VI.), so picturesquely situated, is no longer an inn, though the house, or part of it, still remains. It used to exhibit a fine old swinging sign.

"Blue Jimmy" (Stanza X.) was a notorious horse-stealer of Wessex in those days, who appropriated more than a hundred horses before he was caught, among others one belonging to a neighbour of the writer's grandfather. He was hanged at the now demolished Ivel-chester or Ilchester jail above mentioned—that building formerly of so many sinister associations in the minds of the local peasantry, and the continual haunt of fever, which at last led to its condemnation. Its site is now an innocent-looking green meadow.

April 1902.

THE DUEL

"I am here to time, you see;
The glade is well-screened—eh?—against alarm;
   Fit place to vindicate by my arm
   The honour of my spotless wife,
   Who scorns your libel upon her life
     In boasting intimacy!

   "'All hush-offerings you'll spurn,
My husband. Two must come; one only go,'
   She said. 'That he'll be you I know;
   To faith like ours Heaven will be just,
   And I shall abide in fullest trust
     Your speedy glad return.'"

   "Good. Here am also I;
And we'll proceed without more waste of words
   To warm your cockpit. Of the swords
   Take you your choice. I shall thereby
   Feel that on me no blame can lie,
     Whatever Fate accords."

   So stripped they there, and fought,
And the swords clicked and scraped, and the onsets sped;
   Till the husband fell; and his shirt was red
   With streams from his heart's hot cistern. Nought
   Could save him now; and the other, wrought
     Maybe to pity, said:

   "Why did you urge on this?
Your wife assured you; and 't had better been
   That you had let things pass, serene
   In confidence of long-tried bliss,
   Holding there could be nought amiss
     In what my words might mean."

Then, seeing nor ruth nor rage
Could move his foeman more—now Death's deaf thrall—
He wiped his steel, and, with a call
Like turtledove to dove, swift broke
Into the copse, where under an oak
His horse cropt, held by a page.

"All's over, Sweet," he cried
To the wife, thus guised; for the young page was she.
"'Tis as we hoped and said 't would be.
He never guessed. . . . We mount and ride
To where our love can reign uneyed.
He's clay, and we are free.

THE CARRIER

"There's a seat, I see, still empty?"
    Cried the hailer from the road;
"No, there is not!" said the carrier,
    Quickening his horse and load.

"—They say you are in the grave, Jane;
    But still you ride with me!"
And he looked towards the vacant space
    He had kept beside his knee.

And the passengers murmured: "'Tis where his wife
    In journeys to and fro
Used always to sit; but nobody does
    Since those long years ago."

Rumble-mumble went the van
    Past Sidwell Church and wall,
Till Exon Towers were out of scan,
    And night lay over all.

AN EAST-END CURATE

A small blind street off East Commercial Road;
   Window, door; window, door;
   Every house like the one before,
Is where the curate, Mr. Dowle, has found a pinched abode.
Spectacled, pale, moustache straw-coloured, and with a long thin face,
Day or dark his lodgings' narrow doorstep does he pace.

A bleached pianoforte, with its drawn silk plaitings faded,
Stands in his room, its keys much yellowed, cyphering, and abraded,
"Novello's Anthems" lie at hand, and also a few glees,
And "Laws of Heaven for Earth" in a frame upon the wall one sees.

He goes through his neighbours' houses as his own, and none regards,
And opens their back-doors off-hand, to look for them in their yards:
A man is threatening his wife on the other side of the wall,
But the curate lets it pass as knowing the history of it all.

Freely within his hearing the children skip and laugh and say:
   "There's Mister Dow-well! There's Mister Dow-well!" in their play;
   And the long, pallid, devoted face notes not,
But stoops along abstractedly, for good, or in vain, God wot!

WAITING BOTH

A star looks down at me,
And says: "Here I and you
Stand, each in our degree:
What do you mean to do,—
   Mean to do?"

I say: "For all I know,
Wait, and let Time go by,
Till my change come."—"Just so,"
The star says: "So mean I:—
   So mean I."

THE SOMETHING THAT SAVED HIM

It was when
Whirls of thick waters laved me
    Again and again,
That something arose and saved me;
    Yea, it was then.

In that day
Unseeing the azure went I
    On my way,
And to white winter bent I,
    Knowing no May.

Reft of renown,
Under the night clouds beating
    Up and down,
In my needfulness greeting
    Cit and clown.

Long there had been
Much of a murky colour
    In the scene,
Dull prospects meeting duller;
    Nought between.

Last, there loomed
A closing-in blind alley,
    Though there boomed
A feeble summons to rally
    Where it gloomed.

The clock rang;
The hour brought a hand to deliver;
    I upsprang,
And looked back at den, ditch and river,
    And sang.

"ACCORDING TO THE MIGHTY WORKING"

I

When moiling seems at cease
    In the vague void of night-time,
    And heaven's wide roomage stormless
    Between the dusk and light-time,
    And fear at last is formless,
We call the allurement Peace.

II

Peace, this hid riot, Change,
    This revel of quick-cued mumming,
    This never truly being,
    This evermore becoming,
    This spinner's wheel onfleeing
Outside perception's range.

1917.

A NIGHT IN NOVEMBER

I marked when the weather changed,
And the panes began to quake,
And the winds rose up and ranged,
That night, lying half-awake.

Dead leaves blew into my room,
And alighted upon my bed,
And a tree declared to the gloom
Its sorrow that they were shed.

One leaf of them touched my hand,
And I thought that it was you
There stood as you used to stand,
And saying at last you knew!

(?) 1913.

THE FALLOW DEER AT THE LONELY HOUSE

One without looks in to-night
    Through the curtain-chink
From the sheet of glistening white;
One without looks in to-night
    As we sit and think
    By the fender-brink.

We do not discern those eyes
    Watching in the snow;
Lit by lamps of rosy dyes
We do not discern those eyes
    Wondering, aglow,
    Fourfooted, tiptoe.

THE SELFSAME SONG

A bird sings the selfsame song,
With never a fault in its flow,
That we listened to here those long
    Long years ago.

A pleasing marvel is how
A strain of such rapturous rote
Should have gone on thus till now
    Unchanged in a note!

—But it's not the selfsame bird.—
No: perished to dust is he. . . .
As also are those who heard
    That song with me.

NEAR LANIVET, 1872

There was a stunted handpost just on the crest,
    Only a few feet high:
She was tired, and we stopped in the twilight-time for her rest,
    At the crossways close thereby.

She leant back, being so weary, against its stem,
    And laid her arms on its own,
Each open palm stretched out to each end of them,
    Her sad face sideways thrown.

Her white-clothed form at this dim-lit cease of day
    Made her look as one crucified
In my gaze at her from the midst of the dusty way,
    And hurriedly "Don't," I cried.

I do not think she heard. Loosing thence she said,
    As she stepped forth ready to go,
"I am rested now.—Something strange came into my head;
    I wish I had not leant so!"

And wordless we moved onward down from the hill
    In the west cloud's murked obscure,
And looking back we could see the handpost still
    In the solitude of the moor.

"It struck her too," I thought, for as if afraid
    She heavily breathed as we trailed;
Till she said, "I did not think how 'twould look in the shade,
    When I leant there like one nailed."

I, lightly: "There's nothing in it. For *you*, anyhow!"
    —"O I know there is not," said she . . .
"Yet I wonder . . . If no one is bodily crucified now,
    In spirit one may be!"

And we dragged on and on, while we seemed to see
    In the running of Time's far glass
Her crucified, as she had wondered if she might be
    Some day.—Alas, alas!

THE GARDEN SEAT

Its former green is blue and thin,
And its once firm legs sink in and in;
Soon it will break down unaware,
Soon it will break down unaware.

At night when reddest flowers are black
Those who once sat thereon come back;
Quite a row of them sitting there,
Quite a row of them sitting there.

With them the seat does not break down,
Nor winter freeze them, nor floods drown.
For they are as light as upper air,
They are as light as upper air!

NIGHT-TIME IN MID-FALL

It is a storm-strid night, winds footing swift
    Through the blind profound;
  I know the happenings from their sound;
Leaves totter down still green, and spin and drift;
The tree-trunks rock to their roots, which wrench and lift
The loam where they run onward underground.

The streams are muddy and swollen; eels migrate
    To a new abode;
  Even cross, 'tis said, the turnpike-road;
(Men's feet have felt their crawl, home-coming late):
The westward fronts of towers are saturate,
Church-timbers crack, and witches ride abroad.

A SHEEP FAIR

The day arrives of the autumn fair,
　　And torrents fall,
Though sheep in throngs are gathered there,
　　Ten thousand all,
Sodden, with hurdles round them reared:
And, lot by lot, the pens are cleared,
And the auctioneer wrings out his beard,
And wipes his book, bedrenched and smeared,
And rakes the rain from his face with the edge of his hand,
　　As torrents fall.

The wool of the ewes is like a sponge
　　With the daylong rain:
Jammed tight, to turn, or lie, or lunge,
　　They strive in vain.
Their horns are soft as finger-nails,
Their shepherds reek against the rails,
The tied dogs soak with tucked-in tails,
The buyers' hat-brims fill like pails,
Which spill small cascades when they shift their stand
　　In the daylong rain.

POSTSCRIPT

Time has trailed lengthily since met
　　At Pummery Fair
Those panting thousands in their wet
　　And woolly wear:
And every flock long since has bled,
And all the dripping buyers have sped,
And the hoarse auctioneer is dead,
Who "Going—going!" so often said
As he consigned to doom each meek, mewed band
　　At Pummery Fair.

SNOW IN THE SUBURBS

Every branch big with it,
    Bent every twig with it;
Every fork like a white web-foot;
    Every street and pavement mute:
Some flakes have lost their way, and grope back upward, when
Meeting those meandering down they turn and descend again.
    The palings are glued together like a wall,
    And there is no waft of wind with the fleecy fall.

    A sparrow enters the tree,
        Whereon immediately
    A snow-lump thrice his own slight size
    Descends on him and showers his head and eyes.
        And overturns him,
        And near inurns him,
    And lights on a nether twig, when its brush
Starts off a volley of other lodging lumps with a rush.

    The steps are a blanched slope,
        Up which, with feeble hope,
    A black cat comes, wide-eyed and thin;
        And we take him in.

FRAGMENT

At last I entered a long dark gallery,
   Catacomb-lined; and ranged at the side
   Were the bodies of men from far and wide
Who, motion past, were nevertheless not dead.

  "The sense of waiting here strikes strong;
Everyone's waiting, waiting, it seems to me;
   What are you waiting for so long?—
     What is to happen?" I said.

"O we are waiting for one called God," said they,
   "(Though by some the Will, or Force, or Laws;
   And, vaguely, by some, the Ultimate Cause;)
Waiting for him to see us before we are clay.
   Yes; waiting, waiting, for God *to know it*." . . .

  "To know what?" questioned I.
"To know how things have been going on earth and below it:
   It is clear he must know some day."
   I thereon asked them why.

"Since he made us humble pioneers
Of himself in consciousness of Life's tears,
It needs no mighty prophecy
To tell that what he could mindlessly show
His creatures, he himself will know

"By some still close-cowled mystery
We have reached feeling faster than he,
But he will overtake us anon,
   If the world goes on."

CYNIC'S EPITAPH

A race with the sun as he downed
    I ran at evetide,
Intent who should first gain the ground
    And there hide.

He beat me by some minutes then,
    But I triumphed anon,
For when he'd to rise up again
    I stayed on.

IN DEATH DIVIDED

I

I shall rot here, with those whom in their day
    You never knew,
And alien ones who, ere they chilled to clay,
    Met not my view,
Will in your distant grave-place ever neighbour you.

II

No shade of pinnacle or tree or tower,
    While earth endures,
Will fall on my mound and within the hour
    Steal on to yours;
One robin never haunt our two green covertures.

III

Some organ may resound on Sunday noons
    By where you lie,
Some other thrill the panes with other tunes
    Where moulder I;
No selfsame chords compose our common lullaby.

IV

The simply-cut memorial at my head
    Perhaps may take
A rustic form, and that above your bed
    A stately make;
No linking symbol show thereon for our tale's sake.

V

And in the monotonous moils of strained, hard-run
    Humanity,
The eternal tie which binds us twain in one
    No eye will see
Stretching across the miles that sever you from me.

189–.

IN TENEBRIS

"Considerabam ad dexteram, et videbam; et non erat qui cognosceret
me. . . . Non est qui requirat animam meam."—*Ps.* cxli.

When the clouds' swoln bosoms echo back the shouts of the many and strong
That things are all as they best may be, save a few to be right ere long,
And my eyes have not the vision in them to discern what to these is so clear,
The blot seems straightway in me alone; one better he were not here.

The stout upstanders say, All's well with us: ruers have nought to rue!
And what the potent say so oft, can it fail to be somewhat true?
Breezily go they, breezily come; their dust smokes around their career,
Till I think I am one born out of due time, who has no calling here.

Their dawns bring lusty joys, it seems; their evenings all that is sweet;
Our times are blessed times, they cry: Life shapes it as is most meet,
And nothing is much the matter; there are many smiles to a tear;
Then what is the matter is I, I say. Why should such an one be here? . . .

Let him in whose ears the low-voiced Best is killed by the clash of the First,
Who holds that if way to the Better there be, it exacts a full look at the Worst,
Who feels that delight is a delicate growth cramped by crookedness, custom,
    and fear,
Get him up and be gone as one shaped awry; he disturbs the order here.

1895–96.

"I HAVE LIVED WITH SHADES"

I

I have lived with Shades so long,
And talked to them so oft,
Since forth from cot and croft
I went mankind among,
        That sometimes they
        In their dim style
        Will pause awhile
        To hear my say;

II

And take me by the hand,
And lead me through their rooms
In the To-be, where Dooms
Half-wove and shapeless stand:
        And show from there
        The dwindled dust
        And rot and rust
        Of things that were.

III

"Now turn," they said to me
One day: "Look whence we came,
And signify his name
Who gazes thence at thee."—
        —"Nor name nor race
        Know I, or can,"
        I said, "Of man
        So commonplace.

IV

"He moves me not at all;
I note no ray or jot
Of rareness in his lot,
Or star exceptional.
        Into the dim
        Dead throngs around

He'll sink, nor sound
Be left of him."

v

"Yet," said they, "his frail speech,
Hath accents pitched like thine—
Thy mould and his define
A likeness each to each—
But go! Deep pain
Alas, would be
His name to thee,
And told in vain!"

February 2, 1899.

A POET

Attentive eyes, fantastic heed,
Assessing minds, he does not need,
Nor urgent writs to sup or dine,
Nor pledges in the rosy wine.

For loud acclaim he does not care
By the august or rich or fair,
Nor for smart pilgrims from afar,
Curious on where his hauntings are.

But soon or later, when you hear
That he has doffed this wrinkled gear,
Some evening, at the first star-ray,
Come to his graveside, pause and say:

"Whatever his message—glad or grim—
Two bright-souled women clave to him";
Stand and say that while day decays;
It will be word enough of praise.

July 1914.

PART III

War Poems, and Lyrics from "The Dynasts"

EMBARCATION

(Southampton Docks: October 1899)

Here, where Vespasian's legions struck the sands,
And Cerdic with his Saxons entered in,
And Henry's army leapt afloat to win
Convincing triumphs over neighbour lands,

Vaster battalions press for further strands,
To argue in the selfsame bloody mode
Which this late age of thought, and pact, and code,
Still fails to mend.—Now deckward tramp the bands,

Yellow as autumn leaves, alive as spring;
And as each host draws out upon the sea
Beyond which lies the tragical To-be,
None dubious of the cause, none murmuring,

Wives, sisters, parents, wave white hands and smile,
As if they knew not that they weep the while.

DEPARTURE
(Southampton Docks: October 1899)

While the far farewell music thins and fails,
And the broad bottoms rip the bearing brine—
All smalling slowly to the gray sea-line—
And each significant red smoke-shaft pales,

Keen sense of severance everywhere prevails,
Which shapes the late long tramp of mounting men
To seeming words that ask and ask again:
"How long, O striving Teutons, Slavs, and Gaels

Must your wroth reasonings trade on lives like these,
That are as puppets in a playing hand?—
When shall the saner softer polities
Whereof we dream, have sway in each proud land
And patriotism, grown Godlike, scorn to stand
Bondslave to realms, but circle earth and seas?"

THE GOING OF THE BATTERY

WIVES' LAMENT

(November 2, 1899)

I

O it was sad enough, weak enough, mad enough—
Light in their loving as soldiers can be—
First to risk choosing them, leave alone losing them
Now, in far battle, beyond the South Sea! ...

II

Rain came down drenchingly; but we unblenchingly
Trudged on beside them through mirk and through mire,
They stepping steadily—only too readily!—
Scarce as if stepping brought parting-time nigher.

III

Great guns were gleaming there, living things seeming there,
Cloaked in their tar-cloths, upmouthed to the night;
Wheels wet and yellow from axle to felloe,
Throats blank of sound, but prophetic to sight.

IV

Gas-glimmers drearily, blearily, eerily
Lit our pale faces outstretched for one kiss,
While we stood prest to them, with a last quest to them
Not to court perils that honour could miss.

V

Sharp were those sighs of ours, blinded these eyes of ours,
When at last moved away under the arch
All we loved. Aid for them each woman prayed for them,
Treading back slowly the track of their march.

VI

Someone said: "Nevermore will they come: evermore
Are they now lost to us." O it was wrong!
Though may be hard their ways, some Hand will guard their ways,
Bear them through safely, in brief time or long.

VII

—Yet, voices haunting us, daunting us, taunting us,
Hint in the night-time when life beats are low
Other and graver things. . . . Hold we to braver things,
Wait we in trust, what Time's fulness shall show.

DRUMMER HODGE

I

They throw in Drummer Hodge, to rest
  Uncoffined—just as found:
His landmark is a kopje-crest
  That breaks the veldt around;
And foreign constellations west
  Each night above his mound.

II

Young Hodge the Drummer never knew—
  Fresh from his Wessex home—
The meaning of the broad Karoo,
  The Bush, the dusty loam,
And why uprose to nightly view
  Strange stars amid the gloam.

III

Yet portion of that unknown plain
  Will Hodge for ever be;
His homely Northern breast and brain
  Grow to some Southern tree,
And strange-eyed constellations reign
  His stars eternally.

THE MAN HE KILLED

"Had he and I but met
By some old ancient inn,
We should have sat us down to wet
Right many a nipperkin!

"But ranged as infantry,
And staring face to face,
I shot at him as he at me,
And killed him in his place.

"I shot him dead because—
Because he was my foe,
Just so: my foe of course he was;
That's clear enough; although

"He thought he'd 'list, perhaps,
Off-hand like—just as I—
Was out of work—had sold his traps—
No other reason why.

"Yes; quaint and curious war is!
You shoot a fellow down
You'd treat if met where any bar is,
Or help to half-a-crown."

1902.

THE SOULS OF THE SLAIN

I

The thick lids of Night closed upon me
    Alone at the Bill
    Of the Isle by the Race[1]—
Many-caverned, bald, wrinkled of face—
And with darkness and silence the spirit was on me
    To brood and be still.

II

No wind fanned the flats of the ocean,
    Or promontory sides,
    Or the ooze by the strand,
    Or the bent-bearded slope of the land,
Whose base took its rest amid everlong motion
    Of criss-crossing tides.

III

Soon from out of the Southward seemed nearing
    A whirr, as of wings
    Waved by mighty-vanned flies,
    Or by night-moths of measureless size,
And in softness and smoothness well-nigh beyond hearing
    Of corporal things.

IV

And they bore to the bluff, and alighted—
    A dim-discerned train
    Of sprites without mould,
    Frameless souls none might touch or might hold—
On the ledge by the turreted lantern, far-sighted
    By men of the main.

V

And I heard them say "Home!" and I knew them
    For souls of the felled
    On the earth's nether bord

1. The "Race" is the turbulent sea-area off the Bill of Portland, where contrary tides meet.

Under Capricorn, whither they'd warred,
And I neared in my awe, and gave heedfulness to them
 With breathings inheld.

VI

Then, it seemed, there approached from the northward
 A senior soul-flame
 Of the like filmy hue:
And he met them and spake: "Is it you,
O my men?" Said they, "Aye! We bear homeward and hearthward
 To feast on our fame!"

VII

"I've flown there before you," he said then:
 "Your households are well;
 But—your kin linger less
On your glory and war-mightiness
Than on dearer things."—"Dearer?" cried these from the dead then,
 "Of what do they tell?"

VIII

"Some mothers muse sadly, and murmur
 Your doings as boys—
 Recall the quaint ways
Of your babyhood's innocent days.
Some pray that, ere dying, your faith had grown firmer,
 And higher your joys.

IX

A father broods: 'Would I had set him
 To some humble trade,
 And so slacked his high fire,
And his passionate martial desire;
And told him no stories to woo him and whet him
 To this dire crusade!'"

X

"And, General, how hold out our sweet-hearts,
 Sworn loyal as doves?"
 —"Many mourn; many think
It is not unattractive to prink
Them in sables for heroes. Some fickle and fleet hearts
 Have found them new loves."

177

XI

"And our wives?" quoth another resignedly,
  "Dwell they on our deeds?"
  —"Deeds of home; that live yet
Fresh as new—deeds of fondness or fret;
Ancient words that were kindly expressed or unkindly,
  These, these have their heeds."

XII

—"Alas! then it seems that our glory
  Weighs less in their thought
  Than our old homely acts,
And the long-ago commonplace facts
Of our lives—held by us as scarce part of our story,
  And rated as nought!"

XIII

Then bitterly some: "Was it wise now
  To raise the tomb-door
  For such knowledge? Away!"
But the rest: "Fame we prized till to-day;
Yet that hearts keep us green for old kindness we prize now
  A thousand times more!"

XIV

Thus speaking, the trooped apparitions
  Began to disband
  And resolve them in two:
Those whose record was lovely and true
Bore to northward for home: those of bitter traditions
  Again left the land,

XV

And, towering to seaward in legions,
  They paused at a spot
  Overbending the Race—
That engulphing, ghast, sinister place—
Whither headlong they plunged, to the fathomless regions
  Of myriads forgot.

XVI

And the spirits of those who were homing
   Passed on, rushingly,
     Like the Pentecost Wind;
   And the whirr of their wayfaring thinned
And surceased on the sky, and but left in the gloaming
   Sea-mutterings and me.

December 1899.

"MEN WHO MARCH AWAY"
(Song of the Soldiers)

What of the faith and fire within us
    Men who march away
    Ere the barn-cocks say
    Night is growing gray,
Leaving all that here can win us;
What of the faith and fire within us
    Men who march away?

Is it a purblind prank, O think you,
    Friend with the musing eye,
    Who watch us stepping by
    With doubt and dolorous sigh?
Can much pondering so hoodwink you!
Is it a purblind prank, O think you,
    Friend with the musing eye?

Nay. We well see what we are doing,
    Though some may not see—
    Dalliers as they be—
    England's need are we;
Her distress would leave us rueing:
Nay. We well see what we are doing,
    Though some may not see!

In our heart of hearts believing
    Victory crowns the just,
    And that braggarts must
    Surely bite the dust,
Press we to the field ungrieving,
In our heart of hearts believing
    Victory crowns the just.

Hence the faith and fire within us
    Men who march away
    Ere the barn-cocks say

Night is growing gray,
Leaving all that here can win us;
Hence the faith and fire within us
Men who march away.

September 5, 1914.

BEFORE MARCHING AND AFTER
(In Memoriam F. W. G.)

Orion swung southward aslant
Where the starved Egdon pine-trees had thinned,
The Pleiads aloft seemed to pant
With the heather that twitched in the wind;
But he looked on indifferent to sights such as these,
Unswayed by love, friendship, home joy or home sorrow,
And wondered to what he would march on the morrow.

The crazed household-clock with its whirr
Rang midnight within as he stood,
He heard the low sighing of her
Who had striven from his birth for his good;
But he still only asked the spring starlight, the breeze,
What great thing or small thing his history would borrow
From that Game with Death he would play on the morrow.

When the heath wore the robe of late summer,
And the fuchsia-bells, hot in the sun,
Hung red by the door, a quick comer
Brought tidings that marching was done
For him who had joined in that game over-seas
Where Death stood to win, though his name was to borrow
A brightness therefrom not to fade on the morrow.

September 1915.

JEZREEL

ON ITS SEIZURE BY THE ENGLISH UNDER ALLENBY, SEPTEMBER 1918

Did they catch as it were in a Vision at shut of the day—
When their cavalry smote through the ancient Esdraelon Plain,
And they crossed where the Tishbite stood forth in his enemy's way—
His gaunt mournful Shade as he bade the King haste off amain?

On war-men at this end of time—even on Englishmen's eyes—
Who slay with their arms of new might in that long-ago place,
Flashed he who drove furiously? . . . Ah, did the phantom arise
Of that queen, of that proud Tyrian woman who painted her face?

Faintly marked they the words "Throw her down!" from the Night eerily,
Spectre-spots of the blood of her body on some rotten wall?
And the thin note of pity that came: "A King's daughter is she,"
As they passed where she trodden was once by the chargers' footfall?

Could such be the hauntings of men of to-day, at the cease
Of pursuit, at the dusk-hour, ere slumber their senses could seal?
Enghosted seers, kings—one on horseback who asked "Is it peace?" . . .
Yea, strange things and spectral may men have beheld in Jezreel!

September 24, 1918.

IN TIME OF "THE BREAKING OF NATIONS"[1]

I

Only a man harrowing clods
    In a slow silent walk
With an old horse that stumbles and nods
    Half asleep as they stalk.

II

Only thin smoke without flame
    From the heaps of couch-grass;
Yet this will go onward the same
    Though Dynasties pass.

III

Yonder a maid and her wight
    Come whispering by;
War's annals will cloud into night
    Ere their story die.

1915.

1. Jer. li. 20.

From "The Dynasts"

THE NIGHT OF TRAFALGÁR
(Boatman's Song)

I

In the wild October night-time, when the wind raved round the land,
And the Back-sea met the Front-sea, and our doors were blocked with sand,
And we heard the drub of Dead-man's Bay, where bones of thousands are,
We knew not what the day had done for us at Trafalgár.
Had done,
Had done,
For us at Trafalgár!

II

"Pull hard, and make the Nothe, or down we go!" one says, says he.
We pulled; and bedtime brought the storm; but snug at home slept we.
Yet all the while our gallants after fighting through the day,
Were beating up and down the dark, sou'-west of Cadiz Bay.
The dark,
The dark,
Sou'-west of Cadiz Bay!

III

The victors and the vanquished then the storm it tossed and tore,
As hard they strove, those worn-out men, upon that surly shore;
Dead Nelson and his half-dead crew, his foes from near and far,
Were rolled together on the deep that night at Trafalgár
The deep,
The deep,
That night at Trafalgár!

ALBUERA

They come, beset by riddling hail;
They sway like sedges in a gale;
They fail, and win, and win, and fail. Albuera!

They gain the ground there, yard by yard,
Their brows and hair and lashes charred,
Their blackened teeth set firm and hard.

Their mad assailants rave and reel,
And face, as men who scorn to feel,
The close-lined, three-edged prongs of steel.

Till faintness follows closing-in,
When, faltering headlong down, they spin
Like leaves. But those pay well who win Albuera.

Out of six thousand souls that sware
To hold the mount, or pass elsewhere,
But eighteen hundred muster there.

Pale Colonels, Captains, ranksmen lie,
Facing the earth or facing sky;—
They strove to live, they stretch to die.

Friends, foemen, mingle; heap and heap.—
Hide their hacked bones, Earth!—deep, deep, deep,
Where harmless worms caress and creep.

Hide their hacked bones, Earth!—deep, deep, deep,
Where harmless worms caress and creep.—
What man can grieve? what woman weep?
Better than waking is to sleep! Albuera!

HUSSAR'S SONG

BUDMOUTH DEARS

I

When we lay where Budmouth Beach is,
O, the girls were fresh as peaches,
With their tall and tossing figures and their eyes of blue and brown!
And our hearts would ache with longing
As we paced from our sing-songing,
With a smart *Clink! Clink!* up the Esplanade and down.

II

They distracted and delayed us
By the pleasant pranks they played us,
And what marvel, then, if troopers, even of regiments of renown,
On whom flashed those eyes divine, O,
Should forget the countersign, O,
As we tore *Clink! Clink!* back to camp above the town.

III

Do they miss us much, I wonder,
Now that war has swept us sunder,
And we roam from where the faces smile to where the faces frown?
And no more behold the features
Of the fair fantastic creatures,
And no more *Clink! Clink!* past the parlours of the town?

IV

Shall we once again there meet them?
Falter fond attempts to greet them?
Will the gay sling-jacket glow again beside the muslin gown?—
Will they archly quiz and con us
With a sideway glance upon us,
While our spurs *Clink! Clink!* up the Esplanade and down?

'MY LOVE'S GONE A-FIGHTING'
(*Country-girl's Song*)

I

My Love's gone a-fighting
   Where war-trumpets call,
The wrongs o' men righting
   Wi' carbine and ball,
And sabre for smiting,
   And charger, and all!

II

Of whom does he think there
   Where war-trumpets call?
To whom does he drink there,
   Wi' carbine and ball
On battle's red brink there,
   And charger, and all?

III

Her, whose voice he hears humming
   Where war-trumpets call,
"I wait, Love, thy coming
   Wi' carbine and ball,
And bandsmen a-drumming
   Thee, charger and all!"

THE EVE OF WATERLOO
(*Chorus of Phantoms*)

The eyelids of eve fall together at last,
And the forms so foreign to field and tree
Lie down as though native, and slumber fast!

Sore are the thrills of misgiving we see
In the artless champaign at this harlequinade,
Distracting a vigil where calm should be!

The green seems opprest, and the Plain afraid
Of a Something to come, whereof these are the proofs,—
Neither earthquake, nor storm, nor eclipse's shade!

Yea, the coneys are scared by the thud of hoofs,
And their white scuts flash at their vanishing heels,
And swallows abandon the hamlet-roofs.

The mole's tunnelled chambers are crushed by wheels,
The lark's eggs scattered, their owners fled;
And the hedgehog's household the sapper unseals.

The snail draws in at the terrible tread,
But in vain; he is crushed by the felloe-rim;
The worm asks what can be overhead,

And wriggles deep from a scene so grim,
And guesses him safe; for he does not know
What a foul red flood will be soaking him!

Beaten about by the heel and toe
Are butterflies, sick of the day's long rheum,
To die of a worse than the weather-foe.

Trodden and bruised to a miry tomb
Are ears that have greened but will never be gold,
And flowers in the bud that will never bloom.

So the season's intent, ere its fruit unfold,
Is frustrate, and mangled, and made succumb,
Like a youth of promise struck stark and cold! . . .

And what of these who to-night have come?
—The young sleep sound; but the weather awakes
In the veterans, pains from the past that numb;

Old stabs of Ind, old Peninsular aches,
Old Friedland chills, haunt their moist mud bed;
Cramps from Austerlitz; till their slumber breaks

And each soul sighs as he shifts his head
On the loam he's to lease with the other dead
From to-morrow's mist-fall till Time be sped!

CHORUS OF THE PITIES
(After the Battle)

SEMICHORUS I

To Thee whose eye all Nature owns,
Who hurlest Dynasts from their thrones,[1]
And liftest those of low estate
We sing, with Her men consecrate!

II

Yea, Great and Good, Thee, Thee we hail,
Who shak'st the strong, Who shield'st the frail,
Who hadst not shaped such souls as we
If tendermercy lacked in Thee!

I

Though times be when the mortal moan
Seems unascending to Thy throne,
Though seers do not as yet explain
Why Suffering sobs to Thee in vain;

II

We hold that Thy unscanted scope
Affords a food for final Hope,
That mild-eyed Prescience ponders nigh
Life's loom, to lull it by-and-by.

I

Therefore we quire to highest height
The Wellwiller, the kindly Might
That balances the Vast for weal,
That purges as by wounds to heal.

II

The systemed suns the skies enscroll
Obey Thee in their rhythmic roll,
Ride radiantly at Thy command,
Are darkened by Thy Masterhand!

1. καθεῖλε ΔΥΝΆΣΤΑΣ ἀπὸ θρόνων.—*Magnificat.*

I

And these pale panting multitudes
Seen surging here, their moils, their moods,
All shall "fulfil their joy" in Thee,
In Thee abide eternally!

II

Exultant adoration give
The Alone, through Whom all living live,
The Alone, in Whom all dying die,
Whose means the End shall justify! Amen.

LAST CHORUS

SEMICHORUS I OF THE YEARS

Last as first the question rings
Of the Will's long travailings;
    Why the All-mover,
    Why the All-prover
Ever urges on and measures out the chordless chime of Things.[1]

II

Heaving dumbly
As we deem,
Moulding numbly
As in dream,
Apprehending not how fare the sentient subjects of Its scheme.

SEMICHORUS I OF THE PITIES

Nay;—shall not Its blindness break?
Yea, must not Its heart awake,
    Promptly tending
    To Its mending
In a genial germing purpose, and for loving-kindness' sake?

II

Should It never
Curb or cure
Aught whatever
Those endure
Whom It quickens, let them darkle to extinction swift and sure.

CHORUS

But—a stirring thrills the air
Like to sounds of joyance there
    That the rages
    Of the ages
Shall be cancelled, and deliverance offered from the darts that were,
Consciousness the Will informing, till It fashion all things fair!

---

1. Hor. *Epis.* i. 12.

Additional Poems

from Wessex Poems

A CONFESSION TO A FRIEND IN TROUBLE

Your troubles shrink not, though I feel them less
Here, far away, than when I tarried near;
I even smile old smiles—with listlessness—
Yet smiles they are, not ghastly mockeries mere.

A thought too strange to house within my brain
Haunting its outer precincts I discern:
—That I will not show zeal again to learn
Your griefs, and, sharing them, renew my pain. . . .

It goes, like murky bird or buccaneer
That shapes its lawless figure on the main,
And staunchness tends to banish utterly
The unseemly instinct that had lodgment here;
Yet, comrade old, can bitterer knowledge be
Than that, though banned, such instinct was in me!

1866.

SHE, TO HIM

I

When you shall see me in the toils of Time,
My lauded beauties carried off from me,
My eyes no longer stars as in their prime,
My name forgot of Maiden Fair and Free;

When, in your being, heart concedes to mind,
And judgment, though you scarce its process know,
Recalls the excellencies I once enshrined,
And you are irked that they have withered so;

Remembering mine the loss is, not the blame,
That Sportsman Time but rears his brood to kill,
Knowing me in my soul the very same—
One who would die to spare you touch of ill!—
Will you not grant to old affection's claim
The hand of friendship down Life's sunless hill?

1866.

SAN SEBASTIAN
(August 1813)
With Thoughts of Sergeant M—— (Pensioner), Who Died 185–

"Why, Sergeant, stray on the Ivel Way,
As though at home there were spectres rife?
From first to last 'twas a proud career!
And your sunny years with a gracious wife
    Have brought you a daughter dear.

"I watched her to-day; a more comely maid,
As she danced in her muslin bowed with blue,
Round a Hintock maypole never gayed."
—"Aye, aye; I watched her this day, too,
    As it happens," the Sergeant said.

"My daughter is now," he again began,
"Of just such an age as one I knew
When we of the Line, the Forlorn-hope van,
On an August morning—a chosen few—
    Stormed San Sebastian.

"She's a score less three; so about was *she*—
The maiden I wronged in Peninsular days. . . .
You may prate of your prowess in lusty times,
But as years gnaw inward you blink your bays,
    And see too well your crimes!

"We'd stormed it at night, by the flapping light
Of burning towers, and the mortar's boom:
We'd topped the breach; but had failed to stay,
For our files were misled by the baffling gloom;
    And we said we'd storm by day.

"So, out of the trenches, with features set,
On that hot, still morning, in measured pace,
Our column climbed; climbed higher yet,
Past the fauss'bray, scarp, up the curtain-face,
    And along the parapet.

"From the battered hornwork the cannoneers
Hove crashing balls of iron fire;
On the shaking gap mount the volunteers
In files, and as they mount expire
    Amid curses, groans, and cheers.

"Five hours did we storm, five hours re-form,
As Death cooled those hot blood pricked on;
Till our cause was helped by a woe within:
They were blown from the summit we'd leapt upon,
    And madly we entered in.

"On end for plunder, 'mid rain and thunder
That burst with the lull of our cannonade,
We vamped the streets in the stifling air—
Our hunger unsoothed, our thirst unstayed—
    And ransacked the buildings there.

"From the shady vaults of their walls of white
We rolled rich puncheons of Spanish grape,
Till at length, with the fire of the wine alight,
I saw at a doorway a fair fresh shape—
    A woman, a sylph, or sprite.

"Afeard she fled, and with heated head
I pursued to the chamber she called her own;
—When might is right no qualms deter,
And having her helpless and alone
    I wreaked my will on her.

"She raised her beseeching eyes to me,
And I heard the words of prayer she sent
In her own soft language. . . . Fatefully
I copied those eyes for my punishment
    In begetting the girl you see!

"So, to-day I stand with a God-set brand
Like Cain's, when he wandered from kindred's ken. . . .
I served through the war that made Europe free;
I wived me in peace-year. But, hid from men,
    I bear that mark on me.

"Maybe we shape our offspring's guise
From fancy, or we know not what,
And that no deep impression dies,—
For the mother of my child is not
    The mother of her eyes.

"And I nightly stray on the Ivel Way
As though at home there were spectres rife;
I delight me not in my proud career;
And 'tis coals of fire that a gracious wife
    Should have brought me a daughter dear!"

A SIGN-SEEKER

I mark the months in liveries dank and dry,
  The noontides many-shaped and hued;
    I see the nightfall shades subtrude,
And hear the monotonous hours clang negligently by.

I view the evening bonfires of the sun
  On hills where morning rains have hissed;
    The eyeless countenance of the mist
Pallidly rising when the summer droughts are done.

I have seen the lightning-blade, the leaping star,
  The cauldrons of the sea in storm,
    Have felt the earthquake's lifting arm,
And trodden where abysmal fires and snow-cones are.

I learn to prophesy the hid eclipse,
  The coming of eccentric orbs;
    To mete the dust the sky absorbs,
To weigh the sun, and fix the hour each planet dips.

I witness fellow earth-men surge and strive;
  Assemblies meet, and throb, and part;
    Death's sudden finger, sorrow's smart;
—All the vast various moils that mean a world alive.

But that I fain would wot of shuns my sense—
  Those sights of which old prophets tell,
    Those signs the general word so well
As vouchsafed their unheed, denied my long suspense

In graveyard green, where his pale dust lies pent
  To glimpse a phantom parent, friend,
    Wearing his smile, and "Not the end!"
Outbreathing softly: that were blest enlightenment;

Or, if a dead Love's lips, whom dreams reveal
  When midnight imps of King Decay

Delve sly to solve me back to clay,
Should leave some print to prove her spirit-kisses real;

Or, when Earth's Frail lie bleeding of her Strong,
  If some Recorder, as in Writ,
  Near to the weary scene should flit
And drop one plume as pledge that Heaven inscrolls the wrong.

—There are who, rapt to heights of trancelike trust,
  These tokens claim to feel and see,
  Read radiant hints of times to be—
Of heart to heart returning after dust to dust.

Such scope is granted not to lives like mine . . .
  I have lain in dead men's beds, have walked
  The tombs of those with whom I had talked,
Called many a gone and goodly one to shape a sign,

And panted for response. But none replies;
  No warnings loom, nor whisperings
  To open out my limitings,
And Nescience mutely muses: When a man falls he lies.

MY CICELY
(17–)

"Alive?"—And I leapt in my wonder,
    Was faint of my joyance,
And grasses and grove shone in garments
    Of glory to me.

"She lives, in a plenteous well-being,
    To-day as aforehand;
The dead bore the name—though a rare one—
    The name that bore she."

She lived . . . I, afar in the city
    Of frenzy-led factions,
Had squandered green years and maturer
    In bowing the knee

To Baals illusive and specious,
    Till chance had there voiced me
That one I loved vainly in nonage
    Had ceased her to be.

The passion the planets had scowled on,
    And change had let dwindle,
Her death-rumour smartly relifted
    To full apogee.

I mounted a steed in the dawning
    With acheful remembrance,
And made for the ancient West Highway
    To far Exonb'ry.

Passing heaths, and the House of Long Sieging,
    I neared the thin steeple
That tops the fair fane of Poore's olden
    Episcopal see;

And, changing anew my blown bearer,
    I traversed the downland

Whereon the bleak hill-graves of Chieftains
  Bulge barren of tree;

And still sadly onward I followed
  That Highway the Icen,
Which trails its pale riband down Wessex
  By lynchet and lea.

Along through the Stour-bordered Forum
  Where Legions had wayfared,
And where the slow river-face glasses
  Its green canopy,

And by Weatherbury Castle, and thencefrom
  Through Casterbridge held I
Still on, to entomb her my mindsight
  Saw stretched pallidly.

No highwayman's trot blew the night-wind
  To me so life-weary,
But only the creak of a gibbet
  Or waggoner's jee.

Triple-ramparted Maidon gloomed grayly
  Above me from southward,
And north the hill-fortress of Eggar.
  And square Pummerie.

The Nine-Pillared Cromlech, the Bride-streams,
  The Axe, and the Otter
I passed, to the gate of the city
  Where Exe scents the sea;

Till, spent, in the graveacre pausing,
  I learnt 'twas not *my* Love
To whom Mother Church had just murmured
  A last lullaby.

—"Then, where dwells the Canon's kinswoman,
  My friend of aforetime?"

I asked, to disguise my heart-heavings
   And new ecstasy.

"She wedded."—"Ah!"—"Wedded beneath her—
   She keeps the stage-hostel
Ten miles hence, beside the great Highway—
   The famed Lions-Three.

"Her spouse was her lackey—no option
   'Twixt wedlock and worse things;
A lapse over-sad for a lady
   Of her pedigree!"

I shuddered, said nothing, and wandered
   To shades of green laurel:
More ghastly than death were these tidings
   Of life's irony!

For, on my ride down I had halted
   Awhile at the Lions,
And her—her whose name had once opened
   My heart as a key—

I'd looked on, unknowing, and witnessed
   Her jests with the tapsters,
Her liquor-fired face, her thick accents
   In naming her fee.

"O God, why this seeming derision!"
   I cried in my anguish:
"O once Loved, O fair Unforgotten—
   That Thing—meant it thee!

"Inurned and at peace, lost but sainted,
   Were grief I could compass;
Depraved—'tis for Christ's poor dependent
   A cruel decree!"

I backed on the Highway; but passed not
   The hostel. Within there
Too mocking to Love's re-expression
   Was Time's repartee!

Uptracking where Legions had wayfared
    By cromlechs unstoried,
And lynchets, and sepultured Chieftains,
    In self-colloquy,

A feeling stirred in me and strengthened
    That *she* was not my Love,
But she of the garth, who lay rapt in
    Her long reverie.

And thence till to-day I persuade me
    That this was the true one;
That Death stole intact her young dearness
    And innocency.

Frail-witted, illuded they call me;
    I may be. Far better
To dream than to own the debasement
    Of sweet Cicely.

Moreover I rate it unseemly
    To hold that kind Heaven
Could work such device—to her ruin
    And my misery.

So, lest I disturb my choice vision,
    I shun the West Highway,
Even now, when the knaps ring with rhythms
    From blackbird and bee;

And feel that with slumber half-conscious
    She rests in the church-hay,
Her spirit unsoiled as in youth-time
    When lovers were we.

THE IVY-WIFE

I longed to love a full-boughed beech
    And be as high as he:
I stretched an arm within his reach,
    And signalled unity.
But with his drip he forced a breach,
    And tried to poison me.

I gave the grasp of partnership
    To one of other race—
A plane: he barked him strip by strip
    From upper bough to base;
And me therewith; for gone my grip,
    My arms could not enlace.

In new affection next I strove
    To coll an ash I saw,
And he in trust received my love;
    Till with my soft green claw
I cramped and bound him as I wove . . .
    Such was my love: ha-ha!

By this I gained his strength and height
    Without his rivalry.
But in my triumph I lost sight
    Of afterhaps. Soon he,
Being bark-bound, flagged, snapped, fell outright,
    And in his fall felled me!

NATURE'S QUESTIONING

When I look forth at dawning, pool,
    Field, flock, and lonely tree,
    All seem to gaze at me
Like chastened children sitting silent in a school;

    Their faces dulled, constrained, and worn,
        As though the master's ways
        Through the long teaching days
Had cowed them till their early zest was overborne.

    Upon them stirs in lippings mere
        (As if once clear in call,
        But now scarce breathed at all)—
"We wonder, ever wonder, why we find us here!

    "Has some Vast Imbecility,
        Mighty to build and blend,
        But impotent to tend,
Framed us in jest, and left us now to hazardry?

    "Or come we of an Automaton
        Unconscious of our pains? . . .
        Or are we live remains
Of Godhead dying downwards, brain and eye now gone?

    "Or is it that some high Plan betides,
        As yet not understood,
        Of Evil stormed by Good,
We the Forlorn Hope over which Achievement strides?"

    Thus things around. No answerer I. . . .
        Meanwhile the winds, and rains,
        And Earth's old glooms and pains
Are still the same, and Life and Death are neighbours nigh.

THE IMPERCIPIENT
(At a Cathedral Service)

That with this bright believing band
    I have no claim to be,
That faiths by which my comrades stand
    Seem fantasies to me,
And mirage-mists their Shining Land,
    Is a strange destiny.

Why thus my soul should be consigned
    To infelicity,
Why always I must feel as blind
    To sights my brethren see,
Why joys they've found I cannot find.
    Abides a mystery.

Since heart of mine knows not that ease
    Which they know; since it be
That He who breathes All's Well to these
    Breathes no All's-Well to me,
My lack might move their sympathies
    And Christian charity!

I am like a gazer who should mark
    An inland company
Standing upfingered, with, "Hark! hark!
    The glorious distant sea!"
And feel, "Alas, 'tis but yon dark
    And wind-swept pine to me!"

Yet I would bear my shortcomings
    With meet tranquillity,
But for the charge that blessed things
    I'd liefer not have be.
O, doth a bird deprived of wings
    Go earth-bound wilfully!

     . . . . .

Enough. As yet disquiet clings
    About us. Rest shall we.

from Poems of the Past and the Present

A WIFE IN LONDON
(*December 1899*)

I

She sits in the tawny vapour
  That the Thames-side lanes have uprolled,
  Behind whose webby fold on fold
Like a waning taper
  The street-lamp glimmers cold.

A messenger's knock cracks smartly,
  Flashed news is in her hand
  Of meaning it dazes to understand
Though shaped so shortly:
  He—has fallen—in the far South Land. . . .

II

'Tis the morrow; the fog hangs thicker,
  The postman nears and goes:
  A letter is brought whose lines disclose
By the firelight flicker
  His hand, whom the worm now knows:

Fresh—firm—penned in highest feather—
  Page-full of his hoped return,
  And of home-planned jaunts by brake and burn
In the summer weather,
  And of new love that they would learn.

DOOM AND SHE

I

There dwells a mighty pair—
Slow, statuesque, intense—
Amid the vague Immense:
None can their chronicle declare,
Nor why they be, nor whence.

II

Mother of all things made,
Matchless in artistry,
Unlit with sight is she.—
And though her ever well-obeyed
Vacant of feeling he.

III

The Matron mildly asks—
A throb in every word—
"Our clay-made creatures, lord.
How fare they in their mortal tasks
Upon Earth's bounded bord?

IV

"The fate of those I bear,
Dear lord, pray turn and view,
And notify me true;
Shapings that eyelessly I dare
Maybe I would undo.

V

"Sometimes from lairs of life
Methinks I catch a groan,
Or multitudinous moan,
As though I had schemed a world of strife,
Working by touch alone."

VI

"World-weaver!" he replies,
"I scan all thy domain;
But since nor joy nor pain

218

It lies in me to recognize,
  Thy questionings are vain.

VII

"World-weaver! what *is* Grief?
And what are Right, and Wrong,
And Feeling, that belong
To creatures all who owe thee fief?
  Why is Weak worse than Strong?" . . .

VIII

—Unanswered, curious, meek,
  She broods in sad surmise. . . .
—Some say they have heard her sighs
On Alpine height or Polar peak
  When the night tempests rise.

THE BULLFINCHES

Brother Bulleys, let us sing
From the dawn till evening!—
For we know not that we go not
When to-day's pale pinions fold
Where they be that sang of old.

When I flew to Blackmoor Vale,
Whence the green-gowned faeries hail,
Roosting near them I could hear them
Speak of queenly Nature's ways,
Means, and moods,—well known to fays.

All we creatures, nigh and far
(Said they there), the Mother's are;
Yet she never shows endeavour
To protect from warrings wild
Bird or beast she calls her child.

Busy in her handsome house
Known as Space, she falls a-drowse;
Yet, in seeming, works on dreaming,
While beneath her groping hands
Fiends make havoc in her bands.

How her hussif'ry succeeds
She unknows or she unheeds,
All things making for Death's taking!
—So the green-gowned faeries say
Living over Blackmoor way.

Come then, brethren, let us sing,
From the dawn till evening!—
For we know not that we go not
When the day's pale pinions fold
Where those be that sang of old.

GOD-FORGOTTEN

I towered far, and lo! I stood within
  The presence of the Lord Most High,
Sent thither by the sons of Earth, to win
    Some answer to their cry.

  —"The Earth, sayest thou? The Human race?
  By Me created? Sad its lot?
Nay: I have no remembrance of such place:
    Such world I fashioned not."—

  —"O Lord, forgive me when I say
  Thou spakest the word that made it all."—
"The Earth of men—let me bethink me. . . . Yea!
    I dimly do recall

  "Some tiny sphere I built long back
  (Mid millions of such shapes of mine)
So named . . . It perished, surely—not a wrack
    Remaining, or a sign?

  "It lost my interest from the first,
  My aims therefor succeeding ill;
Haply it died of doing as it durst?"—
    "Lord, it existeth still."—

  "Dark, then, its life! For not a cry
  Of aught it bears do I now hear;
Of its own act the threads were snapt whereby
    Its plaints had reached mine ear.

  "It used to ask for gifts of good,
  Till came its severance, self-entailed,
When sudden silence on that side ensued,
    And has till now prevailed.

  "All other orbs have kept in touch;
  Their voicings reach me speedily:

Thy people took upon them overmuch
    In sundering them from me!

"And it is strange—though sad enough—
    Earth's race should think that one whose call
Frames, daily, shining spheres of flawless stuff
    Must heed their tainted ball! . . .

"But sayest it is by pangs distraught,
    And strife, and silent suffering?—
Sore grieved am I that injury should be wrought
    Even on so poor a thing!

"Thou shouldst have learnt that *Not to Mend*
    For Me could mean but *Not to Know*:
Hence, Messengers! and straightway put an end
    To what men undergo." . . .

Homing at dawn, I thought to see
    One of the Messengers standing by.
—Oh, childish thought! . . . Yet often it comes to me
    When trouble hovers nigh.

TO FLOWERS FROM ITALY IN WINTER

Sunned in the South, and here to-day;
　—If all organic things
Be sentient, Flowers, as some men say,
　What are your ponderings?

How can you stay, nor vanish quite
　From this bleak spot of thorn,
And birch, and fir, and frozen white
　Expanse of the forlorn?

Frail luckless exiles hither brought!
　Your dust will not regain
Old sunny haunts of Classic thought.
　When you shall waste and wane;

But mix with alien earth, be lit
　With frigid Boreal flame,
And not a sign remain in it
　To tell man whence you came.

HIS IMMORTALITY

I

I saw a dead man's finer part
Shining within each faithful heart
Of those bereft. Then said I: "This must be
   His immortality."

II

I looked there as the seasons wore,
And still his soul continuously bore
A life in theirs. But less its shine excelled
   Than when I first beheld.

III

His fellow-yearsmen passed, and then
In later hearts I looked for him again;
And found him—shrunk, alas! into a thin
   And spectral mannikin.

IV

Lastly I ask—now old and chill—
If aught of him remain unperished still;
And find, in me alone, a feeble spark,
   Dying amid the dark.

February 1899.

AN AUGUST MIDNIGHT

I

A shaded lamp and a waving blind,
And the beat of a clock from a distant floor:
On this scene enter—winged, horned, and spined—
A longlegs, a moth, and a dumbledore;
While 'mid my page there idly stands
A sleepy fly, that rubs its hands . . .

II

Thus meet we five, in this still place,
At this point of time, at this point in space.
—My guests besmear my new-penned line,
Or bang at the lamp and fall supine.
"God's humblest, they!" I muse. Yet why?
They know Earth-secrets that know not I.

Max Gate, 1899.

A MAN

(In Memory of H. of M.)

I

In Casterbridge there stood a noble pile,
Wrought with pilaster, bay, and balustrade
In tactful times when shrewd Eliza swayed.—
 On burgher, squire, and clown
It smiled the long street down for near a mile.

II

But evil days beset that domicile;
The stately beauties of its roof and wall
Passed into sordid hands. Condemned to fall
 Were cornice, quoin, and cove,
And all that art had wove in antique style.

III

Among the hired dismantlers entered there
One till the moment of his task untold.
When charged therewith he gazed, and answered bold:
 "Be needy I or no,
I will not help lay low a house so fair!

IV

"Hunger is hard. But since the terms be such—
No wage, or labour stained with the disgrace
Of wrecking what our age cannot replace
 To save its tasteless soul—
I'll do without your dole. Life is not much!"

V

Dismissed with sneers he packed his tools and went,
And wandered workless; for it seemed unwise
To close with one who dared to criticize
 And carp on points of taste:
Rude men should work where placed, and be content.

VI

Years whiled. He aged, sank, sickened; and was not:
And it was said, "A man intractable

And curst is gone." None sighed to hear his knell,
    None sought his churchyard-place;
His name, his rugged face, were soon forgot.

VII

The stones of that fair hall lie far and wide,
And but a few recall its ancient mould;
Yet when I pass the spot I long to hold
    As truth what fancy saith:
"His protest lives where deathless things abide!"

THE RUINED MAID

"O 'melia, my dear, this does everything crown!
Who could have supposed I should meet you in Town?
And whence such fair garments, such prosperi-ty?"—
"O didn't you know I'd been ruined?" said she.

—"You left us in tatters, without shoes or socks,
Tired of digging potatoes, and spudding up docks;
And now you've gay bracelets and bright feathers three!"—
"Yes: that's how we dress when we're ruined," said she.

—"At home in the barton you said 'thee' and 'thou,'
And 'thik oon,' and 'theäs oon,' and 't'other'; but now
Your talking quite fits 'ee for high compa-ny!"—
"Some polish is gained with one's ruin," said she.

—"Your hands were like paws then, your face blue and bleak
But now I'm bewitched by your delicate cheek,
And your little gloves fit as on any la-dy!"—
"We never do work when we're ruined," said she.

—"You used to call home-life a hag-ridden dream,
And you'd sigh, and you'd sock; but at present you seem
To know not of megrims or melancho-ly!"—
"True. One's pretty lively when ruined," said she.

—"I wish I had feathers, a fine sweeping gown,
And a delicate face, and could strut about Town!"—
"My dear—a raw country girl, such as you be,
Cannot quite expect that. You ain't ruined," said she.

Westbourne Park Villas, 1866.

THE RESPECTABLE BURGHER ON "THE HIGHER CRITICISM"

Since Reverend Doctors now declare
That clerks and people must prepare
To doubt if Adam ever were;
To hold the flood a local scare;
To argue, though the stolid stare,
That everything had happened ere
The prophets to its happening sware;
That David was no giant-slayer,
Nor one to call a God-obeyer
In certain details we could spare,
But rather was a debonair
Shrewd bandit, skilled as banjo-player:
That Solomon sang the fleshly Fair,
And gave the Church no thought whate'er,
That Esther with her royal wear,
And Mordecai, the son of Jair,
And Joshua's triumphs, Job's despair,
And Balaam's ass's bitter blare;
Nebuchadnezzar's furnace-flare,
And Daniel and the den affair,
And other stories rich and rare,
Were writ to make old doctrine wear
Something of a romantic air:
That the Nain widow's only heir,
And Lazarus with cadaverous glare
(As done in oils by Piombo's care)
Did not return from Sheol's lair:
That Jael set a fiendish snare,
That Pontius Pilate acted square,
That never a sword cut Malchus' ear;
And (but for shame I must forbear)
That —— —— did not reappear! . . .
—Since thus they hint, nor turn a hair,
All churchgoing will I forswear,
And sit on Sundays in my chair,
And read that moderate man Voltaire.

IN TENEBRIS I
"Percussus sum sicut foenum, et aruit cor meum."—*Ps.* ci.

Wintertime nighs;
But my bereavement-pain
It cannot bring again:
Twice no one dies.

Flower-petals flee;
But, since it once hath been,
No more that severing scene
Can harrow me.

Birds faint in dread:
I shall not lose old strength
In the lone frost's black length:
Strength long since fled!

Leaves freeze to dun;
But friends can not turn cold
This season as of old
For him with none.

Tempests may scath;
But love can not make smart
Again this year his heart
Who no heart hath.

Black is night's cope;
But death will not appal
One who, past doubtings all,
Waits in unhope.

IN TENEBRIS III

"Heu mihi, quia incolatus meus prolongatus est! Habitavi cum
habitantibus Cedar; multum incola fuit anima mea."—*Ps.* cxix.

There have been times when I well might have passed and the ending have
    come—
Points in my path when the dark might have stolen on me, artless, unrueing—
Ere I had learnt that the world was a welter of futile doing:
Such had been times when I well might have passed, and the ending have come!

Say, on the noon when the half-sunny hours told that April was nigh,
And I upgathered and cast forth the snow from the crocus-border,
Fashioned and furbished the soil into a summer-seeming order,
Glowing in gladsome faith that I quickened the year thereby.

Or on that loneliest of eves when afar and benighted we stood,
She who upheld me and I, in the midmost of Egdon together,
Confident I in her watching and ward through the blackening heather,
Deeming her matchless in might and with measureless scope endued.

Or on that winter-wild night when, reclined by the chimney-nook quoin,
Slowly a drowse overgat me, the smallest and feeblest of folk there,
Weak from my baptism of pain; when at times and anon I awoke there—
Heard of a world wheeling on, with no listing or longing to join.

Even then I while unweeting that vision could vex or that knowledge could numb,
That sweets to the mouth in the belly are bitter, and tart, and untoward,
Then, on some dim-coloured scene should my briefly raised curtain have lowered,
Then might the Voice that is law have said "Cease!" and the ending have come.

1896.

from Time's Laughingstocks

THE FARM-WOMAN'S WINTER

I

If seasons all were summers,
   And leaves would never fall,
And hopping casement-comers
   Were foodless not at all,
And fragile folk might be here
   That white winds bid depart;
Then one I used to see here
   Would warm my wasted heart!

II

One frail, who, bravely tilling
   Long hours in gripping gusts,
Was mastered by their chilling,
   And now his ploughshare rusts.
So savage winter catches
   The breath of limber things,
And what I love he snatches,
   And what I love not, brings.

AUTUMN IN KING'S HINTOCK PARK

Here by the baring bough
　　Raking up leaves,
Often I ponder how
　　Springtime deceives,—
I, an old woman now,
　　Raking up leaves.

Here in the avenue
　　Raking up leaves,
Lords' ladies pass in view,
　　Until one heaves
Sighs at life's russet hue,
　　Raking up leaves!

Just as my shape you see
　　Raking up leaves,
I saw, when fresh and free,
　　Those memory weaves
Into grey ghosts by me,
　　Raking up leaves.

Yet, Dear, though one may sigh,
　　Raking up leaves,
New leaves will dance on high—
　　Earth never grieves!—
Will not, when missed am I
　　Raking up leaves.

1901.

1967

In five-score summers! All new eyes,
New minds, new modes, new fools, new wise;
New woes to weep, new joys to prize;

With nothing left of me and you
In that live century's vivid view
Beyond a pinch of dust or two;

A century which, if not sublime,
Will show, I doubt not, at its prime,
A scope above this blinkered time.

—Yet what to me how far above?
For I would only ask thereof
That thy worm should be my worm, Love!

16 Westbourne Park Villas, 1867.

AT WAKING

When night was lifting,
And dawn had crept under its shade,
  Amid cold clouds drifting
Dead-white as a corpse outlaid,
    With a sudden scare
    I seemed to behold
    My Love in bare
    Hard lines unfold.

  Yea, in a moment,
An insight that would not die
  Killed her old endowment
Of charm that had capped all nigh,
    Which vanished to none
    Like the gilt of a cloud,
    And showed her but one
    Of the common crowd.

  She seemed but a sample
Of earth's poor average kind,
  Lit up by no ample
Enrichments of mien or mind.
    I covered my eyes
    As to cover the thought,
    And unrecognize
    What the morn had taught.

  O vision appalling
When the one believed-in thing
  Is seen falling, falling,
With all to which hope can cling.
    Off: it is not true;
    For it cannot be
    That the prize I drew
    Is a blank to me!

Weymouth, 1869.

238

IN THE VAULTED WAY

In the vaulted way, where the passage turned
To the shadowy corner that none could see,
You paused for our parting,—plaintively;
Though overnight had come words that burned
My fond frail happiness out of me.

And then I kissed you,—despite my thought
That our spell must end when reflection came
On what you had deemed me, whose one long aim
Had been to serve you; that what I sought
Lay not in a heart that could breathe such blame.

But yet I kissed you; whereon you again
As of old kissed me. Why, why was it so?
Do you cleave to me after that light-tongued blow?
If you scorned me at eventide, how love then?
The thing is dark, Dear. I do not know.

THE END OF THE EPISODE

Indulge no more may we
In this sweet-bitter pastime:
The love-light shines the last time
  Between you, Dear, and me.

There shall remain no trace
Of what so closely tied us,
And blank as ere love eyed us
  Will be our meeting-place.

The flowers and thymy air,
Will they now miss our coming?
The dumbles thin their humming
  To find we haunt not there?

Though fervent was our vow,
Though ruddily ran our pleasure,
Bliss has fulfilled its measure,
  And sees its sentence now.

Ache deep; but make no moans:
Smile out; but stilly suffer:
The paths of love are rougher
  Than thoroughfares of stones.

THE CONFORMERS

Yes; we'll wed, my little fay,
   And you shall write you mine,
And in a villa chastely gray
   We'll house, and sleep, and dine
   But those night-screened, divine
   Stolen trysts of heretofore,
We of choice ecstasies and fine
     Shall know no more.

The formal-faced cohue
   Will then no more upbraid
With smiting smiles and whisperings two
   Who have thrown less loves in shade.
   We shall no more evade
   The searching light of the sun,
Our game of passion will be played,
     Our dreaming done.

We shall not go in stealth
   To rendezvous unknown,
But friends will ask me of your health,
   And you about my own.
   When we abide alone,
   No leapings each to each,
But syllables in frigid tone
     Of household speech.

When down to dust we glide
   Men will not say askance,
As now: "How all the country side
   Rings with their mad romance!"
   But as they graveward glance
   Remark: "In them we lose
A worthy pair, who helped advance
     Sound parish views."

A DREAM QUESTION
"It shall be dark unto you, that ye shall not divine." Micah iii. 6.

I asked the Lord: "Sire, is this true
Which hosts of theologians hold,
That when we creatures censure you
For shaping griefs and ails untold
(Deeming them punishments undue)
You rage, as Moses wrote of old?

When we exclaim: 'Beneficent
He is not, for he orders pain,
Or, if so, not omnipotent:
To a mere child the thing is plain!'
Those who profess to represent
You, cry out: 'Impious and profane!'"

He: "Save me from my friends, who deem
That I care what my creatures say!
Mouth as you list: sneer, rail, blaspheme,
O manikin, the livelong day,
Not one grief-groan or pleasure-gleam
Will you increase or take away.

"Why things are thus, whoso derides,
May well remain my secret still . . . .
A fourth dimension, say the guides,
To matter is conceivable.
Think some such mystery resides
Within the ethic of my will."

A WIFE AND ANOTHER

"War ends, and he's returning
   Early; yea,
The evening next to-morrow's!"—
   —This I say
To her, whom I suspiciously survey,

  Holding my husband's letter
   To her view.—
She glanced at it but lightly,
   And I knew
That one from him that day had reached her too.

  There was no time for scruple;
   Secretly
I filched her missive, conned it,
   Learnt that he
Would lodge with her ere he came home to me.

  To reach the port before her,
   And, unscanned,
There wait to intercept them
   Soon I planned:
That, in her stead, *I* might before him stand.

  So purposed, so effected;
   At the inn
Assigned, I found her hidden:—
   O that sin
Should bear what she bore when I entered in!

  Her heavy lids grew laden
   With despairs,
Her lips made soundless movements
   Unawares,
While I peered at the chamber hired as theirs.

  And as beside its doorway,
   Deadly hued,

One inside, one withoutside
    We two stood,
He came—my husband—as she knew he would.

No pleasurable triumph
    Was that sight!
The ghastly disappointment
    Broke them quite.
What love was theirs, to move them with such might!

"Madam, forgive me!" said she,
    Sorrow bent,
"A child—I soon shall bear him. . . .
    Yes—I meant
To tell you—that he won me ere he went."

Then, as it were, within me
    Something snapped,
As if my soul had largened:
    Conscience-capped,
I saw myself the snarer—them the trapped.

"My hate dies, and I promise,
    Grace-beguiled,"
I said, "to care for you, be
    Reconciled;
And cherish, and take interest in the child."

Without more words I pressed him
    Through the door
Within which she stood, powerless
    To say more,
And closed it on them, and downstairward bore.

"He joins his wife—my sister,"
    I, below,
Remarked in going—lightly—
    Even as though
All had come right, and we had arranged it so.

As I, my road retracing,
Left them free,
The night alone embracing
Childless me,
I held I had not stirred God wrothfully.

NEW YEAR'S EVE

"I have finished another year," said God,
   "In grey, green, white, and brown;
I have strewn the leaf upon the sod,
Sealed up the worm within the clod,
   And let the last sun down."

"And what's the good of it?" I said,
   "What reasons made you call
From formless void this earth we tread,
When nine-and-ninety can be read
   Why nought should be at all?

"Yea, Sire; why shaped you us, 'who in
   This tabernacle groan'—
If ever a joy be found herein,
Such joy no man had wished to win
   If he had never known!"

Then he: "My labours—logicless—
   You may explain; not I:
Sense-sealed I have wrought, without a guess
That I evolved a Consciousness
   To ask for reasons why.

"Strange that ephemeral creatures who
   By my own ordering are,
Should see the shortness of my view,
Use ethic tests I never knew,
   Or made provision for!"

He sank to raptness as of yore,
   And opening New Year's Day
Wove it by rote as theretofore,
And went on working evermore
   In his unweeting way.

1906.

from Satires of Circumstance

CHANNEL FIRING

That night your great guns, unawares,
Shook all our coffins as we lay,
And broke the chancel window-squares,
We thought it was the Judgment-day

And sat upright. While drearisome
Arose the howl of wakened hounds:
The mouse let fall the altar-crumb,
The worms drew back into the mounds,

The glebe cow drooled. Till God called, "No;
It's gunnery practice out at sea
Just as before you went below;
The world is as it used to be:

"All nations striving strong to make
Red war yet redder. Mad as hatters
They do no more for Christés sake
Than you who are helpless in such matters.

"That this is not the judgment-hour
For some of them's a blessed thing,
For if it were they'd have to scour
Hell's floor for so much threatening. . . .

"Ha, ha. It will be warmer when
I blow the trumpet (if indeed
I ever do; for you are men,
And rest eternal sorely need)."

So down we lay again. "I wonder,
Will the world ever saner be,"
Said one, "than when He sent us under
In our indifferent century!"

And many a skeleton shook his head.
"Instead of preaching forty year,"

My neighbour Parson Thirdly said,
"I wish I had stuck to pipes and beer."

Again the guns disturbed the hour,
Roaring their readiness to avenge,
As far inland as Stourton Tower,
And Camelot, and starlit Stonehenge.

April 1914.

THE FACE AT THE CASEMENT

If ever joy leave
An abiding sting of sorrow,
So befell it on the morrow
 Of that May eve. . . .

The travelled sun dropped
To the north-west, low and lower.
The pony's trot grew slower,
 Until we stopped.

"This cosy house just by
I must call at for a minute,
A sick man lies within it
 Who soon will die.

"He wished to—marry me,
So I am bound, when I drive near him,
To inquire, if but to cheer him,
 How he may be."

A message was sent in,
And wordlessly we waited,
Till some one came and stated
 The bulletin.

And that the sufferer said,
For her call no words could thank her;
As his angel he must rank her
 Till life's spark fled.

Slowly we drove away,
When I turned my head, although not
Called to: why I turned I know not
 Even to this day:

And lo, there in my view
Pressed against an upper lattice
Was a white face, gazing at us
 As we withdrew.

And well did I divine
It to be the man's there dying,
Who but lately had been sighing
    For her pledged mine.

    Then I deigned a deed of hell;
It was done before I knew it;
What devil made me do it
    I cannot tell!

    Yes, while he gazed above,
I put my arm about her
That he might see, nor doubt her
    My plighted Love.

    The pale face vanished quick,
As if blasted, from the casement,
And my shame and self-abasement
    Began their prick.

    And they prick on, ceaselessly,
For that stab in Love's fierce fashion
Which, unfired by lover's passion,
    Was foreign to me.

    She smiled at my caress,
But why came the soft embowment
Of her shoulder at that moment
    She did not guess.

    Long long years has he lain
In thy garth, O sad Saint Cleather:
What tears there, bared to weather,
    Will cleanse that stain!

    Love is long-suffering, brave,
Sweet, prompt, precious as a jewel;
But jealousy is cruel,
    Cruel as the grave!

A PLAINT TO MAN

When you slowly emerged from the den of Time,
And gained percipience as you grew,
And fleshed you fair out of shapeless slime,

Wherefore, O Man, did there come to you
The unhappy need of creating me—
A form like your own—for praying to?

My virtue, power, utility,
Within my maker must all abide,
Since none in myself can ever be,

One thin as a phasm on a lantern-slide
Shown forth in the dark upon some dim sheet,
And by none but its showman vivified.

"Such a forced device," you may say, "is meet
For easing a loaded heart at whiles:
Man needs to conceive of a mercy-seat

Somewhere above the gloomy aisles
Of this wailful world, or he could not bear
The irk no local hope beguiles."

—But since I was framed in your first despair
The doing without me has had no play
In the minds of men when shadows scare;

And now that I dwindle day by day
Beneath the deicide eyes of seers
In a light that will not let me stay,

And to-morrow the whole of me disappears,
The truth should be told, and the fact be faced
That had best been faced in earlier years:

The fact of life with dependence placed
On the human heart's resource alone,
In brotherhood bonded close and graced

With loving-kindness fully blown,
And visioned help unsought, unknown.

1909–10.

GOD'S FUNERAL

I

I saw a slowly-stepping train—
Lined on the brows, scoop-eyed and bent and hoar—
Following in files across a twilit plain
A strange and mystic form the foremost bore.

II

And by contagious throbs of thought
Or latent knowledge that within me lay
And had already stirred me, I was wrought
To consciousness of sorrow even as they.

III

The fore-borne shape, to my blurred eyes,
At first seemed man-like, and anon to change
To an amorphous cloud of marvellous size,
At times endowed with wings of glorious range.

IV

And this phantasmal variousness
Ever possessed it as they drew along:
Yet throughout all it symboled none the less
Potency vast and loving-kindness strong.

V

Almost before I knew I bent
Towards the moving columns without a word;
They, growing in bulk and numbers as they went,
Struck out sick thoughts that could be overheard:—

VI

"O man-projected Figure, of late
Imaged as we, thy knell who shall survive?
Whence came it we were tempted to create
One whom we can no longer keep alive?

VII

"Framing him jealous, fierce, at first,
We gave him justice as the ages rolled,
Will to bless those by circumstance accurst,
And longsuffering, and mercies manifold.

VIII

"And, tricked by our own early dream
And need of solace, we grew self-deceived,
Our making soon our maker did we deem,
And what we had imagined we believed.

IX

"Till, in Time's stayless stealthy swing,
Uncompromising rude reality
Mangled the Monarch of our fashioning,
Who quavered, sank; and now has ceased to be.

X

"So, toward our myth's oblivion,
Darkling, and languid-lipped, we creep and grope
Sadlier than those who wept in Babylon,
Whose Zion was a still abiding hope.

XI

"How sweet it was in years far hied
To start the wheels of day with trustful prayer,
To lie down liegely at the eventide
And feel a blest assurance he was there!

XII

"And who or what shall fill his place?
Whither will wanderers turn distracted eyes
For some fixed star to stimulate their pace
Towards the goal of their enterprise?" . . .

XIII

Some in the background then I saw,
Sweet women, youths, men, all incredulous,
Who chimed: "This is a counterfeit of straw,
This requiem mockery! Still he lives to us!"

XIV

I could not buoy their faith: and yet
Many I had known: with all I sympathized;
And though struck speechless, I did not forget
That what was mourned for, I, too, long had prized.

XV

Still, how to bear such loss I deemed
The insistent question for each animate mind,
And gazing, to my growing sight there seemed
A pale yet positive gleam low down behind,

XVI

Whereof, to lift the general night,
A certain few who stood aloof had said,
"See you upon the horizon that small light—
Swelling somewhat?" Each mourner shook his head.

XVII

And they composed a crowd of whom
Some were right good, and many nigh the best. . . .
Thus dazed and puzzled 'twixt the gleam and gloom
Mechanically I followed with the rest.

1908–10.

"AH, ARE YOU DIGGING ON MY GRAVE?"

"Ah, are you digging on my grave,
   My loved one?—planting rue?"
—"No: yesterday he went to wed
One of the brightest wealth has bred.
'It cannot hurt her now' he said,
   'That I should not be true.'"

"Then who is digging on my grave?
   My nearest dearest kin?"
—"Ah, no: they sit and think, 'What use!
What good will planting flowers produce?
No tendance of her mound can loose
   Her spirit from Death's gin.'"

"But some one digs upon my grave?
   My enemy?—prodding sly?"
—"Nay: when she heard you had passed the Gate
That shuts on all flesh soon or late,
She thought you no more worth her hate,
   And cares not where you lie."

"Then, who is digging on my grave?
   Say—since I have not guessed!"
—"O it is I, my mistress dear,
Your little dog, who still lives near,
And much I hope my movements here
   Have not disturbed your rest?"

"Ah, yes! *You* dig upon my grave . . .
   Why flashed it not on me
That one true heart was left behind!
What feeling do we ever find
To equal among human kind
   A dog's fidelity!"

"Mistress, I dug upon your grave
   To bury a bone, in case
I should be hungry near this spot
When passing on my daily trot.
I am sorry, but I quite forgot
   It was your resting-place."

THE YEAR'S AWAKENING

How do you know that the pilgrim track
Along the belting zodiac
Swept by the sun in his seeming rounds
Is traced by now to the Fishes' bounds
And into the Ram, when weeks of cloud
Have wrapt the sky in a clammy shroud,
And never as yet a tinct of spring
Has shown in the Earth's apparelling;
   O vespering bird, how do you know,
     How do you know?

How do you know, deep underground,
Hid in your bed from sight and sound,
Without a turn in temperature,
With weather life can scarce endure,
That light has won a fraction's strength,
And day put on some moments' length,
Whereof in merest rote will come,
Weeks hence, mild airs that do not numb;
   O crocus root, how do you know,
     How do you know?

February 1910.

UNDER THE WATERFALL

"Whenever I plunge my arm, like this,
In a basin of water, I never miss
The sweet sharp sense of a fugitive day
Fetched back from its thickening shroud of gray.
    Hence the only prime
    And real love-rhyme
    That I know by heart,
    And that leaves no smart,
Is the purl of a little valley fall
About three spans wide and two spans tall
Over a table of solid rock,
And into a scoop of the self-same block;
The purl of a runlet that never ceases
In stir of kingdoms, in wars, in peaces;
With a hollow boiling voice it speaks
And has spoken since hills were turfless peaks."

"And why gives this the only prime
Idea to you of a real love-rhyme?
And why does plunging your arm in a bowl
Full of spring water, bring throbs to your soul?"

"Well, under the fall, in a crease of the stone,
Though where precisely none ever has known,
Jammed darkly, nothing to show how prized,
And by now with its smoothness opalized,
    Is a drinking-glass:
    For, down that pass
    My lover and I
    Walked under a sky
Of blue with a leaf-wove awning of green,
In the burn of August, to paint the scene,
And we placed our basket of fruit and wine
By the runlet's rim, where we sat to dine;
And when we had drunk from the glass together,

Arched by the oak-copse from the weather,
I held the vessel to rinse in the fall,
Where it slipped, and sank, and was past recall,
Though we stooped and plumbed the little abyss
With long bared arms. There the glass still is.
And, as said, if I thrust my arm below
Cold water in basin or bowl, a throe
From the past awakens a sense of that time,
And the glass we used, and the cascade's rhyme.
The basin seems the pool, and its edge
The hard smooth face of the brook-side ledge,
And the leafy pattern of china-ware
The hanging plants that were bathing there.

"By night, by day, when it shines or lours,
There lies intact that chalice of ours,
And its presence adds to the rhyme of love
Persistently sung by the fall above.
No lip has touched it since his and mine
In turns therefrom sipped lovers' wine."

YOUR LAST DRIVE

Here by the moorway you returned,
And saw the borough lights ahead
That lit your face—all undiscerned
To be in a week the face of the dead,
And you told of the charm of that haloed view
That never again would beam on you.

And on your left you passed the spot
Where eight days later you were to lie,
And be spoken of as one who was not;
Beholding it with a heedless eye
As alien from you, though under its tree
You soon would halt everlastingly.

I drove not with you. . . . Yet had I sat
At your side that eve I should not have seen
That the countenance I was glancing at
Had a last-time look in the flickering sheen,
Nor have read the writing upon your face,
"I go hence soon to my resting-place;

"You may miss me then. But I shall not know
How many times you visit me there,
Or what your thoughts are, or if you go
There never at all. And I shall not care.
Should you censure me I shall take no heed,
And even your praises no more shall need."

True: never you'll know. And you will not mind
But shall I then slight you because of such?
Dear ghost, in the past did you ever find
The thought "What profit," move me much?
Yet abides the fact, indeed, the same,—
You are past love, praise, indifference, blame.

December 1912.

THE WALK

You did not walk with me
Of late to the hill-top tree
  By the gated ways,
  As in earlier days;
  You were weak and lame,
  So you never came,
And I went alone, and I did not mind,
Not thinking of you as left behind.

I walked up there to-day
Just in the former way;
  Surveyed around
  The familiar ground
  By myself again:
  What difference, then?
Only that underlying sense
Of the look of a room on returning thence.

RAIN ON A GRAVE

Clouds spout upon her
   Their waters amain
   In ruthless disdain,—
Her who but lately
   Had shivered with pain
As at touch of dishonour
If there had lit on her
So coldly, so straightly
   Such arrows of rain:

One who to shelter
   Her delicate head
Would quicken and quicken
   Each tentative tread
If drops chanced to pelt her
   That summertime spills
   In dust-paven rills
When thunder-clouds thicken
   And birds close their bills.

Would that I lay there
   And she were housed here!
Or better, together
Were folded away there
Exposed to one weather
We both,—who would stray there
When sunny the day there
   Or evening was clear
   At the prime of the year.

Soon will be growing
   Green blades from her mound.
And daisies be showing
   Like stars on the ground,
Till she form part of them—

Ay—the sweet heart of them,
Loved beyond measure
With a child's pleasure
    All her life's round.

Jan. 31, 1913.

WITHOUT CEREMONY

It was your way, my dear,
To vanish without a word
When callers, friends, or kin
Had left, and I hastened in
To rejoin you, as I inferred.

And when you'd a mind to career
Off anywhere—say to town—
You were all on a sudden gone
Before I had thought thereon,
Or noticed your trunks were down.

So, now that you disappear
For ever in that swift style,
Your meaning seems to me
Just as it used to be:
"Good-bye is not worth while!"

LAMENT

How she would have loved
A party to-day!—
Bright-hatted and gloved,
With table and tray
And chairs on the lawn
Her smiles would have shone
With welcomings. . . . But
She is shut, she is shut
   From friendship's spell
   In the jailing shell
   Of her tiny cell.

Or she would have reigned
At a dinner to-night
With ardours unfeigned,
And a generous delight;
All in her abode
She'd have freely bestowed
On her guests. . . . But alas.
She is shut under grass
   Where no cups flow,
   Powerless to know
   That it might be so.

And she would have sought
With a child's eager glance
The shy snowdrops brought
By the new year's advance,
And peered in the rime
Of Candlemas-time
For crocuses . . . chanced
It that she were not tranced
   From sights she loved best;
   Wholly possessed
   By an infinite rest!

And we are here staying
Amid these stale things,
Who care not for gaying,
And those junketings
That used so to joy her,
And never to cloy her
As us they cloy! . . . But
She is shut, she is shut
   From the cheer of them, dead
   To all done and said
   In her yew-arched bed.

THE HAUNTER

He does not think that I haunt here nightly:
  How shall I let him know
That whither his fancy sets him wandering
  I, too, alertly go?—

Hover and hover a few feet from him
  Just as I used to do,
But cannot answer the words he lifts me—
  Only listen thereto!

When I could answer he did not say them:
  When I could let him know
How I would like to join in his journeys
  Seldom he wished to go.
Now that he goes and wants me with him
  More than he used to do,
Never he sees my faithful phantom
  Though he speaks thereto.

Yes, I companion him to places
  Only dreamers know,
Where the shy hares print long paces,
  Where the night rooks go;
Into old aisles where the past is all to him,
  Close as his shade can do,
Always lacking the power to call to him,
  Near as I reach thereto!

What a good haunter I am, O tell him!
  Quickly make him know
If he but sigh since my loss befell him
  Straight to his side I go.
Tell him a faithful one is doing
  All that love can do
Still that his path may be worth pursuing,
  And to bring peace thereto.

HIS VISITOR

I come across from Mellstock while the moon wastes weaker
To behold where I lived with you for twenty years and more:
I shall go in the gray, at the passing of the mail-train,
And need no setting open of the long familiar door
     As before.

The change I notice in my once own quarters!
A formal-fashioned border where the daisies used to be,
The rooms new painted, and the pictures altered,
And other cups and saucers, and no cosy nook for tea
     As with me.

I discern the dim faces of the sleep-wrapt servants;
They are not those who tended me through feeble hours and strong
But strangers quite, who never knew my rule here,
Who never saw me painting, never heard my softling song
     Float along.

So I don't want to linger in this re-decked dwelling,
I feel too uneasy at the contrasts I behold,
And I make again for Mellstock to return here never,
And rejoin the roomy silence, and the mute and manifold
     Souls of old.

1913.

A CIRCULAR

As "legal representative"
I read a missive not my own,
On new designs the senders give
   For clothes, in tints as shown.

Here figure blouses, gowns for tea,
And presentation-trains of state,
Charming ball-dresses, millinery,
   Warranted up to date.

And this gay-pictured, spring-time shout
Of Fashion, hails what lady proud?
Her who before last year ebbed out
   Was costumed in a shroud.

A DREAM OR NO

Why go to Saint-Juliot? What's Juliot to me?
    Some strange necromancy
    But charmed me to fancy
That much of my life claims the spot as its key.

Yes. I have had dreams of that place in the West,
    And a maiden abiding
    Thereat as in hiding;
Fair-eyed and white-shouldered, broad-browed and brown-tressed.

And of how, coastward bound on a night long ago,
    There lonely I found her,
    The sea-birds around her,
And other than nigh things uncaring to know.

So sweet her life there (in my thought has it seemed)
    That quickly she drew me
    To take her unto me,
And lodge her long years with me. Such have I dreamed.

But nought of that maid from Saint-Juliot I see;
    Can she ever have been here,
    And shed her life's sheen here,
The woman I thought a long housemate with me?

Does there even a place like Saint-Juliot exist?
    Or a Vallency Valley
    With stream and leafed alley,
Or Beeny, or Bos with its flounce flinging mist?

February 1913.

A DEATH-DAY RECALLED

Beeny did not quiver,
　Juliot grew not gray,
Thin Vallency's river
　Held its wonted way.
Bos seemed not to utter
　Dimmest note of dirge,
Targan mouth a mutter
　To its creamy surge.

Yet though these, unheeding,
　Listless, passed the hour
Of her spirit's speeding,
　She had, in her flower,
Sought and loved the places—
　Much and often pined
For their lonely faces
　When in towns confined.

Why did not Vallency
　In his purl deplore
One whose haunts were whence he
　Drew his limpid store?
Why did Bos not thunder,
　Targan apprehend
Body and Breath were sunder
　Of their former friend?

PLACES

Nobody says: Ah, that is the place
Where chanced, in the hollow of years ago,
What none of the Three Towns cared to know—
The birth of a little girl of grace—
The sweetest the house saw, first or last;
    Yet it was so
    On that day long past.

Nobody thinks: There, there she lay
In a room by the Hoe, like the bud of a flower.
And listened, just after the bedtime hour,
To the stammering chimes that used to play
The quaint Old Hundred-and-Thirteenth tune
    In Saint Andrew's tower
    Night, morn, and noon.

Nobody calls to mind that here
Upon Boterel Hill, where the waggoners skid,
With cheeks whose airy flush outbid
Fresh fruit in bloom, and free of fear,
She cantered down, as if she must fall
    (Though she never did),
    To the charm of all.

Nay: one there is to whom these things,
That nobody else's mind calls back,
Have a savour that scenes in being lack,
And a presence more than the actual brings;
To whom to-day is beneaped and stale,
    And its urgent clack
    But a vapid tale.

        Plymouth, March 1913.

THE SPELL OF THE ROSE

"I mean to build a hall anon,
    And shape two turrets there,
    And a broad newelled stair,
And a cool well for crystal water;
        Yes; I will build a hall anon.
        Plant roses love shall feed upon,
            And apple-trees and pear."

He set to build the manor-hall,
    And shaped the turrets there,
    And the broad newelled stair,
And the cool well for crystal water;
        He built for me that manor-hall,
        And planted many trees withal,
            But no rose anywhere.

And as he planted never a rose
    That bears the flower of love,
    Though other flowers throve
Some heart-bane moved our souls to sever
        Since he had planted never a rose;
        And misconceits raised horrid shows,
            And agonies came thereof.

"I'll mend these miseries," then said I,
    And so, at dead of night,
    I went and, screened from sight,
That nought should keep our souls in severance
        I set a rose-bush. "This," said I,
        "May end divisions dire and wry,
            And long-drawn days of blight."

But I was called from earth—yea, called
    Before my rose-bush grew;
    And would that now I knew
What feels he of the tree I planted,

And whether, after I was called
To be a ghost, he, as of old,
Gave me his heart anew!

Perhaps now blooms that queen of trees
I set but saw not grow,
And he, beside its glow—
Eyes couched of the mis-vision that blurred me—
Ay, there beside that queen of trees
He sees me as I was, though sees
Too late to tell me so!

ST. LAUNCE'S REVISITED

Slip back, Time!
Yet again I am nearing
Castle and keep, uprearing
   Gray, as in my prime.

At the inn
Smiling nigh, why is it
Not as on my visit
   When hope and I were twin?

Groom and jade
Whom I found here, moulder;
Strange the tavern-holder,
   Strange the tap-maid.

Here I hired
Horse and man for bearing
Me on my wayfaring
   To the door desired.

Evening gloomed
As I journeyed forward
To the faces shoreward,
   Till their dwelling loomed.

If again
Towards the Atlantic sea there
I should speed, they'd be there
   Surely now as then? . . .

Why waste thought,
When I know them vanished
Under earth; yea, banished
   Ever into nought!

THE RE-ENACTMENT

Between the folding sea-downs,
   In the gloom
Of a wailful wintry nightfall,
   When the boom
Of the ocean, like a hammering in a hollow tomb,

   Throbbed up the copse-clothed valley
      From the shore
To the chamber where I darkled,
      Sunk and sore
With gray ponderings why my Loved one had not come before

   To salute me in the dwelling
      That of late
I had hired to waste a while in—
      Dim of date,
Quaint, and remote—wherein I now expectant sate;

   On the solitude, unsignalled,
      Broke a man
Who, in air as if at home there,
      Seemed to scan
Every fire-flecked nook of the apartment span by span,

   A stranger's and no lover's
      Eyes were these,
Eyes of a man who measures
      What he sees
But vaguely, as if wrapt in filmy phantasies.

   Yea, his bearing was so absent
      As he stood,
It bespoke a chord so plaintive
      In his mood,
That soon I judged he would not wrong my quietude.

   "Ah—the supper is just ready!"
      Then he said,

"And the years'-long-binned Madeira
       Flashes red!"
(There was no wine, no food, no supper-table spread.)

   "You will forgive my coming,
       Lady fair?
   I see you as at that time
       Rising there,
The self-same curious querying in your eyes and air.

   "Yet no. How so? You wear not
       The same gown,
   Your locks show woful difference,
       Are not brown:
What, is it not as when I hither came from town?

   "And the place. . . . But you seem other—
       Can it be?
   What's this that Time is doing
       Unto me?
You dwell here, unknown woman? . . . Whereabouts, then is she?

   "And the house-things are much shifted.—
       Put them where
   They stood on this night's fellow;
       Shift her chair:
Here was the couch: and the piano should be there."

   I indulged him, verily nerve-strained
       Being alone,
   And I moved the things as bidden,
       One by one,
And feigned to push the old piano where he had shown.

   "Aha—now I can see her!
       Stand aside:
   Don't thrust her from the table
       Where, meek-eyed,
She makes attempt with matron-manners to preside.

"She serves me: now she rises,
    Goes to play. . . .
But you obstruct her, fill her
    With dismay,
And all-embarrassed, scared, she vanishes away!"

And, as 'twere useless longer
    To persist,
He sighed, and sought the entry
    Ere I wist,
And retreated, disappearing soundless in the mist.

That here some mighty passion
    Once had burned,
Which still the walls enghosted,
    I discerned,
And that by its strong spell mine might be overturned.

I sat depressed; till, later,
    My Love came;
But something in the chamber
    Dimmed our flame,—
An emanation, making our due words fall tame,

As if the intenser drama
    Shown me there
Of what the walls had witnessed
    Filled the air,
And left no room for later passion anywhere.

So came it that our fervours
    Did quite fail
Of future consummation—
    Being made quail
By the weird witchery of the parlour's hidden tale,

Which I, as years passed, faintly
    Learnt to trace,—
One of sad love, born full-winged

In that place
Where the predestined sorrowers first stood face to face.

  And as that month of winter
    Circles round,
  And the evening of the date-day
    Grows embrowned,
I am conscious of those presences, and sit spellbound.

  There, often—lone, forsaken—
    Queries breed
  Within me; whether a phantom
    Had my heed
On that strange night, or was it some wrecked heart indeed?

HAD YOU WEPT

Had you wept; had you but neared me with a hazed uncertain ray,
Dewy as the face of the dawn, in your large and luminous eye,
Then would have come back all the joys the tidings had slain that day,
And a new beginning, a fresh fair heaven, have smoothed the things awry.
But you were less feebly human, and no passionate need for clinging
Possessed your soul to overthrow reserve when I came near;
Ay, though you suffer as much as I from storms the hours are bringing
Upon your heart and mine, I never see you shed a tear.

The deep strong woman is weakest, the weak one is the strong;
The weapon of all weapons best for winning, you have not used;
Have you never been able, or would you not, through the evil times and long?
Has not the gift been given you, or such gift have you refused?
When I bade me not absolve you on that evening or the morrow,
Why did you not make war on me with those who weep like rain?
You felt too much, so gained no balm for all your torrid sorrow,
And hence our deep division, and our dark undying pain.

IN THE BRITISH MUSEUM

"What do you see in that time-touched stone,
      When nothing is there
But ashen blankness, although you give it
      A rigid stare?

"You look not quite as if you saw,
      But as if you heard,
Parting your lips, and treading softly
      As mouse or bird.

"It is only the base of a pillar, they'll tell you,
      That came to us
From a far old hill men used to name
      Areopagus."

—"I know no art, and I only view
      A stone from a wall,
But I am thinking that stone has echoed
      The voice of Paul;

"Paul as he stood and preached beside it
      Facing the crowd,
A small gaunt figure with wasted features,
      Calling out loud

"Words that in all their intimate accents
      Pattered upon
That marble front, and were wide reflected,
      And then were gone.

"I'm a labouring man, and know but little,
      Or nothing at all;
But I can't help thinking that stone once echoed
      The voice of Paul."

THE MOON LOOKS IN

I

I have risen again,
And awhile survey
By my chilly ray
Through your window-pane
Your upturned face,
As you think, "Ah—she
Now dreams of me
In her distant place!"

II

I pierce her blind
In her far-off home:
She fixes a comb,
And says in her mind,
"I start in an hour;
Whom shall I meet?
Won't the men be sweet,
And the women sour!"

SEEN BY THE WAITS

Through snowy woods and shady
    We went to play a tune
To the lonely manor-lady
    By the light of the Christmas moon.

We violed till, upward glancing
    To where a mirror leaned,
It showed her airily dancing,
    Deeming her movements screened;

Dancing alone in the room there,
    Thin-draped in her robe of night;
Her postures, glassed-in the gloom there,
    Were a strange phantasmal sight.

She had learnt (we heard when homing)
    That her roving spouse was dead:
Why she had danced in the gloaming
    We thought, but never said.

IN CHURCH

"And now to God the Father," he ends,
And his voice thrills up to the topmost tiles:
Each listener chokes as he bows and bends,
And emotion pervades the crowded aisles.
Then the preacher glides to the vestry-door,
And shuts it, and thinks he is seen no more.

The door swings softly ajar meanwhile,
And a pupil of his in the Bible class,
Who adores him as one without gloss or guile,
Sees her idol stand with a satisfied smile
And re-enact at the vestry-glass
Each pulpit gesture in deft dumb-show
That had moved the congregation so.

IN THE CEMETERY

"You see those mothers squabbling there?"
Remarks the man of the cemetery.
"One says in tears, *''Tis mine lies here!'*
Another, *'Nay, mine, you Pharisee!'*
Another, *'How dare you move my flowers*
And put your own on this grave of ours!'
But all their children were laid therein
At different times, like sprats in a tin.

"And then the main drain had to cross,
And we moved the lot some nights ago,
And packed them away in the general foss
With hundreds more. But their folks don't know,
And as well cry over a new-laid drain
As anything else, to ease your pain!"

OUTSIDE THE WINDOW

"My stick!" he says, and turns in the lane
To the house just left, whence a vixen voice
Comes out with the firelight through the pane,
And he sees within that the girl of his choice
Stands rating her mother with eyes aglare
For something said while he was there.

"At last I behold her soul undraped!"
Thinks the man who had loved her more than himself;
"My God!—'tis but narrowly I have escaped.—
My precious porcelain proves it delf."
His face has reddened like one ashamed,
And he steals off, leaving his stick unclaimed.

OVER THE COFFIN

They stand confronting, the coffin between,
His wife of old, and his wife of late,
And the dead man whose they both had been
Seems listening aloof, as to things past date.
—"I have called," says the first. "Do you marvel or not?"
"In truth," says the second, "I do—somewhat."

"Well, there was a word to be said by me! . . .
I divorced that man because of you—
It seemed I must do it, boundenly;
But now I am older, and tell you true,
For life is little, and dead lies he;
I would I had let alone you two!
And both of us, scorning parochial ways,
Had lived like the wives in the patriarchs' days."

from Moments of Vision

"WE SAT AT THE WINDOW"
(*Bournemouth, 1875*)

We sat at the window looking out,
And the rain came down like silken strings
That Swithin's day. Each gutter and spout
Babbled unchecked in the busy way
   Of witless things:
Nothing to read, nothing to see
Seemed in that room for her and me
   On Swithin's day.

We were irked by the scene, by our own selves; yes.
For I did not know, nor did she infer
How much there was to read and guess
By her in me, and to see and crown
   By me in her.
Wasted were two souls in their prime,
And great was the waste, that July time
   When the rain came down.

QUID HIC AGIS?

I

When I weekly knew
An ancient pew,
And murmured there
The forms of prayer
And thanks and praise
In the ancient ways,
And heard read out
During August drought
That chapter from Kings
Harvest-time brings;
—How the prophet, broken
By griefs unspoken,
Went heavily away
To fast and to pray,
And, while waiting to die.
The Lord passed by,
And a whirlwind and fire
Drew nigher and nigher,
And a small voice anon
Bade him up and be gone, —
I did not apprehend
As I sat to the end
And watched for her smile
Across the sunned aisle,
That this tale of a seer
Which came once a year
Might, when sands were heaping,
Be like a sweat creeping,
Or in any degree
Bear on her or on me!

II

When later, by chance
Of circumstance,

It befel me to read
On a hot afternoon
At the lectern there
The selfsame words
As the lesson decreed,
To the gathered few
From the hamlets near—
Folk of flocks and herds
Sitting half aswoon,
Who listened thereto
As women and men
Not overmuch
Concerned at such—
So, like them then,
I did not see
What drought might be
With me, with her,
As the Kalendar
Moved on, and Time
Devoured our prime.

III

But now, at last,
When our glory has passed,
And there is no smile
From her in the aisle,
But where it once shone
A marble, men say,
With her name thereon
Is discerned to-day;
And spiritless
In the wilderness
I shrink from sight
And desire the night,
(Though, as in old wise,
I might still arise,
Go forth, and stand
And prophesy in the land),

I feel the shake
Of wind and earthquake,
And consuming fire
Nigher and nigher,
And the voice catch clear,
"What doest thou here?"

The Spectator: 1916. During the War

THE CHANGE

Out of the past there rises a week—
   Who shall read the years O!—
Out of the past there rises a week
   Enringed with a purple zone.
Out of the past there rises a week
   When thoughts were strung too thick to speak,
And the magic of its lineaments remains with me alone.

In that week there was heard a singing—
   Who shall spell the years, the years!—
In that week there was heard a singing,
   And the white owl wondered why.
In that week, yea, a voice was ringing,
   And forth from the casement were candles flinging
Radiance that fell on the deodar and lit up the path thereby.

Could that song have a mocking note?—
   Who shall unroll the years O!—
Could that song have a mocking note
   To the white owl's sense as it fell?
Could that song have a mocking note
   As it trilled out warm from the singer's throat,
And who was the mocker and who the mocked when two felt all was well?

In a tedious trampling crowd yet later—
   Who shall bare the years, the years!—
In a tedious trampling crowd yet later,
   When silvery singings were dumb;
In a crowd uncaring what time might fate her,
   Mid murks of night I stood to await her,
And the twanging of iron wheels gave out the signal that she was come.

She said with a travel-tired smile—
   Who shall lift the years O!—
She said with a travel-tired smile,
   Half scared by scene so strange;

She said, outworn by mile on mile,
The blurred lamps wanning her face the while,
"O Love, I am here; I am with you!" . . . Ah, that there should have come a change!

O the doom by someone spoken—
    Who shall unseal the years, the years!—
O the doom that gave no token,
    When nothing of bale saw we:
O the doom by someone spoken,
O the heart by someone broken,
The heart whose sweet reverberances are all time leaves to me.

Jan.–Feb. 1913.

"BY THE RUNIC STONE"
(Two who became a story)

By the Runic Stone
  They sat, where the grass sloped down,
And chattered, he white-hatted, she in brown,
    Pink-faced, breeze-blown.

Rapt there alone
  In the transport of talking so
In such a place, there was nothing to let them know
    What hours had flown.

And the die thrown
  By them heedlessly there, the dent
It was to cut in their encompassment,
    Were, too, unknown.

It might have strown
  Their zest with qualms to see,
As in a glass, Time toss their history
    From zone to zone!

TRANSFORMATIONS

Portion of this yew
Is a man my grandsire knew,
Bosomed here at its foot:
This branch may be his wife,
A ruddy human life
Now turned to a green shoot.

These grasses must be made
Of her who often prayed,
Last century, for repose;
And the fair girl long ago
Whom I often tried to know
May be entering this rose.

So, they are not underground,
But as nerves and veins abound
In the growths of upper air,
And they feel the sun and rain,
And the energy again
That made them what they were!

THE LAST SIGNAL
(*Oct. 11, 1886*)
A Memory of William Barnes

Silently I footed by an uphill road
　That led from my abode to a spot yew-boughed;
Yellowly the sun sloped low down to westward,
　　And dark was the east with cloud.

Then, amid the shadow of that livid sad east,
　Where the light was least, and a gate stood wide,
Something flashed the fire of the sun that was facing it,
　　Like a brief blaze on that side.

Looking hard and harder I knew what it meant—
　The sudden shine sent from the livid east scene;
It meant the west mirrored by the coffin of my friend there,
　　Turning to the road from his green,

To take his last journey forth—he who in his prime
　Trudged so many a time from that gate athwart the land!
Thus a farewell to me he signalled on his grave-way,
　　As with a wave of his hand.

Winterborne-Came Path.

THE HOUSE OF SILENCE

"That is a quiet place—
That house in the trees with the shady lawn."
"—If, child, you knew what there goes on
You would not call it a quiet place.
Why, a phantom abides there, the last of its race,
    And a brain spins there till dawn."

"But I see nobody there,—
Nobody moves about the green,
Or wanders the heavy trees between."
"—Ah, that's because you do not bear
The visioning powers of souls who dare
    To pierce the material screen.

"Morning, noon, and night,
Mid those funereal shades that seem
The uncanny scenery of a dream,
Figures dance to a mind with sight,
And music and laughter like floods of light
    Make all the precincts gleam.

"It is a poet's bower,
Through which there pass, in fleet arrays,
Long teams of all the years and days,
Of joys and sorrows, of earth and heaven,
That meet mankind in its ages seven,
    An aion in an hour."

"WHY DID I SKETCH?"

Why did I sketch an upland green,
 And put the figure in
 Of one on the spot with me?—
For now that one has ceased to be seen
 The picture waxes akin
 To a wordless irony.

If you go drawing on down or cliff
 Let no soft curves intrude
 Of a woman's silhouette,
But show the escarpments stark and stiff
 As in utter solitude;
 So shall you half forget.

Let me sooner pass from sight of the sky
 Than again on a thoughtless day
 Limn, laugh, and sing, and rhyme
With a woman sitting near, whom I
 Paint in for love, and who may
 Be called hence in my time

   From an old note.

CONJECTURE

If there were in my kalendar
  No Emma, Florence, Mary,
What would be my existence now—
  A hermit's?—wanderer's weary?
    How should I live, and how
    Near would be death, or far?

Could it have been that other eyes,
  Might have uplit my highway?
That fond, sad, retrospective sight
  Would catch from this dim byway
    Prized figures different quite
    From those that now arise?

With how strange aspect would there creep
  The dawn, the night, the daytime,
If memory were not what it is
  In song-time, toil, or pray-time.—
    O were it else than this,
    I'd pass to pulseless sleep!

LOVE THE MONOPOLIST
(*Young Lover's Reverie*)

The train draws forth from the station-yard.
   And with it carries me.
I rise, and stretch out, and regard
   The platform left, and see
An airy slim blue form there standing,
   And know that it is she.

While with strained vision I watch on,
   The figure turns round quite
To greet friends gaily; then is gone. . . .
   The import may be slight,
But why remained she not hard gazing
   Till I was out of sight?

"O do not chat with others there,"
   I brood. "They are not I.
O strain your thoughts as if they were
   Gold bands between us; eye
All neighbour scenes as so much blankness
   Till I again am by!

"A troubled soughing in the breeze
   And the sky overhead
Let yourself feel; and shadeful trees,
   Ripe corn, and apples red,
Read as things barren and distasteful
   While we are separated!

"When I come back uncloak your gloom.
   And let in lovely day;
Then the long dark as of the tomb
   Can well be thrust away
With sweet things I shall have to practise,
   And you will have to say!"

       Begun 1871: finished—

OVERLOOKING THE RIVER STOUR

The swallows flew in the curves of an eight
    Above the river-gleam
    In the wet June's last beam:
Like little crossbows animate
The swallows flew in the curves of an eight
    Above the river-gleam.

Planing up shavings of crystal spray
    A moor-hen darted out
    From the bank thereabout,
And through the stream-shine ripped his way;
Planing up shavings of crystal spray
    A moor-hen darted out.

Closed were the kingcups; and the mead
    Dripped in monotonous green,
    Though the day's morning sheen
Had shown it golden and honeybee'd;
Closed were the kingcups; and the mead
    Dripped in monotonous green.

And never I turned my head, alack,
    While these things met my gaze
    Through the pane's drop-drenched glaze,
To see the more behind my back. . . .
O never I turned, but let, alack,
    These less things hold my gaze!

OLD FURNITURE

I know not how it may be with others
　　Who sit amid relics of householdry
That date from the days of their mothers' mothers,
　　But well I know how it is with me
　　　Continually.

I see the hands of the generations
　　That owned each shiny familiar thing
In play on its knobs and indentations,
　　And with its ancient fashioning
　　　Still dallying:

Hands behind hands, growing paler and paler,
　　As in a mirror a candle-flame
Shows images of itself, each frailer
　　As it recedes, though the eye may frame
　　　Its shape the same.

On the clock's dull dial a foggy finger,
　　Moving to set the minutes right
With tentative touches that lift and linger
　　In the wont of a moth on a summer night,
　　　Creeps to my sight.

On this old viol, too, fingers are dancing—
　　As whilom—just over the strings by the nut,
The tip of a bow receding, advancing
　　In airy quivers, as if it would cut
　　　The plaintive gut.

And I see a face by that box for tinder,
　　Glowing forth in fits from the dark,
And fading again, as the linten cinder
　　Kindles to red at the flinty spark,
　　　Or goes out stark.

Well, well. It is best to be up and doing,
     The world has no use for one to-day
Who eyes things thus—no aim pursuing!
     He should not continue in this stay,
          But sink away.

THE AGEING HOUSE

When the walls were red
That now are seen
To be overspread
With a mouldy green,
A fresh fair head
Would often lean
From the sunny casement
And scan the scene,
While blithely spoke the wind to the little sycamore tree.

But storms have raged
Those walls about,
And the head has aged
That once looked out;
And zest is suaged
And trust grows doubt,
And slow effacement
Is rife throughout,
While fiercely girds the wind at the long-limbed sycamore tree!

THE CAGED GOLDFINCH

Within a churchyard, on a recent grave,
    I saw a little cage
That jailed a goldfinch. All was silence save
    Its hops from stage to stage.

There was inquiry in its wistful eye,
    And once it tried to sing;
Of him or her who placed it there, and why,
    No one knew anything.

THE BALLET

They crush together—a rustling heap of flesh—
Of more than flesh, a heap of souls; and then
    They part, enmesh,
    And crush together again,
Like the pink petals of a too sanguine rose
    Frightened shut just when it blows.

Though all alike in their tinsel livery,
And indistinguishable at a sweeping glance,
    They muster, maybe,
    As lives wide in irrelevance;
A world of her own has each one underneath,
    Detached as a sword from its sheath.

Daughters, wives, mistresses; honest or false, sold, bought;
Hearts of all sizes; gay, fond, gushing, or penned,
    Various in thought
    Of lover, rival, friend;
Links in a one-pulsed chain, all showing one smile,
    Yet severed so many a mile!

THE WIND'S PROPHECY

I travel on by barren farms,
And gulls glint out like silver flecks
Against a cloud that speaks of wrecks,
And bellies down with black alarms.
I say: "Thus from my lady's arms
I go; those arms I love the best!"
The wind replies from dip and rise,
"Nay; toward her arms thou journeyest."

A distant verge morosely gray
Appears, while clots of flying foam
Break from its muddy monochrome,
And a light blinks up far away.
I sigh: "My eyes now as all day
Behold her ebon loops of hair!"
Like bursting bonds the wind responds,
"Nay, wait for tresses flashing fair!"

From tides the lofty coastlands screen
Come smitings like the slam of doors,
Or hammerings on hollow floors,
As the swell cleaves through caves unseen.
Say I: "Though broad this wild terrene.
Her city home is matched of none!"
From the hoarse skies the wind replies:
"Thou shouldst have said her sea-bord one."

The all-prevailing clouds exclude
The one quick timorous transient star;
The waves outside where breakers are
Huzza like a mad multitude.
"Where the sun ups it, mist-imbued,"
I cry, "there reigns the star for me!"
The wind outshrieks from points and peaks:
"Here, westward, where it downs, mean ye!"

Yonder the headland, vulturine,
Snores like old Skrymer in his sleep,
And every chasm and every steep
Blackens as wakes each pharos-shine.
"I roam, but one is safely mine,"
I say. "God grant she stay my own!"
Low laughs the wind as if it grinned:
"Thy Love is one thou'st not yet known."

Rewritten from an old copy.

DURING WIND AND RAIN

They sing their dearest songs—
He, she, all of them—yea,
Treble and tenor and bass,
    And one to play;
With the candles mooning each face. . . .
    Ah, no; the years O!
How the sick leaves reel down in throngs!

They clear the creeping moss—
Elders and juniors—aye,
Making the pathways neat
    And the garden gay;
And they build a shady seat. . . .
    Ah, no; the years, the years;
See, the white storm-birds wing across.

They are blithely breakfasting all—
Men and maidens—yea,
Under the summer tree,
    With a glimpse of the bay,
While pet fowl come to the knee. . . .
    Ah, no; the years O!
And the rotten rose is ript from the wall.

They change to a high new house,
He, she, all of them—aye,
Clocks and carpets and chairs
    On the lawn all day,
And brightest things that are theirs. . . .
    Ah, no; the years, the years;
Down their carved names the rain-drop ploughs.

MOLLY GONE

No more summer for Molly and me;
    There is snow on the tree,
And the blackbirds plump large as the rooks are, almost,
    And the water is hard
Where they used to dip bills at the dawn ere her figure was lost
    To these coasts, now my prison close-barred.

No more planting by Molly and me
    Where the beds used to be
Of sweet-william; no training the clambering rose
    By the framework of fir
Now bowering the pathway, whereon it swings gaily and blows
    As if calling commendment from her.

No more jauntings by Molly and me
    To the town by the sea,
Or along over Whitesheet to Wynyard's green Gap,
    Catching Montacute Crest
To the right against Sedgmoor, and Corton-Hill's far-distant cap,
    And Pilsdon and Lewsdon to west.

No more singing by Molly to me
    In the evenings when she
Was in mood and in voice, and the candles were lit,
    And past the porch-quoin
The rays would spring out on the laurels; and dumbledores hit
    On the pane, as if wishing to join.

Where, then, is Molly, who's no more with me?
    —As I stand on this lea,
Thinking thus, there's a many-flamed star in the air,
    That tosses a sign
That her glance is regarding its face from her home, so that there
    Her eyes may have meetings with mine.

THE PEDESTRIAN

AN INCIDENT OF 1883

"Sir, will you let me give you a ride?
Nox venit, and the heath is wide."
—My phaeton-lantern shone on one
  Young, fair, even fresh,
  But burdened with flesh:
A leathern satchel at his side,
His breathings short, his coat undone.

'Twas as if his corpulent figure slopped
With the shake of his walking when he stopped,
And, though the night's pinch grew acute,
  He wore but a thin
  Wind-thridded suit,
Yet well-shaped shoes for walking in,
Artistic beaver, cane gold-topped.

"Alas, my friend," he said with a smile,
"I am daily bound to foot ten mile—
Wet, dry, or dark—before I rest.
  Six months to live
  My doctors give
Me as my prospect here, at best,
Unless I vamp my sturdiest!"

His voice was that of a man refined,
A man, one well could feel, of mind,
Quite winning in its musical ease;
  But in mould maligned
  By some disease;
And I asked again. But he shook his head;
Then, as if more were due, he said:—

"A student was I—of Schopenhauer,
Kant, Hegel,—and the fountained bower
Of the Muses, too, knew my regard:

But ah—I fear me
The grave gapes near me! . . .
Would I could this gross sheath discard,
And rise an ethereal shape, unmarred!"

How I remember him!—his short breath,
His aspect, marked for early death,
As he dropped into the night for ever;
        One caught in his prime
        Of high endeavour;
From all philosophies soon to sever
Through an unconscienced trick of Time!

"WHO'S IN THE NEXT ROOM?"

"Who's in the next room?—who?
  I seemed to see
Somebody in the dawning passing through,
  Unknown to me."
"Nay: you saw nought. He passed invisibly."

"Who's in the next room?—who?
  I seem to hear
Somebody muttering firm in a language new
  That chills the ear."
"No: you catch not his tongue who has entered there."

"Who's in the next room?—who?
  I seem to feel
His breath like a clammy draught, as if it drew
  From the Polar Wheel."
"No: none who breathes at all does the door conceal."

"Who's in the next room?—who?
  A figure wan
With a message to one in there of something due?
  Shall I know him anon?"
"Yea he; and he brought such; and you'll know him anon."

AT A COUNTRY FAIR

At a bygone Western country fair
I saw a giant led by a dwarf
With a red string like a long thin scarf;
How much he was the stronger there
    The giant seemed unaware.

And then I saw that the giant was blind,
And the dwarf a shrewd-eyed little thing;
The giant, mild, timid, obeyed the string
As if he had no independent mind,
    Or will of any kind.

Wherever the dwarf decided to go
At his heels the other trotted meekly,
(Perhaps—I know not—reproaching weakly)
Like one Fate bade that it must be so,
    Whether he wished or no.

Various sights in various climes
I have seen, and more I may see yet,
But that sight never shall I forget,
And have thought it the sorriest of pantomimes,
    If once, a hundred times!

HE REVISITS HIS FIRST SCHOOL

I should not have shown in the flesh,
I ought to have gone as a ghost;
It was awkward, unseemly almost,
Standing solidly there as when fresh,
    Pink, tiny, crisp-curled,
    My pinions yet furled
From the winds of the world.

After waiting so many a year
To wait longer, and go as a sprite
From the tomb at the mid of some night
Was the right, radiant way to appear;
    Not as one wanzing weak
    From life's roar and reek,
    His rest still to seek:

Yea, beglimpsed through the quaint quarried glass
Of green moonlight, by me greener made,
When they'd cry, perhaps, "There sits his shade
In his olden haunt—just as he was
    When in Walkingame he
    Conned the grand Rule-of-Three
    With the bent of a bee."

But to show in the afternoon sun,
With an aspect of hollow-eyed care,
When none wished to see me come there,
Was a garish thing, better undone.
    Yes; wrong was the way;
    But yet, let me say,
    I may right it—some day.

MIDNIGHT ON THE GREAT WESTERN

In the third-class seat sat the journeying boy,
    And the roof-lamp's oily flame
Played down on his listless form and face,
Bewrapt past knowing to what he was going,
    Or whence he came.

In the band of his hat the journeying boy
    Had a ticket stuck; and a string
Around his neck bore the key of his box,
That twinkled gleams of the lamp's sad beams
    Like a living thing.

What past can be yours, O journeying boy
    Towards a world unknown,
Who calmly, as if incurious quite
On all at stake, can undertake
    This plunge alone?

Knows your soul a sphere, O journeying boy,
    Our rude realms far above,
Whence with spacious vision you mark and mete
This region of sin that you find you in,
    But are not of?

IN A WAITING-ROOM

On a morning sick as the day of doom
  With the drizzling gray
  Of an English May,
There were few in the railway waiting-room.
About its walls were framed and varnished
Pictures of liners, fly-blown, tarnished.
  The table bore a Testament
  For travellers' reading, if suchwise bent.

I read it on and on,
  And, thronging the Gospel of Saint John,
  Were figures—additions, multiplications—
By some one scrawled, with sundry emendations;
  Not scoffingly designed,
  But with an absent mind,—
  Plainly a bagman's counts of cost,
  What he had profited, what lost;
And whilst I wondered if there could have been
  Any particle of a soul
  In that poor man at all,
  To cypher rates of wage
  Upon that printed page,
  There joined in the charmless scene
And stood over me and the scribbled book
  (To lend the hour's mean hue
  A smear of tragedy too)
A soldier and wife, with haggard look
Subdued to stone by strong endeavour;
  And then I heard
  From a casual word
They were parting as they believed for ever.

  But next there came
  Like the eastern flame
Of some high altar, children—a pair—

Who laughed at the fly-blown pictures there.
"Here are the lovely ships that we,
Mother, are by and by going to see!
When we get there it's 'most sure to be fine,
And the band will play, and the sun will shine!"
It rained on the skylight with a din
As we waited and still no train came in;
But the words of the child in the squalid room
Had spread a glory through the gloom.

PATHS OF FORMER TIME

No; no;
It must not be so:
They are the ways we do not go.

Still chew
The kine, and moo
In the meadows we used to wander through;

Still purl
The rivulets and curl
Towards the weirs with a musical swirl;

Haymakers
As in former years
Rake rolls into heaps that the pitchfork rears;

Wheels crack
On the turfy track
The waggon pursues with its toppling pack.

"Why then shun—
Since summer's not done—
All this because of the lack of one?"

Had you been
Sharer of that scene
You would not ask while it bites in keen

Why it is so
We can no more go
By the summer paths we used to know!

1913.

THE SHADOW ON THE STONE

I went by the Druid stone
That broods in the garden white and lone,
And I stopped and looked at the shifting shadows
That at some moments fall thereon
From the tree hard by with a rhythmic swing,
And they shaped in my imagining
To the shade that a well-known head and shoulders
Threw there when she was gardening.

I thought her behind my back,
Yea, her I long had learned to lack,
And I said: "I am sure you are standing behind me,
Though how do you get into this old track?"
And there was no sound but the fall of a leaf
As a sad response; and to keep down grief
I would not turn my head to discover
That there was nothing in my belief.

Yet I wanted to look and see
That nobody stood at the back of me;
But I thought once more: "Nay, I'll not unvision
A shape which, somehow, there may be."
So I went on softly from the glade,
And left her behind me throwing her shade,
As she were indeed an apparition—
My head unturned lest my dream should fade.

Begun 1913: finished 1916.

THE CHOIRMASTER'S BURIAL

He often would ask us
That, when he died,
After playing so many
To their last rest,
If out of us any
Should here abide,
And it would not task us,
We would with our lutes
Play over him
By his grave-brim
The psalm he liked best—
The one whose sense suits
"Mount Ephraim"—
And perhaps we should seem
To him, in Death's dream,
Like the seraphim.

As soon as I knew
That his spirit was gone
I thought this his due,
And spoke thereupon.
"I think," said the vicar,
"A read service quicker
Than viols out-of-doors
In these frosts and hoars.
That old-fashioned way
Requires a fine day,
And it seems to me
It had better not be."

Hence, that afternoon,
Though never knew he
That his wish could not be,
To get through it faster
They buried the master
Without any tune.

But 'twas said that, when
At the dead of next night,
The vicar looked out,
There struck on his ken
Thronged roundabout,
Where the frost was graying
The headstoned grass,
A band all in white
Like the saints in church-glass,
Singing and playing
The ancient stave
By the choirmaster's grave.

Such the tenor man told
When he had grown old.

WHILE DRAWING IN A CHURCHYARD

"It is sad that so many of worth,
  Still in the flesh," soughed the yew,
"Misjudge their lot whom kindly earth
    Secludes from view.

"They ride their diurnal round
  Each day-span's sum of hours
In peerless ease, without jolt or bound
    Or ache like ours.

"If the living could but hear
  What is heard by my roots as they creep
Round the restful flock, and the things said there
    No one would weep."

"'Now set among the wise,'
  They say: 'Enlarged in scope,
That no God trumpet us to rise
    We truly hope.'"

I listened to his strange tale
  In the mood that stillness brings,
And I grew to accept as the day wore pale
    That show of things.

"FOR LIFE I HAD NEVER CARED GREATLY"

For Life I had never cared greatly,
    As worth a man's while;
      Peradventures unsought,
    Peradventures that finished in nought,
Had kept me from youth and through manhood till lately
      Unwon by its style.

In earliest years—why I know not—
    I viewed it askance;
      Conditions of doubt,
    Conditions that leaked slowly out,
May haply have bent me to stand and to show not
      Much zest for its dance.

With symphonies soft and sweet colour
    It courted me then,
      Till evasions seemed wrong,
    Till evasions gave in to its song,
And I warmed, until living aloofly loomed duller
      Than life among men.

Anew I found nought to set eyes on,
    When, lifting its hand,
      It uncloaked a star,
    Uncloaked it from fog-damps afar,
And showed its beams burning from pole to horizon
      As bright as a brand.

And so, the rough highway forgetting,
    I pace hill and dale
      Regarding the sky,
    Regarding the vision on high,
And thus re-illumed have no humour for letting
      My pilgrimage fait.

HIS COUNTRY

I journeyed from my native spot
  Across the south sea shine,
And found that people in hall and cot
Laboured and suffered each his lot
  Even as I did mine.

**He travels southward, and
looks around;**

Thus noting them in meads and marts
  It did not seem to me
That my dear country with its hearts,
Minds, yearnings, worse and better parts
  Had ended with the sea.

and cannot discover the boundary

I further and further went anon,
  As such I still surveyed,
And further yet—yea, on and on,
And all the men I looked upon
  Had heart-strings fellow-made.

of his native country;

I traced the whole terrestrial round,
  Homing the other side;
Then said I, "What is there to bound
My denizenship? It seems I have found
  Its scope to be world-wide."

**or where his duties to his
fellow-creatures end;**

I asked me: "Whom have I to fight,
  And whom have I to dare,
And whom to weaken, crush, and blight?
My country seems to have kept in sight
  On my way everywhere."

nor who are his enemies.

1913.

from Late Lyrics and Earlier

GOING AND STAYING

I

The moving sun-shapes on the spray,
The sparkles where the brook was flowing,
Pink faces, plightings, moonlit May,
These were the things we wished would stay;
    But they were going.

II

Seasons of blankness as of snow,
The silent bleed of a world decaying,
The moan of multitudes in woe,
These were the things we wished would go;
    But they were staying.

III

Then we looked closelier at Time,
And saw his ghostly arms revolving
To sweep off woeful things with prime,
Things sinister with things sublime
    Alike dissolving.

HER SONG

I sang that song on Sunday,
    To witch an idle while,
I sang that song on Monday,
    As fittest to beguile:
I sang it as the year outwore,
      And the new slid in;
I thought not what might shape before
    Another would begin.

I sang that song in summer,
    All unforeknowingly,
To him as a new-comer
    From regions strange to me:
I sang it when in afteryears
      The shades stretched out,
And paths were faint; and flocking fears
    Brought cup-eyed care and doubt.

Sings he that song on Sundays
    In some dim land afar,
On Saturdays, or Mondays,
    As when the evening star
Glimpsed in upon his bending face,
      And my hanging hair,
And time untouched me with a trace
    Of soul-smart or despair?

"AND THERE WAS A GREAT CALM"
(On the Signing of the Armistice, Nov. 11, 1918)

I

There had been years of Passion—scorching, cold,
And much Despair, and Anger heaving high,
Care whitely watching, Sorrows manifold,
Among the young, among the weak and old,
And the pensive Spirit of Pity whispered, "Why?"

II

Men had not paused to answer. Foes distraught
Pierced the thinned peoples in a brute-like blindness,
Philosophies that sages long had taught,
And Selflessness, were as an unknown thought,
And "Hell!" and "Shell!" were yapped at Lovingkindness.

III

The feeble folk at home had grown full-used
To "dug-outs," "snipers," "Huns," from the war-adept
In the mornings heard, and at evetides perused;
To day-dreamt men in millions, when they mused—
To nightmare-men in millions when they slept.

IV

Waking to wish existence timeless, null,
Sirius they watched above where armies fell;
He seemed to check his flapping when, in the lull
Of night a boom came thencewise, like the dull
Plunge of a stone dropped into some deep well.

V

So, when old hopes that earth was bettering slowly
Were dead and damned, there sounded "War is done!"
One morrow. Said the bereft, and meek, and lowly,
"Will men some day be given to grace? yea, wholly,
And in good sooth, as our dreams used to run?"

VI

Breathless they paused. Out there men raised their glance
To where had stood those poplars lank and lopped,

As they had raised it through the four years' dance
Of Death in the now familiar flats of France;
And murmured, "Strange, this! How? All firing stopped?"

VII

Aye; all was hushed. The about-to-fire fired not,
The aimed-at moved away in trance-lipped song.
One checkless regiment slung a clinching shot
And turned. The Spirit of Irony smirked out, "What?
Spoil peradventures woven of Rage and Wrong?"

VIII

Thenceforth no flying fires inflamed the gray,
No hurtlings shook the dewdrop from the thorn,
No moan perplexed the mute bird on the spray;
Worn horses mused: "We are not whipped to-day";
No weft-winged engines blurred the moon's thin horn.

IX

Calm fell. From Heaven distilled a clemency;
There was peace on earth, and silence in the sky;
Some could, some could not, shake off misery:
The Sinister Spirit sneered: "It had to be!"
And again the Spirit of Pity whispered, "Why?"

"IF IT'S EVER SPRING AGAIN"
(Song)

If it's ever spring again,
    Spring again,
I shall go where went I when
Down the moor-cock splashed, and hen,
Seeing me not, amid their flounder,
Standing with my arm around her;
If it's ever spring again,
    Spring again,
I shall go where went I then.

If it's ever summer-time,
    Summer-time,
With the hay crop at the prime,
And the cuckoos—two—in rhyme,
As they used to be, or seemed to,
We shall do as long we've dreamed to,
If it's ever summer-time,
    Summer-time,
With the hay, and bees achime.

THE TWO HOUSES

In the heart of night,
When farers were not near,
The left house said to the house on the right,
"I have marked your rise, O smart newcomer here."

Said the right, cold-eyed:
"Newcomer here I am,
Hence haler than you with your cracked old hide,
Loose casements, wormy beams, and doors that jam.

"Modern my wood,
My hangings fair of hue;
While my windows open as they should,
And water-pipes thread all my chambers through.

"Your gear is gray,
Your face wears furrows untold."
"—Yours might," mourned the other, "if you held, brother,
The Presences from aforetime that I hold.

"You have not known
Men's lives, deaths, toils, and teens;
You are but a heap of stick and stone:
A new house has no sense of the have-beens.

"Void as a drum
You stand: I am packed with these,
Though, strangely, living dwellers who come
See not the phantoms all my substance sees!

"Visible in the morning
Stand they, when dawn drags in;
Visible at night; yet hint or warning
Of these thin elbowers few of the inmates win.

"Babes new-brought-forth
Obsess my rooms; straight-stretched

Lank corpses, ere outborne to earth;
Yea, throng they as when first from the Byss upfetched.

    "Dancers and singers
      Throb in me now as once;
Rich-noted throats and gossamered flingers
Of heels; the learned in love-lore and the dunce.

    "Note here within
      The bridegroom and the bride,
Who smile and greet their friends and kin,
And down my stairs depart for tracks untried.

    "Where such inbe,
      A dwelling's character
Takes theirs, and a vague semblancy
To them in all its limbs, and light, and atmosphere.

    "Yet the blind folk
      My tenants, who come and go
In the flesh mid these, with souls unwoke,
Of such sylph-like surrounders do not know."

    "—Will the day come,"
      Said the new one, awestruck, faint,
  "When I shall lodge shades dim and dumb—
And with such spectral guests become acquaint?"

    "—That will it, boy;
      Such shades will people thee,
  Each in his misery, irk, or joy,
And print on thee their presences as on me."

"I WORKED NO WILE TO MEET YOU"
(Song)

I worked no wile to meet you,
  My sight was set elsewhere,
I sheered about to shun you,
  And lent your life no care.
I was unprimed to greet you
  At such a date and place,
Constraint alone had won you
  Vision of my strange face!

You did not seek to see me
  Then or at all, you said,
—Meant passing when you neared me,
  But stumbling-blocks forbade.
You even had thought to flee me.
  By other mindings moved;
No influent star endeared me,
  Unknown, unrecked, unproved!

What, then, was there to tell us
  The flux of flustering hours
Of their own tide would bring us
  By no device of ours
To where the daysprings well us
  Heart-hydromels that cheer,
Till Time enearth and swing us
  Round with the turning sphere.

AT THE RAILWAY STATION, UPWAY

"There is not much that I can do,
  For I've no money that's quite my own!"
  Spoke up the pitying child—
A little boy with a violin
At the station before the train came in,—
"But I can play my fiddle to you,
And a nice one 'tis, and good in tone!"

  The man in the handcuffs smiled;
The constable looked, and he smiled, too,
  As the fiddle began to twang;
And the man in the handcuffs suddenly sang
      With grimful glee:
      "This life so free
      Is the thing for me!"
And the constable smiled, and said no word,
As if unconscious of what he heard;
And so they went on till the train came in—
The convict, and boy with the violin.

SIDE BY SIDE

So there sat they,
The estranged two,
Thrust in one pew
By chance that day;
Placed so, breath-nigh,
Each comer unwitting
Who was to be sitting
In touch close by.

Thus side by side
Blindly alighted,
They seemed united
As groom and bride,
Who'd not communed
For many years—
Lives from twain spheres
With hearts distuned.

Her fringes brushed
His garment's hem
As the harmonies rushed
Through each of them:
Her lips could be heard
In the creed and psalms,
And their fingers neared
At the giving of alms.

And women and men,
The matins ended,
By looks commended
Them, joined again.
Quickly said she,
"Don't undeceive them—
Better thus leave them":
"Quite so," said he.

Slight words!—the last
Between them said,
  Those two, once wed,
  Who had not stood fast.
  Diverse their ways
  From the western door,
  To meet no more
  In their span of days.

MISMET

I

He was leaning by a face,
He was looking into eyes,
And he knew a trysting-place,
And he heard seductive sighs;
  But the face,
  And the eyes,
  And the place,
  And the sighs,
Were not, alas, the right ones—the ones meet for him—
Though fine and sweet the features, and the feelings all abrim.

II

She was looking at a form,
She was listening for a tread,
She could feel a waft of charm
When a certain name was said;
  But the form,
  And the tread,
  And the charm,
  And name said,
Were the wrong ones for her, and ever would be so,
While the heritor of the right it would have saved her soul to know!

VOICES FROM THINGS GROWING IN A CHURCHYARD

These flowers are I, poor Fanny Hurd,
    Sir or Madam,
A little girl here sepultured.
Once I flit-fluttered like a bird
Above the grass, as now I wave
In daisy shapes above my grave,
    All day cheerily,
    All night eerily!

—I am one Bachelor Bowring, "Gent,"
    Sir or Madam;
In shingled oak my bones were pent;
Hence more than a hundred years I spent
In my feat of change from a coffin-thrall
To a dancer in green as leaves on a wall,
    All day cheerily,
    All night eerily!

—I, these berries of juice and gloss,
    Sir or Madam,
Am clean forgotten as Thomas Voss;
Thin-urned, I have burrowed away from the moss
That covers my sod, and have entered this yew,
And turned to clusters ruddy of view,
    All day cheerily,
    All night eerily!

—The Lady Gertrude, proud, high-bred,
    Sir or Madam,
Am I—this laurel that shades your head;
Into its veins I have stilly sped,
And made them of me; and my leaves now shine,
As did my satins superfine,
    All day cheerily,
    All night eerily!

—I, who as innocent withwind climb,
    Sir or Madam,
Am one Eve Greensleeves, in olden time
Kissed by men from many a clime,
Beneath sun, stars, in blaze, in breeze,
As now by glowworms and by bees,
    All day cheerily,
    All night eerily![1]

—I'm old Squire Audeley Grey, who grew,
    Sir or Madam,
Aweary of life, and in scorn withdrew;
Till anon I clambered up anew
As ivy-green, when my ache was stayed,
And in that attire I have longtime gayed
    All day cheerily,
    All night eerily!

—And so these maskers breathe to each
    Sir or Madam
Who lingers there, and their lively speech
Affords an interpreter much to teach,
As their murmurous accents seem to come
Thence hitheraround in a radiant hum,
    All day cheerily,
    All night eerily!

1. It was said her real name was Eve Travillian or Trevelyan; and that she was the handsome mother of two or three illegitimate children, *circa* 1784–85.

BY HENSTRIDGE CROSS AT THE YEAR'S END
(From this centuries-old cross-road the highway leads east to London, north to Bristol
and Bath, west to Exeter and the Land's End, and south to the Channel coast.)

Why go the east road now? . . .
That way a youth went on a morrow
After mirth, and he brought back sorrow
   Painted upon his brow:
Why go the east road now?

Why go the north road now?
Torn, leaf-strewn, as if scoured by foemen,
Once edging fiefs of my forefolk yeomen,
   Fallows fat to the plough:
Why go the north road now?

Why go the west road now?
Thence to us came she, bosom-burning,
Welcome with joyousness returning. . . .
   She sleeps under the bough:
Why go the west road now?

Why go the south road now?
That way marched they some are forgetting,
Stark to the moon left, past regretting
   Loves who have falsed their vow. . . .
Why go the south road now?

Why go any road now?
White stands the handpost for brisk onbearers,
"Halt!" is the word for wan-cheeked farers
   Musing on Whither, and How. . . .
Why go any road now?

"Yea: we want new feet now"
Answer the stones. "Want chit-chat, laughter:
Plenty of such to go hereafter
   By our tracks, we trow!
We are for new feet now."

During the War.

THE CHAPEL-ORGANIST
(A.D. 185–)

I've been thinking it through, as I play here to-night, to play never again,
By the light of that lowering sun peering in at the window-pane,
And over the back-street roofs, throwing shades from the boys of the chore
In the gallery, right upon me, sitting up to these keys once more. . . .
How I used to hear tongues ask, as I sat here when I was new:
"Who is she playing the organ? She touches it mightily true!"
"She travels from Havenpool Town," the deacon would softly speak,
"The stipend can hardly cover her fare hither twice in the week."
(It fell far short of doing, indeed; but I never told,
For I have craved minstrelsy more than lovers, or beauty, or gold.)

'Twas so he answered at first, but the story grew different later:
"It cannot go on much longer, from what we hear of her now!"
At the meaning wheeze in the words the inquirer would shift his place
Till he could see round the curtain that screened me from people below.
"A handsome girl," he would murmur, upstaring (and so I am).
"But—too much sex in her build; fine eyes, but eyelids too heavy;
A bosom too full for her age; in her lips too voluptuous a dye."
(It may be. But who put it there? Assuredly it was not I.)

I went on playing and singing when this I had heard, and more,
Though tears half-blinded me; yes, I remained going on and on,
Just as I used me to chord and to sing at the selfsame time! . . .
For it's a contralto—my voice is; they'll hear it again here to-night
In the psalmody notes that I love far beyond every lower delight.

Well, the deacon, in fact, that day had learnt new tidings about me;
They troubled his mind not a little, for he was a worthy man.
(He trades as a chemist in High Street, and during the week he had sought
His fellow-deacon, who throve as a bookbinder over the way.)
"These are strange rumours," he said. "We must guard the good name of the
    chapel.
If, sooth, she's of evil report, what else can we do but dismiss her?"
"—But get such another to play here we cannot for double the price!"

It settled the point for the time, and I triumphed awhile in their strait,
And my much-beloved grand semibreves went living on, pending my fate.

At length in the congregation more headshakes and murmurs were rife,
And my dismissal was ruled, though I was not warned of it then.
But a day came when they declared it. The news entered me as a sword;
I was broken; so pallid of face that they thought I should faint, they said.
I rallied. "O, rather than go, I will play you for nothing!" said I.
'Twas in much desperation I spoke it, for bring me to forfeit I could not
Those melodies chorded so richly for which I had laboured and lived.
They paused. And for nothing I played at the chapel through Sundays again,
Upheld by that art which I loved more than blandishments lavished of men.

But it fell that murmurs anew from the flock broke the pastor's peace.
Some member had seen me at Havenpool, comrading close a sea-captain.
(O yes; I was thereto constrained, lacking means for the fare to and fro.)
Yet God knows, if aught He knows ever, I loved the Old-Hundredth, Saint
    Stephen's,
Mount Zion, New Sabbath, Miles-Lane, Holy Rest, and Arabia, and Eaton,
Above all embraces of body by wooers who sought me and won! . . .
Next week 'twas declared I was seen coming home with a swain ere the sun.

The deacons insisted then, strong; and forgiveness I did not implore.
I saw all was lost for me, quite, but I made a last bid in my throbs.
My bent, finding victual in lust, men's senses had libelled my soul,
But the soul should die game, if I knew it! I turned to my masters and said:
"I yield, Gentlemen, without parlance. But—let me just hymn you *once* more!
It's a little thing, Sirs, that I ask; and a passion is music with me!"
They saw that consent would cost nothing, and show as good grace, as knew I,
Though tremble I did, and feel sick, as I paused thereat, dumb for their words.
They gloomily nodded assent, saying, "Yes, if you care to. Once more,
And only once more, understand." To that with a bend I agreed.
—"You've a fixed and a far-reaching look," spoke one who had eyed me awhile.
"I've a fixed and a far-reaching plan, and my look only showed it," I smile.

This evening of Sunday is come—the last of my functioning here.
"She plays as if she were possessed!" they exclaim, glancing upward and round.
"Such harmonies I never dreamt the old instrument capable of!"
Meantime the sun lowers and goes; shades deepen; the lights are turned up,

And the people voice out the last singing: tune Tallis: the Evening Hymn.
(I wonder Dissenters sing Ken: it shows them more liberal in spirit
At this little chapel down here than at certain new others I know.)
I sing as I play. Murmurs some one: "No woman's throat richer than hers!"
"True: in these parts," think I. "But, my man, never more will its richness
  outspread."
And I sing with them onward: "The grave dread as little do I as my bed."

I lift up my feet from the pedals; and then, while my eyes are still wet
From the symphonies born of my fingers, I do that whereon I am set,
And draw from my "full round bosom" (their words; how can *I* help its heave?)
A bottle blue-coloured and fluted—a vinaigrette, they may conceive—
And before the choir measures my meaning, reads aught in my moves to and fro,
I drink from the phial at a draught, and they think it a pick-me-up; so.
Then I gather my books as to leave, bend over the keys as to pray.
When they come to me motionless, stooping, quick death will have whisked me
  away.

"Sure, nobody meant her to poison herself in her haste, after all!"
The deacons will say as they carry me down and the night shadows fall,
"Though the charges were true," they will add. "It's a case red as scarlet withal!"
I have never once minced it. Lived chaste I have not. Heaven knows it above! . . .
But past all the heavings of passion—it's music has been my life-love! . . .
That tune did go well—this last playing! . . . I reckon they'll bury me here. . . .
Not a soul from the seaport my birthplace—will come, or bestow me . . . a tear.

"COULD I BUT WILL"
(Song: *Verses 1, 3, key major; verse 2, key minor*)

Could I but will,
　　Will to my bent,
I'd have afar ones near me still,
And music of rare ravishment,
In strains that move the toes and heels!
And when the sweethearts sat for rest
The unbetrothed should foot with zest
　　Ecstatic reels.

Could I be head,
　　Head-god, "Come, now,
Dear girl," I'd say, "whose flame is fled,
Who liest with linen-banded brow,
Stirred but by shakes from Earth's deep core—"
I'd say to her: "Unshroud and meet
That Love who kissed and called thee Sweet!—
　　Yea, come once more!"

Even half-god power
　　In spinning dooms
Had I, this frozen scene should flower,
And sand-swept plains and Arctic glooms
Should green them gay with waving leaves,
Mid which old friends and I would walk
With weightless feet and magic talk
　　Uncounted eves.

AT THE ENTERING OF THE NEW YEAR

I (OLD STYLE)

Our songs went up and out the chimney,
And roused the home-gone husbandmen;
Our allemands, our heys, poussettings,
Our hands-across and back again,
Sent rhythmic throbbings through the casements
  On to the white highway,
Where nighted farers paused and muttered,
  "Keep it up well, do they!"

The contrabasso's measured booming
Sped at each bar to the parish bounds,
To shepherds at their midnight lambings,
To stealthy poachers on their rounds;
And everybody caught full duly
  The notes of our delight,
As Time unrobed the Youth of Promise
  Hailed by our sanguine sight.

II (NEW STYLE)

We stand in the dusk of a pine-tree limb,
As if to give ear to the muffled peal,
Brought or withheld at the breeze's whim;
But our truest heed is to words that steal
From the mantled ghost that looms in the gray.
And seems, so far as our sense can see,
To feature bereaved Humanity,
As it sighs to the imminent year its say:—

"O stay without, O stay without,
Calm comely Youth, untasked, untired
Though stars irradiate thee about
Thy entrance here is undesired.
Open the gate not, mystic one;
Must we avow what we would close confine?
With thee, good friend, we would have converse none,
  Albeit the fault may not be thine."

December 31. During the War.

346

A PROCESSION OF DEAD DAYS

I see the ghost of a perished day;
I know his face, and the feel of his dawn:
'Twas he who took me far away
   To a spot strange and gray:
Look at me, Day, and then pass on,
But come again: yes, come anon!

Enters another into view;
His features are not cold or white,
But rosy as a vein seen through:
   Too soon he smiles adieu.
Adieu, O ghost-day of delight;
But come and grace my dying sight.

Enters the day that brought the kiss:
He brought it in his foggy hand
To where the mumbling river is,
   And the high clematis;
It lent new colour to the land,
And all the boy within me manned.

Ah, this one. Yes, I know his name,
He is the day that wrought a shine
Even on a precinct common and tame,
   As 'twere of purposed aim.
He shows him as a rainbow sign
Of promise made to me and mine.

The next stands forth in his morning clothes.
And yet, despite their misty blue,
They mark no sombre custom-growths
   That joyous living loathes,
But a meteor act, that left in its queue
A train of sparks my lifetime through.

I almost tremble at his nod—
This next in train—who looks at me

As I were slave, and he were god
   Wielding an iron rod.
I close my eyes; yet still is he
In front there, looking mastery.

In semblance of a face averse
The phantom of the next one comes:
I did not know what better or worse
   Chancings might bless or curse
When his original glossed the thrums
Of ivy, bringing that which numbs.

Yes; trees were turning in their sleep
Upon their windy pillows of gray
When he stole in. Silent his creep
   On the grassed eastern steep. . . .
I shall not soon forget that day,
And what his third hour took away!

HE FOLLOWS HIMSELF

In a heavy time I dogged myself
  Along a louring way,
Till my leading self to my following self
  Said: "Why do you hang on me
    So harassingly?"

"I have watched you, Heart of mine," I cried,
  "So often going astray
And leaving me, that I have pursued,
  Feeling such truancy
    Ought not to be."

He said no more, and I dogged him on
  From noon to the dun of day
By prowling paths, until anew
  He begged: "Please turn and flee!—
    What do you see?"

"Methinks I see a man," said I,
  "Dimming his hours to gray.
I will not leave him while I know
  Part of myself is he
    Who dreams such dree!"

"I go to my old friend's house," he urged,
  "So do not watch me, pray!"
"Well, I will leave you in peace," said I,
  "Though of this poignancy
    You should fight free:

"Your friend, O other me, is dead;
  You know not what you say."
—"That do I! And at his green-grassed door
  By night's bright galaxy
    I bend a knee."

—The yew-plumes moved like mockers' beards
Though only boughs were they,
And I seemed to go; yet still was there,
And am, and there haunt we
Thus bootlessly.

VAGG HOLLOW

Vagg Hollow is a marshy spot on the old Roman Road near Ilchester,
where "things" are seen. Merchandise was formerly fetched inland
from the canal-boats at Load-Bridge by waggons this way.

"What do you see in Vagg Hollow,
Little boy, when you go
In the morning at five on your lonely drive?"
"—I see men's souls, who follow
Till we've passed where the road lies low,
When they vanish at our creaking!

"They are like white faces speaking
Beside and behind the waggon—
One just as father's was when here.
The waggoner drinks from his flagon,
(Or he'd flinch when the Hollow is near)
But he does not give me any.

"Sometimes the faces are many;
But I walk along by the horses,
He asleep on the straw as we jog;
And I hear the loud water-courses,
And the drops from the trees in the fog,
And watch till the day is breaking,

"And the wind out by Tintinhull waking;
I hear in it father's call
As he called when I saw him dying,
And he sat by the fire last Fall,
And mother stood by sighing;
But I'm not afraid at all!"

THE DREAM IS—WHICH?

I am laughing by the brook with her,
    Splashed in its tumbling stir;
And then it is a blankness looms
    As if I walked not there,
Nor she, but found me in haggard rooms,
    And treading a lonely stair.

With radiant cheeks and rapid eyes
    We sit where none espies;
Till a harsh change comes edging in
    As no such scene were there,
But winter, and I were bent and thin,
    And cinder-gray my hair.

We dance in heys around the hall,
    Weightless as thistleball;
And then a curtain drops between,
    As if I danced not there,
But wandered through a mounded green
    To find her, I knew where.

March 1913.

THE MASTER AND THE LEAVES

I

We are budding, Master, budding,
  We of your favourite tree;
March drought and April flooding
  Arouse us merrily,
Our stemlets newly studding;
  And yet you do not see!

II

We are fully woven for summer
  In stuff of limpest green,
The twitterer and the hummer
  Here rest of nights, unseen,
While like a long-roll drummer
  The nightjar thrills the treen.

III

We are turning yellow, Master,
  And next we are turning red,
And faster then and faster
  Shall seek our rooty bed,
All wasted in disaster!
  But you lift not your head.

IV

—"I mark your early going,
  And that you'll soon be clay,
I have seen your summer showing
  As in my youthful day;
But why I seem unknowing
  Is too sunk in to say!"

1917.

LAST WORDS TO A DUMB FRIEND

Pet was never mourned as you,
Purrer of the spotless hue,
Plumy tail, and wistful gaze
While you humoured our queer ways,
Or outshrilled your morning call
Up the stairs and through the hall—
Foot suspended in its fall—
While, expectant, you would stand
Arched, to meet the stroking hand;
Till your way you chose to wend
Yonder, to your tragic end.

Never another pet for me!
Let your place all vacant be;
Better blankness day by day
Than companion torn away.
Better bid his memory fade,
Better blot each mark he made,
Selfishly escape distress
By contrived forgetfulness,
Than preserve his prints to make
Every morn and eve an ache.

From the chair whereon he sat
Sweep his fur, nor wince thereat;
Rake his little pathways out
Mid the bushes roundabout;
Smooth away his talons' mark
From the claw-worn pine-tree bark,
Where he climbed as dusk embrowned,
Waiting us who loitered round.

Strange it is this speechless thing,
Subject to our mastering,
Subject for his life and food

To our gift, and time, and mood;
Timid pensioner of us Powers,
His existence ruled by ours,
Should—by crossing at a breath
Into safe and shielded death,
By the merely taking hence
Of his insignificance—
Loom as largened to the sense,
Shape as part, above man's will,
Of the Imperturbable.

As a prisoner, flight debarred,
Exercising in a yard,
Still retain I, troubled, shaken,
Mean estate, by him forsaken;
And this home, which scarcely took
Impress from his little look,
By his faring to the Dim
Grows all eloquent of him.

Housemate, I can think you still
Bounding to the window-sill,
Over which I vaguely see
Your small mound beneath the tree,
Showing in the autumn shade
That you moulder where you played.

October 2, 1904.

A DRIZZLING EASTER MORNING

And he is risen? Well, be it so. . . .
And still the pensive lands complain,
And dead men wait as long ago,
As if, much doubting, they would know
What they are ransomed from, before
They pass again their sheltering door.

I stand amid them in the rain,
While blusters vex the yew and vane;
And on the road the weary wain
Plods forward, laden heavily;
And toilers with their aches are fain
For endless rest—though risen is he.

ON ONE WHO LIVED AND DIED WHERE HE WAS BORN

When a night in November
  Blew forth its bleared airs
An infant descended
  His birth-chamber stairs
  For the very first time,
  At the still, midnight chime;
All unapprehended
  His mission, his aim.—
Thus, first, one November,
An infant descended
    The stairs.

On a night in November
  Of weariful cares,
A frail aged figure
  Ascended those stairs
  For the very last time:
  All gone his life's prime,
All vanished his vigour,
  And fine, forceful frame:
Thus, last, one November
Ascended that figure
    Upstairs.

On those nights in November—
  Apart eighty years—
The babe and the bent one
  Who traversed those stairs
  From the early first time
  To the last feeble climb—
That fresh and that spent one—
  Were even the same:
Yea, who passed in November
As infant, as bent one,
    Those stairs.

Wise child of November!
　From birth to blanched hairs
Descending, ascending,
　Wealth-wantless, those stairs;
　Who saw quick in time
　As a vain pantomime
Life's tending, its ending,
　The worth of its fame.
Wise child of November,
Descending, ascending
　Those stairs!

"I WAS THE MIDMOST"

I was the midmost of my world
　When first I frisked me free,
For though within its circuit gleamed
　But a small company,
And I was immature, they seemed
　To bend their looks on me.

She was the midmost of my world
　When I went further forth,
And hence it was that, whether I turned
　To south, east, west, or north,
Beams of an all-day Polestar burned
　From that new axe of earth.

Where now is midmost in my world?
　I trace it not at all:
No midmost shows it here, or there,
　When wistful voices call
"We are fain! We are fain!" from everywhere
　On Earth's bewildering ball!

THE WHIPPER-IN

"My father was the whipper-in,—
　　Is still—if I'm not misled?
And now I see, where the hedge is thin,
　　A little spot of red;
　　Surely it is my father
　　Going to the kennel-shed!

"I cursed and fought my father—aye,
　　And sailed to a foreign land;
And feeling sorry, I'm back, to stay,
　　Please God, as his helping hand.
　　Surely it is my father
　　Near where the kennels stand?"

"—True. Whipper-in he used to be
　　For twenty years or more;
And you did go away to sea
　　As youths have done before.
　　Yes, oddly enough that red there
　　Is the very coat he wore.

"But he—he's dead; was thrown somehow,
　　And gave his back a crick,
And though that is his coat, 'tis now
　　The scarecrow of a rick;
　　You'll see when you get nearer—
　　'Tis spread out on a stick.

"You see, when all had settled down
　　Your mother's things were sold,
And she went back to her own town,
　　And the coat, ate out with mould,
　　Is now used by the farmer
　　For scaring, as 'tis old."

THE LAMENT OF THE LOOKING-GLASS

Words from the mirror softly pass
   To the curtains with a sigh:
"Why should I trouble again to glass
   These smileless things hard by,
Since she I pleasured once, alas,
   Is now no longer nigh!"

"I've imaged shadows of coursing cloud,
   And of the plying limb
On the pensive pine when the air is loud
   With its aerial hymn;
But never do they make me proud
   To catch them within my rim!

"I flash back phantoms of the night
   That sometimes flit by me,
I echo roses red and white—
   The loveliest blooms that be—
But now I never hold to sight
   So sweet a flower as she."

RAKE-HELL MUSES

Yes; since she knows not need,
　　Nor walks in blindness,
I may without unkindness
　　This true thing tell:

Which would be truth, indeed,
　　Though worse in speaking,
Were her poor footsteps seeking
　　A pauper's cell.

I judge, then, better far
　　She now have sorrow,
Than gladness that to-morrow
　　Might know its knell.—

It may be men there are
　　Could make of union
A lifelong sweet communion
　　Or passioned spell;

But *I*, to save her name
　　And bring salvation
By altar-affirmation
　　And bridal bell;

I, by whose rash unshame
　　These tears come to her:—
My faith would more undo her
　　Than my farewell!

Chained to me, year by year
　　My moody madness
Would make her olden gladness
　　An intermell.

She'll take the ill that's near,
　　And bear the blaming.

'Twill pass. Full soon her shaming
  They'll cease to yell.

Our unborn, first her moan,
  Will grow her guerdon,
Until from blot and burden
  A joyance swell;

In that therein she'll own
  My good part wholly,
My evil staining solely
  My own vile fell.

Of the disgrace, may be
  "He shunned to share it,
Being false," they'll say. I'll bear it,
  Time will dispel

The calumny, and prove
  This much about me,
That she lives best without me
  Who would live well.

That, this once, not self-love
  But good intention
Pleads that against convention
  We two rebel.

For, is one moonlight dance,
  One midnight passion,
A rock whereon to fashion
  Life's citadel?

Prove they their power to prance
  Life's miles together
From upper slope to nether
  Who trip an ell?

—Years hence, or now apace,
  May tongues be calling

News of my further falling
  Sinward pell-mell:

Then this great good will grace
  Our lives' division,
She's saved from more misprision
  Though I plumb hell.

  189–

AN ANCIENT TO ANCIENTS

Where once we danced, where once we sang,
    Gentlemen,
The floors are sunken, cobwebs hang,
And cracks creep; worms have fed upon
The doors. Yea, sprightlier times were then
Than now, with harps and tabrets gone,
    Gentlemen!

Where once we rowed, where once we sailed
    Gentlemen,
And damsels took the tiller, veiled
Against too strong a stare (God wot
Their fancy, then or anywhen!)
Upon that shore we are clean forgot,
    Gentlemen!

We have lost somewhat, afar and near,
    Gentlemen,
The thinning of our ranks each year
Affords a hint we are nigh undone,
That we shall not be ever again
The marked of many, loved of one,
    Gentlemen.

In dance the polka hit our wish,
    Gentlemen,
The paced quadrille, the spry schottische,
"Sir Roger."—And in opera spheres
The "Girl" (the famed "Bohemian"),
And "Trovatore," held the ears,
    Gentlemen.

This season's paintings do not please,
    Gentlemen,
Like Etty, Mulready, Maclise;
Throbbing romance has waned and wanned;
No wizard wields the witching pen

Of Bulwer, Scott, Dumas, and Sand,
    Gentlemen.

The bower we shrined to Tennyson,
    Gentlemen,
Is roof-wrecked; damps there drip upon
Sagged seats, the creeper-nails are rust,
The spider is sole denizen;
Even she who voiced those rhymes is dust,
    Gentlemen!

We who met sunrise sanguine-souled,
    Gentlemen,
Are wearing weary. We are old;
These younger press; we feel our rout
Is imminent to Aïdes' den,—
That evening shades are stretching out,
    Gentlemen!

And yet, though ours be failing frames.
    Gentlemen,
So were some others' history names,
Who trode their track light-limbed and fast
As these youth, and not alien
From enterprise, to their long last,
    Gentlemen.

Sophocles, Plato, Socrates,
    Gentlemen,
Pythagoras, Thucydides,
Herodotus, and Homer,—yea,
Clement, Augustin, Origen,
Burnt brightlier towards their setting-day,
    Gentlemen.

And ye, red-lipped and smooth-browed; list,
    Gentlemen;
Much is there waits you we have missed;
Much lore we leave you worth the knowing,
Much, much has lain outside our ken:
Nay, rush not: time serves: we are going,
    Gentlemen.

from Human Shows

A BIRD-SCENE AT A RURAL DWELLING

When the inmate stirs, the birds retire discreetly
From the window-ledge, whereon they whistled sweetly
    And on the step of the door,
     In the misty morning hoar;
   But now the dweller is up they flee
   To the crooked neighbouring codlin-tree;
And when he comes fully forth they seek the garden,
And call from the lofty costard, as pleading pardon
    For shouting so near before
    In their joy at being alive:—
Meanwhile the hammering clock within goes five.

I know a domicile of brown and green,
Where for a hundred summers there have been
Just such enactments, just such daybreaks seen.

THE LATER AUTUMN

Gone are the lovers, under the bush
    Stretched at their ease;
    Gone the bees,
Tangling themselves in your hair as they rush
    On the line of your track,
    Leg-laden, back
    With a dip to their hive
    In a prepossessed dive.

Toadsmeat is mangy, frosted, and sere;
    Apples in grass
    Crunch as we pass,
And rot ere the men who make cyder appear.
    Couch-fires abound
    On fallows around,
    And shades far extend
    Like lives soon to end.

Spinning leaves join the remains shrunk and brown
    Of last year's display
    That lie wasting away,
On whose corpses they earlier as scorners gazed down
    From their aery green height:
    Now in the same plight
    They huddle; while yon
    A robin looks on.

GREEN SLATES
(Penpethy)

It happened once, before the duller
  Loomings of life defined them,
I searched for slates of greenish colour
  A quarry where men mined them;

And saw, the while I peered around there,
  In the quarry standing
A form against the slate background there,
  Of fairness eye-commanding.

And now, though fifty years have flown me,
  With all their dreams and duties,
And strange-pipped dice my hand has thrown me,
  And dust are all her beauties,

Green slates—seen high on roofs, or lower
  In waggon, truck, or lorry—
Cry out: "Our home was where you saw her
  Standing in the quarry!"

FOUR IN THE MORNING

At four this day of June I rise:
The dawn-light strengthens steadily;
Earth is a cerule mystery,
As if not far from Paradise
      At four o'clock,

Or else near the Great Nebula,
Or where the Pleiads blink and smile:
(For though we see with eyes of guile
The grisly grin of things by day,
      At four o'clock

They show their best.) . . . In this vale's space
I am up the first, I think. Yet, no,
A whistling? and the to-and-fro
Wheezed whettings of a scythe apace
      At four o'clock? . . .

—Though pleasure spurred, I rose with irk:
Here is one at compulsion's whip
Taking his life's stern stewardship
With blithe uncare, and hard at work
      At four o'clock!

Bockhampton.

IN ST. PAUL'S A WHILE AGO

Summer and winter close commune
On this July afternoon
As I enter chilly Paul's,
With its chasmal classic walls.
—Drifts of gray illumination
From the lofty fenestration
Slant them down in bristling spines that spread
Fan-like upon the vast dust-moted shade.

Moveless here, no whit allied
To the daemonian din outside,
Statues stand, cadaverous, wan,
Round the loiterers looking on
Under the yawning dome and nave,
Pondering whatnot, giddy or grave.
Here a verger moves a chair,
Or a red rope fixes there:—
A brimming Hebe, rapt in her adorning,
Brushes an Artemisia craped in mourning;
Beatrice Benedick piques, coquetting;
All unknowing or forgetting
That strange Jew, Damascus-bound,
Whose name, thereafter travelling round
To this precinct of the world,
Spread here like a flag unfurled:
Anon inspiring architectural sages
To frame this pile, writ his throughout the ages:
Whence also the encircling mart
Assumed his name, of him no part,
And to his vision-seeing mind
Charmless, blank in every kind;
And whose displays, even had they called his eye,
No gold or silver had been his to buy;
Whose haunters, had they seen him stand

On his own steps here, lift his hand
In stress of eager, stammering speech,
And his meaning chanced to reach,
Would have proclaimed him as they passed
An epilept enthusiast.

A LAST JOURNEY

"Father, you seem to have been sleeping fair?"
The child uncovered the dimity-curtained window-square
    And looked out at the dawn,
  And back at the dying man nigh gone,
    And propped up in his chair,
Whose breathing a robin's "chink" took up in antiphon.

    The open fireplace spread
  Like a vast weary yawn above his head,
Its thin blue blower waved against his whitening crown,
    For he could not lie down:
  He raised him on his arms so emaciated:—

  "Yes; I've slept long, my child. But as for rest,
    Well, that I cannot say.
The whole night have I footed field and turnpike way—
    A regular pilgrimage—as at my best
    And very briskest day!

  "'Twas first to Weatherb'ry, to see them there,
    And thence to King's-Stag, where
I joined in a jolly trip to Weydon-Priors Fair:
  I shot for nuts, bought gingerbreads, cream-cheese;
    And, not content with these,
I went to London: heard the watchmen cry the hours.

"I soon was off again, and found me in the bowers
    Of father's apple-trees,
  And he shook the apples down: they fell in showers,
Whereon he turned, smiled strange at me, as ill at ease;
  And then you pulled the curtain; and, ah me,
  I found me back where I wished not to be!"

  'Twas told the child next day: "Your father's dead."
    And, struck, she questioned, "O,

That journey, then, did father really go?—
Buy nuts, and cakes, and travel at night till dawn was red,
And tire himself with journeying, as he said,
To see those old friends that he cared for so?"

SINE PROLE
(Mediaeval Latin Sequence-Metre)

Forth from ages thick in mystery,
Through the morn and noon of history,
　　To the moment where I stand
Has my line wound: I the last one—
Outcome of each spectral past one
　　Of that file, so many-manned!

Nothing in its time-trail marred it:
As one long life I regard it
　　Throughout all the years till now,
When it fain—the close seen coming—
After annals past all plumbing—
　　Makes to Being its parting bow.

Unlike Jahveh's ancient nation,
Little in their line's cessation
　　Moderns see for surge of sighs:
They have been schooled by lengthier vision,
View Life's lottery with misprision,
　　And its dice that fling no prize!

THE BEST SHE COULD

Nine leaves a minute
Swim down shakily;
Each one fain would spin it
Straight to earth; but, see,
How the sharp airs win it
Slantwise away!—Hear it say,
"Now we have finished our summer show
Of what we knew the way to do:
Alas, not much! But, as things go,
As fair as any. And night-time calls,
  And the curtain falls!"

Sunlight goes on shining
As if no frost were here,
Blackbirds seem designing
Where to build next year;
Yet is warmth declining:
And still the day seems to say,
"Saw you how Dame Summer drest?
Of all God taught her she bethought her!
Alas, not much! And yet the best
She could, within the too short time
  Granted her prime."

Nov. 8, 1923.

THE GRAVEYARD OF DEAD CREEDS

I lit upon the graveyard of dead creeds
In wistful wanderings through old wastes of thought,
Where bristled fennish fungi, fruiting nought,
Amid the sepulchres begirt with weeds,

Which stone by stone recorded sanct, deceased
Catholicons that had, in centuries flown,
Physicked created man through his long groan,
Ere they went under, all their potence ceased.

When in a breath-while, lo, their spectres rose
Like wakened winds that autumn summons up:—
"Out of us cometh an heir, that shall disclose
New promise!" cried they. "And the caustic cup

"We ignorantly upheld to men, be filled
With draughts more pure than those we ever distilled,
That shall make tolerable to sentient seers
The melancholy marching of the years."

A LIGHT SNOW-FALL AFTER FROST

On the flat road a man at last appears:
    How much his whitening hairs
Owe to the settling snow's mute anchorage,
And how much to a life's rough pilgrimage,
    One cannot certify.

    The frost is on the wane,
And cobwebs hanging close outside the pane
Pose as festoons of thick white worsted there,
Of their pale presence no eye being aware
    Till the rime made them plain.

    A second man comes by;
His ruddy beard brings fire to the pallid scene:
    His coat is faded green;
    Hence seems it that his mien
    Wears something of the dye
Of the berried holm-trees that he passes nigh.

The snow-feathers so gently swoop that though
    But half an hour ago
The road was brown, and now is starkly white,
A watcher would have failed defining quite
    When it transformed it so.

Near Surbiton.

WINTER NIGHT IN WOODLAND
(Old Time)

The bark of a fox rings, sonorous and long:—
Three barks, and then silentness; "wong, wong, wong!"
In quality horn-like, yet melancholy,
As from teachings of years; for an old one is he.
The hand of all men is against him, he knows; and yet, why?
That he knows not,—will never know, down to his death-halloo cry.

With clap-nets and lanterns off start the bird-baiters,
In trim to make raids on the roosts in the copse,
Where they beat the boughs artfully, while their awaiters
Grow heavy at home over divers warm drops.
The poachers, with swingels, and matches of brimstone, outcreep
To steal upon pheasants and drowse them a-perch and asleep.

Out there, on the verge, where a path wavers through,
Dark figures, filed singly, thrid quickly the view,
Yet heavily laden: land-carriers are they
In the hire of the smugglers from some nearest bay.
Each bears his two "tubs," slung across, one in front, one behind,
To a further snug hiding, which none but themselves are to find.

And then, when the night has turned twelve the air brings
From dim distance, a rhythm of voices and strings:
'Tis the quire, just afoot on their long yearly rounds,
To rouse by worn carols each house in their bounds;
Robert Penny, the Dewys, Mail, Voss, and the rest; till anon
Tired and thirsty, but cheerful, they home to their beds in the dawn,

THE NEW TOY

She cannot leave it alone,
 The new toy;
She pats it, smooths it, rights it, to show it's her own,
As the other train-passengers muse on its temper and tone
 Till she draws from it cries of annoy:—
She feigns to appear as if thinking it nothing so rare
 Or worthy of pride, to achieve
This wonder a child, though with reason the rest of them there
 May so be inclined to believe.

NOBODY COMES

Tree-leaves labour up and down,
 And through them the fainting light
 Succumbs to the crawl of night.
Outside in the road the telegraph wire
 To the town from the darkening land
Intones to travellers like a spectral lyre
 Swept by a spectral hand.

A car comes up, with lamps full-glare,
 That flash upon a tree:
 It has nothing to do with me,
And whangs along in a world of its own,
 Leaving a blacker air;
And mute by the gate I stand again alone,
 And nobody pulls up there.

October 9, 1924.

THE LAST LEAF

"The leaves throng thick above:—
Well, I'll come back, dear Love,
   When they all are down!"

She watched that August tree,
(None now scorned summer as she),
   Till it broidered it brown.

And then October came blowing,
And the leaves showed signs they were going,
   And she saw up through them.

O how she counted them then!
—November left her but ten,
   And started to strew them.

"Ah, when they all are gone,
And the skeleton-time comes on,
   Whom shall I see!"

—When the fifteenth spread its sky
That month, her upturned eye
   Could count but three.

And at the close of the week
A flush flapped over her cheek:
   The last one fell.

But—he did not come. And, at length,
Her hope of him lost all strength,
   And it was as a knell. . . .

When he did come again,
Years later, a husband then,
   Heavy somewhat,

With a smile she reminded him:
And he cried: "Ah, that vow of our whim!—
　Which I forgot,

"As one does!—And was that the tree?
So it was!—Dear me, dear me:
　Yes: I forgot."

THE AËROLITE

I thought a germ of Consciousness
Escaped on an aërolite
    Aions ago
From some far globe, where no distress
Had means to mar supreme delight;

But only things abode that made
The power to feel a gift uncloyed
    Of gladsome glow,
And life unendingly displayed
Emotions loved, desired, enjoyed.

And that this stray, exotic germ
Fell wanderingly upon our sphere,
    After its wingings,
Quickened, and showed to us the worm
That gnaws vitalities native here,

And operated to unblind
Earth's old-established ignorance
    Of stains and stingings,
Which grin no griefs while not opined,
But cruelly tax intelligence.

"How shall we," then the seers said,
"Oust this awareness, this disease
    Called sense, here sown,
Though good, no doubt, where it was bred,
And wherein all things work to please?"

Others cried: "Nay, we rather would,
Since this untoward gift is sent
    For ends unknown,
Limit its registerings to good,
And hide from it all anguishment."

I left them pondering. This was how
(Or so I dreamed) was waked on earth
    The mortal moan
Begot of sentience. Maybe now
Normal unwareness waits rebirth.

"SHE OPENED THE DOOR"

She opened the door of the West to me,
   With its loud sea-lashings,
   And cliff-side clashings
Of waters rife with revelry.

She opened the door of Romance to me,
   The door from a cell
   I had known too well,
Too long, till then, and was fain to flee.

She opened the door of a Love to me,
   That passed the wry
   World-welters by
As far as the arching blue the lea.

She opens the door of the Past to me,
   Its magic lights,
   Its heavenly heights,
When forward little is to see!

1913.

THE HARBOUR BRIDGE

From here, the quay, one looks above to mark
The bridge across the harbour, hanging dark
Against the day's-end sky, fair-green in glow
Over and under the middle archway's bow:
It draws its skeleton where the sun has set,
Yea, clear from cutwater to parapet;
On which mild glow, too, lines of rope and spar
   Trace themselves black as char.

Down here in shade we hear the painters shift
Against the bollards with a drowsy lift,
As moved by the incoming stealthy tide.
High up across the bridge the burghers glide
As cut black-paper portraits hastening on
In conversation none knows what upon:
Their sharp-edged lips move quickly word by word
   To speech that is not heard.

There trails the dreamful girl, who leans and stops,
There presses the practical woman to the shops,
There is a sailor, meeting his wife with a start,
And we, drawn nearer, judge they are keeping apart.
Both pause. She says: "I've looked for you. I thought
We'd make it up." Then no words can be caught.
At last: "Won't you come home?" She moves still nigher:
   "'Tis comfortable, with a fire."

"No," he says gloomily. "And, anyhow,
I can't give up the other woman now:
You should have talked like that in former days,
When I was last home." They go different ways.
And the west dims, and yellow lamplights shine:
And soon above, like lamps more opaline,
White stars ghost forth, that care not for men's wives,
   Or any other lives.

Weymouth.

VAGRANT'S SONG
(With an Old Wessex Refrain)

I

When a dark-eyed dawn
    Crawls forth, cloud-drawn,
And starlings doubt the night-time's close;
    And "three months yet,"
    They seem to fret,
"Before we cease us slaves of snows,
    And sun returns
    To loose the burns,
And this wild woe called Winter goes!"—
    O a hollow tree
    Is as good for me
As a house where the back-brand[1] glows!
Che-hane, mother; che-hane, mother,
    As a house where the back-brand glows!

II

When autumn brings
    A whirr of wings
Among the evergreens around,
    And sundry thrills
    About their quills
Awe rooks, and misgivings abound,
    And the joyless pines
    In leaning lines
Protect from gales the lower ground,
    O a hollow tree
    Is as good for me
As a house of a thousand pound!
Che-hane, mother; che-hane, mother,
    As a house of a thousand pound!

1. "Back-brand"—the log which used to be laid at the back of a wood fire.

HORSES ABOARD

Horses in horsecloths stand in a row
On board the huge ship that at last lets go:
Whither are they sailing? They do not know,
Nor what for, nor how.—
                              They are horses of war,
And are going to where there is fighting afar;
But they gaze through their eye-holes unwitting they are,
And that in some wilderness, gaunt and ghast,
Their bones will bleach ere a year has passed,
And the item be as "war-waste" classed.—
And when the band booms, and the folk say "Good-bye!"
And the shore slides astern, they appear wrenched awry
From the scheme Nature planned for them,—wondering why.

THE MISSED TRAIN

How I was caught
Hieing home, after days of allure,
And forced to an inn—small, obscure—
   At the junction, gloom-fraught.

How civil my face
To get them to chamber me there—
A roof I had scorned, scarce aware
   That it stood at the place.

And how all the night
I had dreams of the unwitting cause
Of my lodgment. How lonely I was:
   How consoled by her sprite!

Thus onetime to me . . .
Dim wastes of dead years bar away
Then from now. But such happenings to-day
   Fall to lovers, may be!

Years, years as shoaled seas,
Truly, stretch now between! Less and less
Shrink the visions then vast in me.—Yes,
   Then in me: Now in these.

THE THING UNPLANNED

The white winter sun struck its stroke on the bridge,
  The meadow-rills rippled and gleamed
As I left the thatched post-office, just by the ridge,
And dropped in my pocket her long tender letter,
With: "This must be snapped! it is more than it seemed;
  And now is the opportune time!"

But against what I willed worked the surging sublime
  Of the thing that I did—the thing better!

A POPULAR PERSONAGE AT HOME

"I live here: 'Wessex' is my name:
I am a dog known rather well:
I guard the house; but how that came
To be my whim I cannot tell.

"With a leap and a heart elate I go
At the end of an hour's expectancy
To take a walk of a mile or so
With the folk I let live here with me.

"Along the path, amid the grass
I sniff, and find out rarest smells
For rolling over as I pass
The open fields towards the dells.

"No doubt I shall always cross this sill,
And turn the corner, and stand steady,
Gazing back for my mistress till
She reaches where I have run already,

"And that this meadow with its brook,
And bulrush, even as it appears
As I plunge by with hasty look,
Will stay the same a thousand years."

Thus "Wessex." But a dubious ray
At times informs his steadfast eye,
Just for a trice, as though to say,
"Yet, will this pass, and pass shall I?"

1924.

A WATERING-PLACE LADY INVENTORIED

A sweetness of temper unsurpassed and unforgettable,
A mole on the cheek whose absence would have been regrettable,
A ripple of pleasant converse full of modulation,
A bearing of inconveniences without vexation,
Till a cynic would find her amiability provoking,
Tempting him to indulge in mean and wicked joking.

Flawlessly oval of face, especially cheek and chin,
With a glance of a quality that beckoned for a glance akin,
A habit of swift assent to any intelligence broken,
Before the fact to be conveyed was fully spoken
And she could know to what her colloquist would win her,—
This from a too alive impulsion to sympathy in her,—
All with a sense of the ridiculous, keen yet charitable;
In brief, a rich, profuse attractiveness unnarratable.

I should have added her hints that her husband prized her but slenderly,
And that (with a sigh) 'twas a pity she'd no one to treat her tenderly.

SHORTENING DAYS AT THE HOMESTEAD

The first fire since the summer is lit, and is smoking into the room:
  The sun-rays thread it through, like woof-lines in a loom.
  Sparrows spurt from the hedge, whom misgivings appal
That winter did not leave last year for ever, after all.
    Like shock-headed urchins, spiny-haired,
    Stand pollard willows, their twigs just bared.

Who is this coming with pondering pace,
  Black and ruddy, with white embossed,
  His eyes being black, and ruddy his face
And the marge of his hair like morning frost?
    It's the cider-maker,
    And appletree-shaker,
  And behind him on wheels, in readiness,
  His mill, and tubs, and vat, and press.

THE PAPHIAN BALL
ANOTHER CHRISTMAS EXPERIENCE OF THE MELLSTOCK QUIRE

We went our Christmas rounds once more,
With quire and viols as theretofore.

Our path was near by Rushy-Pond,
Where Egdon-Heath outstretched beyond.

There stood a figure against the moon,
Tall, spare, and humming a weirdsome tune.

"You tire of Christian carols," he said:
"Come and lute at a ball instead.

"'Tis to your gain, for it ensures
That many guineas will be yours.

"A slight condition hangs on't, true,
But you will scarce say nay thereto:

"That you go blindfold; that anon
The place may not be gossiped on."

They stood and argued with each other:
"Why sing from one house to another

"These ancient hymns in the freezing night,
And all for nought? 'Tis foolish, quite!"

"—'Tis serving God, and shunning evil:
Might not elsedoing serve the devil?"

"But grand pay!" . . . They were lured by his call,
Agreeing to go blindfold all.

They walked, he guiding, some new track,
Doubting to find the pathway back.

In a strange hall they found them when
They were unblinded all again.

Gilded alcoves, great chandeliers,
Voluptuous paintings ranged in tiers,

In brief, a mansion large and rare,
With rows of dancers waiting there.

They tuned and played; the couples danced;
Half-naked women tripped, advanced,

With handsome partners footing fast,
Who swore strange oaths, and whirled them past.

And thus and thus the slow hours wore them:
While shone their guineas heaped before them.

Drowsy at length, in lieu of the dance
"*While Shepherds watched* . . ." they bowed by chance;

And in a moment, at a blink,
There flashed a change; ere they could think

The ball-room vanished and all its crew:
Only the well-known heath they view—

The spot of their crossing overnight,
When wheedled by the stranger's sleight.

There, east, the Christmas dawn hung red.
And dark Rainbarrow with its dead

Bulged like a supine negress' breast
Against Clyffe-Clump's faint far-off crest.

Yea; the rare mansion, gorgeous, bright,
The ladies, gallants, gone were quite.

The heaped-up guineas, too, were gone
With the gold table they were on.

"Why did not grasp we what was owed!"
Cried some, as homeward, shamed, they strode.

Now comes the marvel and the warning:
When they had dragged to church next morning,

With downcast heads and scarce a word,
They were astound at what they heard.

Praises from all came forth in showers
For how they'd cheered the midnight hours.

"We've heard you many times," friends said,
"But like *that* never have you played!

"Rejoice, ye tenants of the earth,
And celebrate your Saviour's birth.

"Never so thrilled the darkness through,
Or more inspired us so to do!" . . .

—The man who used to tell this tale
Was the tenor-viol, Michael Mail;

Yes; Mail the tenor, now but earth!
I give it for what it may be worth.

THE SIX BOARDS

Six boards belong to me:
I do not know where they may be;
If growing green, or lying dry
    In a cockloft nigh.

Some morning I shall claim them,
And who may then possess will aim them
To bring to me those boards I need
    With thoughtful speed.

But though they hurry so
To yield me mine, I shall not know
How well my want they'll have supplied
    When notified.

Those boards and I—how much
In common we, of feel and touch
Shall share thence on,—earth's far core-quakings,
    Hill-shocks, tide-shakings—

Yea, hid where none will note,
The once live tree and man, remote
From mundane hurt as if on Venus, Mars,
    Or furthest stars.

from Winter Words

PROUD SONGSTERS

The thrushes sing as the sun is going,
   And the finches whistle in ones and pairs,
And as it gets dark loud nightingales
     In bushes
Pipe, as they can when April wears,
   As if all Time were theirs.

These are brand-new birds of twelve-months' growing,
Which a year ago, or less than twain,
No finches were, nor nightingales,
     Nor thrushes,
But only particles of grain,
   And earth, and air, and rain.

"I AM THE ONE"

I am the one whom ringdoves see
    Through chinks in boughs
    When they do not rouse
    In sudden dread,
But stay on cooing, as if they said:
    "Oh; it's only he."

I am the passer when up-eared hares,
    Stirred as they eat
    The new-sprung wheat,
    Their munch resume
As if they thought: "He is one for whom
    Nobody cares."

Wet-eyed mourners glance at me
    As in train they pass
    Along the grass
    To a hollowed spot,
And think: "No matter; he quizzes not
    Our misery."

I hear above: "We stars must lend
    No fierce regard
    To his gaze, so hard
    Bent on us thus,—
Must scathe him not. He is one with us
    Beginning and end."

AN UNKINDLY MAY

A shepherd stands by a gate in a white smock-frock:
He holds the gate ajar, intently counting his flock.

The sour spring wind is blurting boisterous-wise,
And bears on it dirty clouds across the skies;
Plantation timbers creak like rusty cranes,
And pigeons and rooks, dishevelled by late rains,
Are like gaunt vultures, sodden and unkempt,
And song-birds do not end what they attempt:
The buds have tried to open, but quite failing
Have pinched themselves together in their quailing.
The sun frowns whitely in eye-trying flaps
Through passing cloud-holes, mimicking audible taps.
"Nature, you're not commendable to-day!"
I think. "Better to-morrow!" she seems to say.

That shepherd still stands in that white smock-frock,
Unnoting all things save the counting his flock.

UNKEPT GOOD FRIDAYS

There are many more Good Fridays
    Than this, if we but knew
The names, and could relate them,
    Of men whom rulers slew
For their goodwill, and date them
As runs the twelvemonth through.

These nameless Christs' Good Fridays,
    Whose virtues wrought their end,
Bore days of bonds and burning,
    With no man to their friend,
Of mockeries, and spurning;
    Yet they are all unpenned.

When they had their Good Fridays
    Of bloody sweat and strain
Oblivion hides. We quote not
    Their dying words of pain,
Their sepulchres we note not,
    Unwitting where they have lain.

No annual Good Fridays
    Gained they from cross and cord,
From being sawn asunder,
    Disfigured and abhorred,
Smitten and trampled under:
    Such dates no hands have scored.

Let be. Let lack Good Fridays
    These Christs of unwrit names;
The world was not even worthy
    To taunt their hopes and aims,
As little of earth, earthy,
    As his mankind proclaims.

Good Friday, 1927.

THE MOUND

For a moment pause:—
Just here it was;
And through the thin thorn hedge, by the rays of the moon,
I can see the tree in the field, and beside it the mound—
Now sheeted with snow—whereon we sat that June
When it was green and round,
And she crazed my mind by what she coolly told—
The history of her undoing,
(As I saw it), but she called "comradeship,"
That bred in her no rueing:
And saying she'd not be bound
For life to one man, young, ripe-yeared, or old,
Left me—an innocent simpleton to her viewing;
For, though my accompt of years outscored her own,
Hers had more hotly flown. . . .
We never met again by this green mound,
To press as once so often lip on lip,
And palter, and pause:—
Yes; here it was!

EVENING SHADOWS

The shadows of my chimneys stretch afar
Across the plot, and on to the privet bower,
And even the shadows of their smokings show,
And nothing says just now that where they are
They will in future stretch at this same hour,
Though in my earthen cyst I shall not know.

And at this time the neighbouring Pagan mound,
Whose myths the Gospel news now supersede,
Upon the greensward also throws its shade,
And nothing says such shade will spread around
Even as to-day when men will no more heed
The Gospel news than when the mound was made.

LYING AWAKE

You, Morningtide Star, now are steady-eyed, over the east,
    I know it as if I saw you;
You, Beeches, engrave on the sky your thin twigs, even the least;
    Had I paper and pencil I'd draw you.

You, Meadow, are white with your counterpane cover of dew,
    I see it as if I were there;
You, Churchyard, are lightening faint from the shade of the yew
    The names creeping out everywhere.

THE LADY IN THE FURS

"I'm a lofty lovely woman,"
  Says the lady in the furs,
In the glance she throws around her
  On the poorer dames and sirs:
"This robe, that cost three figures,
  Yes, is mine," her nod avers.

"True, my money did not buy it,
  But my husband's, from the trade;
And they, they only got it
  From things feeble and afraid
By murdering them in ambush
  With a cunning engine's aid.

"True, my hands, too, did not shape it
  To the pretty cut you see,
But the hands of midnight workers
  Who are strangers quite to me:
It was fitted, too, by dressers
  Ranged around me toilsomely.

"But I am a lovely lady,
  Though sneerers say I shine
By robbing Nature's children
  Of apparel not mine,
And that I am but a broom-stick,
  Like a scarecrow's wooden spine."

1925.

CHILDHOOD AMONG THE FERNS

I sat one sprinkling day upon the lea,
Where tall-stemmed ferns spread out luxuriantly,
And nothing but those tall ferns sheltered me.

The rain gained strength, and damped each lopping frond,
Ran down their stalks beside me and beyond,
And shaped slow-creeping rivulets as I conned,

With pride, my spray-roofed house. And though anon
Some drops pierced its green rafters, I sat on,
Making pretence I was not rained upon.

The sun then burst, and brought forth a sweet breath
From the limp ferns as they dried underneath:
I said: "I could live on here thus till death";

And queried in the green rays as I sate:
"Why should I have to grow to man's estate,
And this afar-noised World perambulate?"

A COUNTENANCE

Her laugh was not in the middle of her face quite,
  As a gay laugh springs,
It was plain she was anxious about some things
  I could not trace quite.
Her curls were like fir-cones—piled up, brown—
  Or rather like tight-tied sheaves:
It seemed they could never be taken down. . . .

And her lips were too full, some might say:
I did not think so. Anyway,
The shadow her lower one would cast
Was green in hue whenever she passed
  Bright sun on midsummer leaves.
Alas, I knew not much of her,
And lost all sight and touch of her!

If otherwise, should I have minded
The shy laugh not in the middle of her mouth quite,
And would my kisses have died of drouth quite
  As love became unblinded?

1884.

"I WATCHED A BLACKBIRD"

I watched a blackbird on a budding sycamore
One Easter Day, when sap was stirring twigs to the core;
  I saw his tongue, and crocus-coloured bill
  Parting and closing as he turned his trill;
  Then he flew down, seized on a stem of hay,
And upped to where his building scheme was under way,
As if so sure a nest were never shaped on spray.

AFTER THE BURIAL

The family had buried him,
    Their bread-bringer, their best:
They had returned to the house, whose hush a dim
    Vague vacancy expressed.

There sat his sons, mute, rigid-faced,
    His daughters, strained, red-eyed,
His wife, whose wan, worn features, vigil-traced,
    Bent over him when he died.

At once a peal bursts from the bells
    Of a large tall tower hard by:
Along the street the jocund clangour swells,
    And upward to the sky.

Probably it was a wedding-peal,
    Or possibly for a birth,
Or townsman knighted for political zeal,
    This resonant mark of mirth.

The mourners, heavy-browed, sat on
    Motionless. Well they heard,
They could not help it; nevertheless thereon
    Spoke not a single word,

Nor window did they close, to numb
    The bells' insistent calls
Of joy; but suffered the harassing din to come
    And penetrate their souls.

AN EVENING IN GALILEE

She looks far west towards Carmel, shading her eyes with her hand,
And she then looks east to the Jordan, and the smooth Tiberias' strand.
"Is my son mad?" she asks; and never an answer has she,
Save from herself, aghast at the possibility.
"He professes as his firm faiths things far too grotesque to be true,
And his vesture is odd—too careless for one of his fair young hue! . . .

"He lays down doctrines as if he were old—aye, fifty at least:
In the Temple he terrified me, opposing the very High-Priest!
Why did he say to me, 'Woman, what have I to do with thee?'
O it cuts to the heart that a child of mine thus spoke to me!
And he said, too, 'Who is my mother?'—when he knows so very well.
He might have said, 'Who is my father?'—and I'd found it hard to tell!
That no one knows but Joseph and—one other, nor ever will;
One who'll not see me again. . . . How it chanced!—I dreaming no ill! . . .

"Would he'd not mix with the lowest folk—like those fishermen—
The while so capable, culling new knowledge, beyond our ken! . . .
That woman of no good character, ever following him,
Adores him if I mistake not: his wish of her is but a whim
Of his madness, it may be, outmarking his lack of coherency;
After his 'Keep the Commandments!' to smile upon such as she!
It is just what all those do who are wandering in their wit.
I don't know—dare not say—what harm may grow from it.

O a mad son is a terrible thing; it even may lead
To arrest, and death! . . . And how he can preach, expound, and read!
"Here comes my husband. Shall I unveil him this tragedy-brink?
No. He has nightmares enough. I'll pray, and think, and think." . . .
She remembers she's never put on any pot for his evening meal,
And pondering a plea looks vaguely to south of her—towards Jezreel.

SEEING THE MOON RISE

We used to go to Froom-hill Barrow
    To see the round moon rise
    Into the heath-rimmed skies,
Trudging thither by plough and harrow
Up the pathway, steep and narrow,
    Singing a song.
Now we do not go there. Why?
    Zest burns not so high!

Latterly we've only conned her
    With a passing glance
    From window or door by chance,
Hoping to go again, high yonder,
As we used, and gaze, and ponder,
    Singing a song.
Thitherward we do not go:
    Feet once quick are slow!

August 1927.

HE NEVER EXPECTED MUCH
[OR] A CONSIDERATION
[*A reflection*] on My Eighty-Sixth Birthday

Well, World, you have kept faith with me,
    Kept faith with me;
Upon the whole you have proved to be
    Much as you said you were.
Since as a child I used to lie
Upon the leaze and watch the sky,
Never, I own, expected I
    That life would all be fair.

'Twas then you said, and since have said,
    Times since have said,
In that mysterious voice you shed
    From clouds and hills around:
"Many have loved me desperately,
Many with smooth serenity,
While some have shown contempt of me
    Till they dropped underground.

"I do not promise overmuch,
    Child; overmuch;
Just neutral-tinted haps and such,"
    You said to minds like mine.
Wise warning for your credit's sake!
Which I for one failed not to take,
And hence could stem such strain and ache
    As each year might assign.

STANDING BY THE MANTELPIECE
(H. M. M., 1873)

This candle-wax is shaping to a shroud
To-night. (They call it that, as you may know)—
By touching it the claimant is avowed,
And hence I press it with my finger—so.

To-night. To me twice night, that should have been
The radiance of the midmost tick of noon,
And close around me wintertime is seen
That might have shone the veriest day of June!

But since all's lost, and nothing really lies
Above but shade, and shadier shade below,
Let me make clear, before one of us dies,
My mind to yours, just now embittered so.

Since you agreed, unurged and full-advised,
And let warmth grow without discouragement,
Why do you bear you now as if surprised,
When what has come was clearly consequent?

Since you have spoken, and finality
Closes around, and my last movements loom,
I say no more: the rest must wait till we
Are face to face again, yonside the tomb.

And let the candle-wax thus mould a shape
Whose meaning now, if hid before, you know,
And how by touch one present claims its drape
And that it's I who press my finger—so.

THAT KISS IN THE DARK

Recall it you?—
Say you do!—
When you went out into the night,
In an impatience that would not wait,
From that lone house in the woodland spot,
And when I, thinking you had gone
For ever and ever from my sight,
Came after, printing a kiss upon
    Black air
    In my despair,
And my two lips lit on your cheek
As you leant silent against a gate,
Making my woman's face flush hot
At what I had done in the dark, unware
You lingered for me but would not speak:
Yes, kissed you, thinking you were not there!
    Recall it you?—
    Say you do!

DRINKING SONG

Once on a time when thought began
   Lived Thales: he
   Was said to see
Vast truths that mortals seldom can;
   It seems without
   A moment's doubt
That everything was made for man.
CHORUS.

   Fill full your cups: feel no distress
   That thoughts so great should now be less!

Earth mid the sky stood firm and flat,
   He held, till came
   A sage by name
Copernicus, and righted that.
   We trod, he told,
   A globe that rolled
Around a sun it warmed it at.
CHORUS.

   Fill full your cups: feel no distress;
   'Tis only one great thought the less!

But still we held, as Time flew by
   And wit increased,
   Ours was, at least,
The only world whose rank was high:
   Till rumours flew
   From folk who knew
Of globes galore about the sky.
CHORUS.

   Fill full your cups: feel no distress;
   'Tis only one great thought the less!

And that this earth, our one estate,
   Was no prime ball,
   The best of all,

But common, mean; indeed, tenth-rate:
  And men, so proud,
  A feeble crowd,
Unworthy any special fate.
             CHORUS.
  Fill full your cups: feel no distress;
  'Tis only one great thought the less!

Then rose one Hume, who could not see,
  If earth were such,
  Required were much
To prove no miracles could be:
  "Better believe
  The eyes deceive
Than that God's clockwork jolts," said he.
             CHORUS.
  Fill full your cups: feel no distress;
  'Tis only one great thought the less!

Next this strange message Darwin brings,
  (Though saying his say
  In a quiet way);
We all are one with creeping things;
  And apes and men
  Blood-brethren,
And likewise reptile forms with stings.
             CHORUS.
  Fill full your cups: feel no distress;
  'Tis only one great thought the less!

And when this philosoph had done
  Came Doctor Cheyne:
  Speaking plain he
Proved no virgin bore a son.
  "Such tale, indeed,
  Helps not our creed,"
He said. "A tale long known to none."

CHORUS.

Fill full your cups: feel no distress;
'Tis only one great thought the less!

And now comes Einstein with a notion—
Not yet quite clear
To many here—
That's there's no time, no space, no motion,
Nor rathe nor late,
Nor square nor straight,
But just a sort of bending-ocean.

CHORUS.

Fill full your cups: feel no distress;
'Tis only one great thought the less!

So here we are, in piteous case:
Like butterflies
Of many dyes
Upon an Alpine glacier's face:
To fly and cower
In some warm bower
Our chief concern in such a place.

CHORUS.

Fill full your cups: feel no distress
At all our great thoughts shrinking less:
We'll do a good deed nevertheless!

A MUSICAL INCIDENT

When I see the room it hurts me
    As with a pricking blade,
Those women being the memoried reason why my cheer deserts me.—
    'Twas thus. One of them played
    To please her friend, not knowing
    That friend was speedily growing,
    Behind the player's chair,
    Somnolent, unaware
    Of any music there.

I saw it, and it distressed me,
    For I had begun to think
I loved the drowsy listener, when this arose to test me
    And tug me from love's brink.
    "Beautiful!" said she, waking
    As the music ceased. "Heart-aching!"
    Though never a note she'd heard
    To judge of as averred—
    Save that of the very last word.

All would have faded in me,
    But that the sleeper brought
News a week thence that her friend was dead. It stirred within me
    Sense of injustice wrought
    That dead player's poor intent—
    So heartily, kindly meant—
    As blandly added the sigher:
    "How glad I am I was nigh her,
    To hear her last tune!"—"Liar!"
    I lipped.—This gave love pause,
    And killed it, such as it was.

DEAD "WESSEX" THE DOG TO THE HOUSEHOLD

Do you think of me at all,
   Wistful ones?
Do you think of me at all
    As if nigh?
Do you think of me at all
At the creep of evenfall,
Or when the sky-birds call
    As they fly?

Do you look for me at times,
   Wistful ones?
Do you look for me at times
    Strained and still?
Do you look for me at times,
When the hour for walking chimes,
On that grassy path that climbs
    Up the hill?

You may hear a jump or trot,
   Wistful ones,
You may hear a jump or trot—
    Mine, as 'twere—
You may hear a jump or trot
On the stair or path or plot;
But I shall cause it not,
    Be not there.

Should you call as when I knew you,
   Wistful ones,
Should you call as when I knew you,
    Shared your home;
Should you call as when I knew you,
I shall not turn to view you,
I shall not listen to you,
    Shall not come.

A PRIVATE MAN ON PUBLIC MEN

When my contemporaries were driving
Their coach through Life with strain and striving,
And raking riches into heaps,
And ably pleading in the Courts
With smart rejoinders and retorts,
Or where the Senate nightly keeps
Its vigils, till their fames were fanned
By rumour's tongue throughout the land,
I lived in quiet, screened, unknown,
Pondering upon some stick or stone,
Or news of some rare book or bird
Latterly bought, or seen, or heard,
Not wishing ever to set eyes on
The surging crowd beyond the horizon,
Tasting years of moderate gladness
Mellowed by sundry days of sadness,
Shut from the noise of the world without,
Hearing but dimly its rush and rout,
Unenvying those amid its roar,
Little endowed, not wanting more.

CHRISTMAS IN THE ELGIN ROOM
BRITISH MUSEUM: EARLY LAST CENTURY

"What is the noise that shakes the night,
And seems to soar to the Pole-star height?"
　　—"Christmas bells,
　　The watchman tells
Who walks this hall that blears us captives with its blight."

"And what, then, mean such clangs, so clear?"
"—'Tis said to have been a day of cheer,
　　And source of grace
　　To the human race
Long ere their woven sails winged us to exile here.

"We are those whom Christmas overthrew
Some centuries after Pheidias knew
　　How to shape us
　　And bedrape us
And to set us in Athena's temple for men's view.

"O it is sad now we are sold—
We gods! for Borean people's gold,
　　And brought to the gloom
　　Of this gaunt room
Which sunlight shuns, and sweet Aurore but enters cold.

"For all these bells, would I were still
Radiant as on Athenai's Hill."
　　—"And I, and I!"
　　The others sigh,
"Before this Christ was known, and we had men's good will."

Thereat old Helios could but nod,
Throbbed, too, the Ilissus River-god,
　　And the torsos there
　　Of deities fair,
Whose limbs were shards beneath some Acropolitan clod:

Demeter too, Poseidon hoar,
Persephone, and many more
   Of Zeus' high breed,—
   All loth to heed
What the bells sang that night which shook them to the core.

    1905 and 1926.

HE RESOLVES TO SAY NO MORE

O my soul, keep the rest unknown!
It is too like a sound of moan
   When the charnel-eyed
   Pale Horse has nighed:
Yea, none shall gather what I hide!

Why load men's minds with more to bear
That bear already ails to spare?
   From now alway
   Till my last day
What I discern I will not say.

Let Time roll backward if it will;
(Magians who drive the midnight quill
   With brain aglow
   Can see it so,)
What I have learnt no man shall know.

And if my vision range beyond
The blinkered sight of souls in bond,
   —By truth made free—
   I'll let all be,
And show to no man what I see.

APPENDIX A
Typography and Titles

The typography in Hardy's *Chosen Poems*, and again in the contents of his *Collected Poems*, gave the titles in all-capitals; words that would normally be lowercase were printed in capitals of a smaller size; and this cascade of large letters, the sizes hardly distinguishable without a conscious effort, can produce at times an emphasis at variance with his likely intention. Thus "IN ST. PAUL'S A WHILE AGO" may suggest a remarkable moment, but when the small capitals are rendered lowercase it appears unremarkable: "In St. Paul's a while ago"—a notation well suited to Hardy's sense of the "crass casualty" of time and circumstance. He conveys a similar prosaic humility in titles that are caption-summaries of the poems they announce: "HE NEVER EXPECTED MUCH" ("He never expected much").

A strong precedent of course existed, more conspicuous on its face but less surprising in its effect, namely the descriptive titles employed by Wordsworth and Coleridge in *Lyrical Ballads:* "Lines left upon a Seat in a Yew-tree which stands near the Lake of Esthwaite, on a desolate part of the shore, yet commanding a beautiful prospect." The titles of *Lyrical Ballads*, however, are deliberately pedestrian and circumstantial, never metaphysical. By contrast, a capital letter, as Hardy used it, might intimate a kind of allegory—a point not necessarily clear in "HE ABJURES LOVE" but quite plain in "He abjures Love." The same goes for his evocation of natural entities that can sometimes carry a more-than-natural sense: "'THE MOON LOOKS IN'" ("'The Moon looks in'"). Take away the all-capitals and the Moon herself becomes an active character.

Conventional typography has been used for the titles in the present selection, in keeping with standard editions of Hardy's poetry that capitalize all parts of speech except articles and prepositions. The following list comprises some poems in which his own occasional practice may have signaled an understatement or irony regarding the contingencies of time, place, and personal consciousness.

> To meet, or otherwise
> The Self-unseeing
> He abjures Love
> Friends beyond
> Her Death and after
> The Something that saved him
> Before Marching and after
> The Moon looks in
> A Death-Day recalled

St. Launce's revisited
Voices from Things growing in a Churchyard
He follows Himself
On One who lived and died where He was born
The Thing unplanned
He never expected much
He resolves to say no more

APPENDIX B
Volumes in Which *Chosen Poems* First Appeared

Wessex Poems and Other Verses (1898)

The Temporary the All
Amabel
Hap
Neutral Tones
She at His Funeral
Her Initials
To Him [She, to Him, II]
Ditty
The Burghers
Her Death and After
Unknowing
Friends Beyond
Thoughts of Phena
In a Wood
To a Motherless Child
At an Inn
In a Eweleaze near Weatherbury
"I Look into My Glass"

Poems of the Past and the Present (1901)

Embarcation
Departure
The Going of the Battery
Drummer Hodge
The Man He Killed
The Souls of the Slain
Shelley's Skylark
Rome. The Vatican: Salle Delle Muse
Rome. At the Pyramid of Cestius near the Graves of Shelley and Keats
On an Invitation to the United States
"I Said to Love"

A Commonplace Day
At a Lunar Eclipse
To Life
The Subalterns
The Sleep-Worker
To an Unborn Pauper Child
To Lizbie Browne
Song of Hope
A Broken Appointment
"How Great my Grief"
"I Need Not Go"
A Spot
The Dream-Follower
Wives in the Sere
The Darkling Thrush
The Self-Unseeing
In Tenebris [In Tenebris II]
"I Have Lived with Shades"

Time's Laughingstocks and Other Verses (1909)

A Trampwoman's Tragedy
The House of Hospitalities
Shut Out That Moon
Reminiscences of a Dancing Man
The Dead Man Walking
The Division
On the Departure Platform
In a Cathedral City
"I Say I'll Seek Her"
In the Mind's Eye
The Night of the Dance
He Abjures Love
Let Me Enjoy
The Ballad-Singer
The Fiddler
A Church Romance
The Dead Quire
The Roman Road
Night in the Old Home

After the Last Breath
She Hears the Storm
The Man He Killed
George Meredith
Yell'ham-Wood's Story

The Dynasts (1910)

The Night of Trafalgar
Albuera
Hussar's Song
"My Love's Gone a-Fighting"
The Eve of Waterloo
Chorus of the Pities
Last Chorus

Satires of Circumstance (1914)

In Front of the Landscape
The Convergence of the Twain
The Ghost of the Past
After the Visit
To Meet, or Otherwise
The Difference
The Sun on the Bookcase
"When I Set Out for Lyonnesse"
Beyond the Last Lamp
Lost Love
"My Spirit Will Not Haunt the Mound"
Wessex Heights
In Death Divided
The Schreckhorn
A Singer Asleep
Before and after Summer
The Going
"I Found Her Out There"
The Voice
After a Journey
Beeny Cliff
At Castle Boterel

The Phantom Horsewoman
Where the Picnic Was
The Coronation
"Regret Not Me"
Exeunt Omnes
A Poet
In the Moonlight

Moments of Vision and Miscellaneous Verses (1917)

At the Word "Farewell"
First Sight of Her and After
Near Lanivet, 1872
Joys of Memory
To the Moon
On a Midsummer Eve
Timing Her
The Blinded Bird
The Duel
"Something Tapped"
The Wound
A Merrymaking in Question
The Oxen
Great Things
Paying Calls
Fragment
The Something That Saved Him
"Men Who March Away"
In Time of "the Breaking of Nations"
Before Marching and After
Afterwards

Late Lyrics and Earlier (1922)

Weathers
Epeisodia
The Garden Seat
"The Curtains Now Are Drawn"
Jezreel
"According to the Mighty Working"

"As 'Twere To-Night"
A Night in November
The Fallow Deer at the Lonely House
The Selfsame Song
The Chimes Play "Life's a Bumper!"
Saying Good-Bye
The Singing Woman
Just the Same
The Last Time

The Famous Tragedy of the Queen of Cornwall (1923)

"Could He but Live for Me"
"Let's Meet Again To-Night, My Fair"

Human Shows, Far Phantasies, Songs, and Trifles (1925)

Waiting Both
"Any Little Old Song"
The Carrier
Lover to Mistress
The Monument-Maker
Come Not; Yet Come!
"Let Me Believe"
An East-End Curate
In St. Paul's a While Ago
Singing Lovers
Night-Time in Mid-Fall
A Sheep Fair
Snow in the Suburbs
Two Lips
Last Love-Word
Cynic's Epitaph
Song to an Old Burden
"Why Do I?"

The present volume contains all of the *Poems of 1912–13*. Hardy included eight in his *Chosen Poems;* the remaining thirteen are printed here among the "Additional Poems." The group originally made a separate section of *Satires of Circumstance,* in the order given on the list below, which for convenient reference also marks the subset that went into *Chosen Poems*.

The Going [*Chosen Poems*]
Your Last Drive
The Walk
Rain on a Grave
"I Found Her Out There" [*Chosen Poems*]
Without Ceremony
Lament
The Haunter
The Voice [*Chosen Poems*]
His Visitor
A Circular
A Dream or No
After a Journey [*Chosen Poems*]
A Death-Day Recalled
Beeny Cliff [*Chosen Poems*]
At Castle Boterel [*Chosen Poems*]
Places
The Phantom Horsewoman [*Chosen Poems*]
The Spell of the Rose
St. Launce's Revisited
Where the Picnic Was [*Chosen Poems*]

NOTES

Chosen Poems of Thomas Hardy

To Meet, or Otherwise
cimmerian: gloomy

Ditty
knap: the summit of a hillock

The Night of the Dance
backbrand: the log laid at the back of a fire

The Division
besom: sweep

In a Eweleaze near Wetherbury
eweleaze: a meadow for sheep (*leaze* being an archaic spelling of "lease")

A Spot
gaingiving: misgiving
sereward: toward a withered state

The Darkling Thrush
coppice: a small thicket of trees grown for lumber

The Going
beetling: ominously overhanging

Beeny Cliff
prinked: adorned

Shut Out That Moon
casement: romantic word for window; specifically, with a hinged opening like a door

"Regret Not Me"
junketings: feasts, merrymaking

In the Mind's Eye
casement: romantic word for window; specifically, with a hinged opening like a door

Amabel
dorp: a village

Reminiscences of a Dancing Man
Almack's: a social club in London with multiple establishments
Willis: former name of Almack's
cremorne: a dance hall
Jullien's: quadrille by Louis-Antoine Jullien, a popular French composer (1812–1860)
yclept: archaic form of *named*
The Argyle: another London social club
moue: a pout, or small grimace

He Abjures Love
daysman: monitor; constant minder
lours: grimly portends

"I Need Not Go"
sough: a sigh

Wives in the Sere
sere: withered; dry

Epeisodia
leaze: meadow or field for grazing

Joys of Memory
copestrees: trees in a copse

Timing Her
Lalage: possibly Lalage Acland, the daughter of John Acland, a friend of Hardy's
vair: lining made of squirrel-fur

Song to an Old Burden
rigadoon: a jumping quickstep dance

To an Unborn Pauper Child
teens: sorrows

Exeunt Omnes
Exeunt omnes: all depart
The poem is dated on Hardy's seventy-third birthday.

Friends Beyond
stillicide: continuous dripping of water
charlock: a weed in the wild mustard family with yellow flowers
grintern: compartment in a granary for threshed corn; from *grinter*, a granary supervisor
Trine: the holy Trinity

In Front of the Landscape
coombe: a deep hollow
nimb: nimbus; halo
leaze: a meadow or pasture

The Convergence of the Twain
salamandrine: salamander-like (the salamander being credited with a mythical power to pass through fire unharmed)

George Meredith
vitiate: archaic spelling of *vitiated;* corrupted, infected

A Singer Asleep
chine: coastal ravine

A Church Romance
Bowing "New Sabbath or "Mount Ephraim": playing on fiddle the hymns of those names

The Oxen
barton: farmyard
coombe: a deep hollow

After the Last Breath
outshapes: outlines the shape of

Night in the Old Home
tristfulness: sadness
sere: withered; dry

On an Invitation to the United States
emprise: a daring enterprise or undertaking
wonning: dwelling in a particular place

The Dead Quire
settle: a high-backed bench
supernal: heavenly
roisterer: merry-maker
leaze: a meadow or pasture

The Burghers
pleasaunce: an enclosed area for pleasant walks
haw: field bordering a house
cicatrize: heal by inducing a scar

The Coronation
Rimmon: alternative name of Baal, the Middle East fertility god
catafalque: decorated platform to support a coffin during funerals

Her Death and After
ruth: compassion; pity for another's misery

A Trampwoman's Tragedy
Marshwood midge: mosquito from the vale of Marshwood
tor: a rocky peak

The Duel
cockpit: a pit in the ground for cockfights

An East-End Curate
glees: short pieces of vocal music for a few male voices

The Something That Saved Him
cit: sophisticate

In Tenebris
Considerabam . . . animam meam: "I looked on my right hand, and beheld; but there was
   no man that would know me. . . . No man cared for my soul"

The Going of the Battery
felloe: iron rim of a wagon wheel

Drummer Hodge
"Drummer Hodge" is a poem of the Second Boer War (1899)
kopje-crest: Afrikaans for the crest of a steep hillock
veldt: open pasture in South Africa
karoo: arid scrubland plateau in South Africa

The Man He Killed
nipperkin: a small quantity of liquor

The Souls of the Slain
prink: primp, tidy up

Additional Poems

San Sebastian
vlanker-light: light emitted by sparks from the fire
fauss-bray: fortification around the main ramparts

My Cicely
Baals: plural of the Middle East fertility god
lynchet: flinty outcropping, from accumulated dirt and stone at the edge of a plowed field

cromlech: megalithic structure, made of large vertical stone blocks arranged in a circle, with horizontal blocks laid above them crosswise; thought to have served as places of worship and memorials for the dead

blee: color

garth: churchyard

The Impercipient

liefer: rather

The Bullfinches

hussif'ry: the business of being a housewife

An August Midnight

dumbledore: bumblebee

A Man

pile: elaborate structure

pilaster: an architectural feature slightly protruding from a wall to create the semblance of a freestanding pillar

bay: the space in a roof between the trusses

The Ruined Maid

spudding up docks: digging up weeds with a spade

barton: farmyard

sock: sigh

megrims: migraines

In Tenebris I

In Tenebris: in darkness

Percussus sum . . . cor meum: "My heart is smitten, and withered like grass"

In Tenebris III

Heu mihi . . . anima mea: "Woe is me, that I sojourn in Mesech, that I dwell in the tents of Kedar! My soul hath long dwelt with him that hateth peace."

quoin: a corner, made by masonry blocks joining a ceiling and a wall, or two walls

The Farm-Woman's Winter

casement corners: corners of a window frame with a hinged opening like a door

The Conformers

fay: fairylike creature; here, diminutive of "faithful one"

cohue: an unruly crowd

Channel Firing

chancel: space around the altar in a church

glebe: church fields

The Face at the Casement
casement: window frame with a hinged opening like a door
garth: churchyard

A Plaint to Man
lantern-slide: photographic slide for projection using a magic lantern

"Ah, Are You Digging on My Grave?"
Death's gin: a cotton gin separates the seed from the usable fiber of cotton; so here with
    Death's gin, the soul from the body

Poems of 1912–13
Veteris vestigia flammae: traces of an unextinguished passion (*Aeneid* 4.23)

Rain on a Grave
amain: all at once

Lament
rime: frost

Places
beneaped: gone aground from high spring tides

St. Launce's Revisited
St. Launce's: Launceton, Cornwall, the termination point of Hardy's train journeys to
    visit Emma Gifford

The Re-Enactment
copse: a small thicket of trees or shrubs

Seen by the Waits
waits: onlookers; in context, the carolers

In the Cemetery
sprats: small edible marine fish

Outside the Window
delf: pottery made in Delft, Holland, cheaper than real porcelain

"We Sat at the Window"
Swithin's Day: July 15 holiday in honor of St. Swithin, a bishop of Winchester in the
    ninth century

Quid Hic Agis?
Quid hic agis: What dost thou here? (from the book of Kings, the Lord's words to Elijah)

The Change
deodar: ornamental subspecies of cedar

"By the Runic Stone"
runic stone: a stone carved with runes, thought to be located near St. Juliot Rectory

Overlooking the River Stour
kingcups: buttercups

The Ageing House
casement: window frame with a hinged opening like a door

The Wind's Prophecy
Pharos-shine: beam from a lighthouse (the Pharos of Alexandria being one of the Seven Wonders of the World)

Molly Gone
Molly was Hardy's sister Mary

The Pedestrian
"Nox venit": night cometh
vamp: stride

He Revisits His First School
wanzing: waning, dwindling
Walkingame: The Tutor's Assistant, by Francis Walkingame, a school primer
Rule of Three: the product of the means equals the product of the extremes; as in 2:3 :: 4:6

In a Waiting-Room
bagman: a traveling salesman

Paths of Former Time
kine: cattle
weirs: dams placed across a stream to raise, divert, or regulate the flow

Going and Staying
plightings: making pledges to marry

The Two Houses
casements: window frames with a hinged opening like a door
teens: sorrows

"I Worked No Wile to Meet You"
sheered: swerved
hydromels: mixed honey and water (a drink like mead)

The Chapel-Organist
semibreves: whole notes

At the Entering of the New Year

allemands: English folk dance steps that move facing partners forward past each other
    with an arm-clasp

heys: dance steps in which two lines of couples parade opposite and alongside each other

pousettings: dance steps that exchange partners between two couples by a diagonal move

casements: window frames with a hinged opening like a door

He Follows Himself

dree: suffering

The Master and the Leaves

nightjar: long-tailed bird akin to the North American nighthawk and whippoorwill

The Whipper-In

whipper-in: caretaker of hunting dogs

Rake-Hell Muses

rake-hell: a libertine scoundrel; a seducer

guerdon: reward

ell: length just over a meter

An Ancient to Ancients

tabrets: small tabors (a kind of frame drum)

Etty, Mulready, Maclise: fashionable early Victorian painters

Aïdes: Hades

A Bird-Scene at a Rural Dwelling

codlin-tree: tree bearing codlin apples

costard: a variety of large apple

The Later Autumn

sere: withered; dry

couch-fires: a fast-spreading coarse weed used for burning

A Last Journey

dimity: a strong cotton fabric

Sine Prole

Sine prole: without offspring

Jahveh: Yahweh (Jehovah), god of the Israelites

The Graveyard of Dead Creeds

catholicons: universal remedies; cure-alls

A Light Snow-Fall after Frost

worsted: a kind of wool cloth

rime: frost

Winter Night in Woodland
copse: a small thicket of trees
swingels: cudgels or flails

The Aërolite
Aërolite: meteorite

The Harbour Bridge
cutwater: wedge-shaped base at the end of a bridge pier
bollards: wooden posts on a quay, used for mooring boats

Vagrant's Song
Che-hane: Dorset expression, evidently meaning "I'm safe and sound"

The Paphian Bull
Paphian: relating to Paphos, a coastal city in Cyprus containing a famous temple of
Venus; hence, given to the worship of Venus

The Mound
palter: trifle, bargain, hang back

Childhood among the Ferns
conned: surveyed

Seeing the Moon Rise
conned: surveyed

He Never Expected Much
leaze: a field or down

Drinking Song
Thales: the first Greek philosopher
Doctor Cheyne: George Cheyne (1671–1743), a disciple of Sir Isaac Newton and theorist
of natural religion

Christmas in the Elgin Room
Elgin Room: room of the British Museum housing the Elgin Marbles from the Parthenon
Pheidias: the greatest of ancient Athenian sculptors

UNCOMMON AND HISTORICALLY
SIGNIFICANT PLACE-NAMES

Areopagus: the Hill of Ares, in Athens, site of the forum in which the highest government
    council held session
Beeny: cliff near Bocastle, in Cornwall
Dundagel: location of Tintagel Castle, a famed headland associated with King Arthur's
    birth
Jezreel: ancient city in Palestine; the Jezreel Valley saw the victory of Gen. Edmund
    Allenby over Ottoman Turks in September 1918
Leucadia: the promontory from which Sappho is said to have thrown herself, from un-
    requited love of Phaon
Lyonnesse: a country fabled in Arthurian legend, now supposed to lie underwater
Mellstock: now Stinsford Parish, in Dorset, where Hardy lived
Ridgeway: the South Dorset Ridgeway, thought to be the oldest road in England
St. Launce's: terminal point of Hardy's train journeys to visit Emma Gifford
San Sebastian: Site of a hard-fought siege during the Napoleonic wars
Schreckhorn: the Matterhorn, a mountain in Switzerland
Stourton Tower: King Alfred's Tower, built in the late eighteenth century to commemorate
    King Alfred's defeat of the Danes in the year 878

ACKNOWLEDGMENTS

John Kulka had the idea for this book several years ago. Our model was an earlier reprint of Hardy's *Chosen Poems*, edited by Francine Shapiro Puk (Ungar, 1978), which included a shorter selection of additional poems. John Donatich at Yale University Press encouraged the project from the start. Beasie Goddu made the endnotes with an acuity that clarified without overburdening the text. Jennifer Banks offered valuable comments on a draft of the introduction and has guided the work to completion with wonderful patience and efficiency. Abigail Storch oversaw logistics and greatly expedited the passage from manuscript to print. Two anonymous readers for Yale University Press gave advice which I have followed in the notes and appendixes. Finally I am grateful to Laura Dooley for her superlative copy editing and to Jeffrey Schier for his vigilant oversight of production and proofs.

INDEX OF TITLES

INDEX OF FIRST LINES